# WHY CONTEXT MATTERS IN EDUCATIONAL LEADERSHIP

*Why Context Matters in Educational Leadership: A New Theoretical Understanding* is unique in the field of educational leadership studies. This book offers a systematic account of educational leadership from the perspective that context matters. It argues that studies of leadership in education can only progress if the importance of context is understood and presents context as a set of constraints under which leadership is exercised.

A theoretical book that offers at last three major challenges to dominant positions in the field in a systematic way, it provides a new, coherent, and more realistic way to think about leadership in context. The chapters offer concrete steps for complex problem-solving in schools and will help schools tailor solutions to local constraints and circumstances.

Written by leading scholars Colin W. Evers and Gabriele Lakomski, this book will be essential reading for students and researchers working in the fields of education, educational administration and leadership.

**Colin W. Evers** is Emeritus Professor of Educational Leadership at the University of New South Wales, Australia. His research focuses on decision making in educational administration, the distribution of leadership in organizational contexts, links between emotion and leadership, and developing a view of educational leadership as critical learning.

**Gabriele Lakomski** is Professor Emeritus in the Melbourne Centre for the Study of Higher Education at the University of Melbourne. Her research interests cover leadership, organizational learning and culture, neuroscience and the emotions, the relation between cognition and emotion, and implications for rational decision-making in organizational contexts.

# WHY CONTEXT MATTERS IN EDUCATIONAL LEADERSHIP

A New Theoretical Understanding

Colin W. Evers
Gabriele Lakomski

LONDON AND NEW YORK

Cover image: © Aitor Diago/Getty Images

First published 2022
by Routledge
2 Park Square, Milton Park, Abingdon, Oxon OX14 4RN

and by Routledge
605 Third Avenue, New York, NY 10158

*Routledge is an imprint of the Taylor & Francis Group, an informa business*

© 2022 Colin W. Evers, Gabriele Lakomski

The right of Colin W. Evers, Gabriele Lakomski to be identified as authors of this work has been asserted in accordance with sections 77 and 78 of the Copyright, Designs and Patents Act 1988.

All rights reserved. No part of this book may be reprinted or reproduced or utilised in any form or by any electronic, mechanical, or other means, now known or hereafter invented, including photocopying and recording, or in any information storage or retrieval system, without permission in writing from the publishers.

*Trademark notice*: Product or corporate names may be trademarks or registered trademarks, and are used only for identification and explanation without intent to infringe.

*British Library Cataloguing-in-Publication Data*
A catalogue record for this book is available from the British Library

*Library of Congress Cataloging-in-Publication Data*
A catalog record has been requested for this book

ISBN: 9781032148830 (hbk)
ISBN: 9781032148847 (pbk)
ISBN: 9781003241577 (ebk)

DOI: 10.4324/9781003241577

Typeset in Bembo
by KnowledgeWorks Global Ltd.

# CONTENTS

*List of Figures*     viii
*List of Tables*     ix
*Preface*     x
*Acknowledgements*     xv

## PART I
## Philosophical foundations

1 Naturalism, educational administration, and leadership:
  An overview     3
  *Introduction 3*
  *Particularity versus generality 4*
  *Naturalism and ethics 8*
  *Naturalising ethics and its critics 10*
  *Cognition, educational administration, and neuroscience 12*
  *Leadership, distributed cognition, and organization 14*
  *Conclusion 17*

2 Methodological individualism and educational leadership     21
  *Introduction 21*
  *The rise of leadership 21*
  *Individuals and structures 23*
  *Against reduction in social explanation 25*
  *The centralized mind, emergence, and self-organization 27*
  *Distributed cognition 31*

*Structured problems   32*
*Conclusion   34*

3  Leader cognition in context     37
*Introduction   37*
*Disembodied cognition   38*
*Self as constructed   41*
*From extended mind to cognitive ecologies   42*
*Cognitive practices and enculturated cognition   46*
*Conclusion   48*

## PART II
## The social context of leadership

4  Leadership, evidence, and inference     57
*Introduction   57*
*Learning from other leaders   58*
*Similarity in classification   59*
*Swans, a duck, and property possession   60*
*Theory-ladenness   62*
*Falsification and theory choice   63*
*Theory and the search for patterns   64*
*Theory and effect size   68*
*Conclusion   71*

5  Developing leadership – from uncertainty to social epistemology     74
*Introduction   74*
*Uncertainty and social prediction: Popper's argument   74*
*Uncertainty and social prediction: Chaos   77*
*Social epistemology: Dewey, Kitcher, and Popper   79*
*Modelling learning organizations and individuals in context   83*
*Organizational and institutional constraints on learning   85*
*Organizational scaffolding of the mind   87*
*Conclusion   89*

6  Learning leadership through problem-solving trajectories     92
*Introduction   92*
*Example of a problems-solutions trajectory   93*
*Defining problems   96*
*Defining tentative theories   98*
*Defining error elimination   100*
*Conclusion   103*

7  Constraints, structure, and reasoning 106
   *Introduction 106*
   *Evidence for human irrationality 106*
   *Some philosophical responses 108*
   *Cultural differences in reasoning 110*
   *Normative cognitive pluralism 112*
   *Problems, solutions, and objectivity 112*
   *Problems of scale 117*
   *Conclusion 121*

## PART III
## Individuals in context – reason, emotion, organization

8  Naturalizing emotion 127
   *Introduction 127*
   *Emotion in education and educational leadership 129*
   *From emotions as essences to emotions as constructions 131*
   *The sociocultural construction of emotions 133*
   *The sociological construction of emotion 134*
   *The semantic pointer theory of emotion 136*
   *The neural construction of emotion 138*
   *Conclusion 140*

9  The role of emotion in educational decision-making 145
   *Introduction 145*
   *Normative versus descriptive accounts of decision-making 146*
   *High reason, classical decision-making, and bounded rationality 147*
   *Emotion enters the equation 150*
   *The somatic marker hypothesis 152*
   *Emotional decision-making 156*
   *Informed intuition 158*
   *Conclusion 159*

10 A naturalistic view of organizations 162
   *Introduction 162*
   *Organizations and environment 164*
   *Epistemological problems 166*
   *From environment to task environment 168*
   *From task environment to activity space and thinking with things 171*
   *Organizations as cognitive systems 173*
   *Conclusion 175*

*Index* 180

# FIGURES

| | | |
|---|---|---|
| 7.1 | Euclid's first proof that $AB^2 = AC^2 + BC^2$ | 113 |
| 7.2 | The Gougu theorem | 114 |
| 7.3 | Galileo's thought experiment | 115 |

# TABLES

1.1  Decision-Making to Solve Absenteeism  7
6.1  An Example of Epistemically Structured Problem-Solving  95

# PREFACE

The title, *Why Context Matters in Educational Leadership: A New Theoretical Understanding*, signals unambiguously that the subject matter of this book is the development and defence of context in educational leadership, and that such treatment offers a new theoretical perspective. In general, we view context as a set of constraints under which leadership is exercised. Leadership is multifaceted and has many goals. We therefore narrow our account of context as the study of those constraints that are to do with leading for the purpose of solving problems. This means that the demand for a solution, a normative requirement, is also part of the constraint set that defines the context in which leadership is exercised, that is, specifically with the aim of solving problems.

We distinguish three main contexts that help specify the constraint set under which problems are defined and their solutions worked out. The first is the physical world as described and understood by natural science. This is to acknowledge that humans, as physical entities, are constrained in their interactions with the physical world by what science reveals about the properties and laws of that world. A further methodological implication of this context is that theories of leadership must cohere with natural science in order to provide realistic accounts of leading. Accounts of what leadership can accomplish that are disconnected from what the physical world will allow, will fail in a fairly fundamental way: they won't provide an adequate framework for problem-solving. Leading cannot be indifferent to the laws governing this context.

Cohering with natural science has consequences for both ontology and epistemology. The ontology required for understanding leadership is that given by natural science. It is possible for theories of leadership to possess different or additional ontological features above those required as posits for the physical world. However, if these play an essential role in the activity of leading, then it is hard to say how they mesh with the causal machinery of physical contexts that make no use of entities beyond those required for natural science. With respect to ontology, our philosophical perspective is scientific realism.

Consequences for epistemology also flow from our realist ontology. Consider a theory of leadership whose justification is thought to reside in its fitting all the available data. An analogous case would be a curve that passes through all the available data points. But an arbitrarily large number of curves will also pass through those same data points. So, empirical adequacy is not sufficient for choosing among all those curves, or theories. Epistemology needs more resources, and in this case, it is the extra-empirical virtue of simplicity. Theories of leadership that don't require an expansion of ontology to achieve explanatory results enjoy the virtue of simplicity over those that do. Simplicity is not the only extra-empirical virtue we countenance. We also include comprehensiveness and coherence. In requiring a theory of leadership to enjoy both empirical and extra-empirical virtues, as well as cohering with natural science, we are defending a naturalistic coherentist epistemology.

A second context is the social. In understanding this context, we are guided by two broad considerations. The first can be regarded as a somewhat static requirement sometimes regarded as originating in a version of new institutional theory. The basic idea is that, say, a system of education within a particular jurisdiction is constrained by both constitutive rules and regulative rules. These rules help define the system's social ontology. Thus, the distinction between a school teacher and someone who is not a school teacher is constitutively defined by contracts of employment, conditions of initial certification and continuing performance, and broader statutory requirements as specified in the jurisdiction's laws. These are rules that constitute, in the sense of defining, what it means to distinguish a school teacher from others. In addition, much of the practice of teaching is controlled by regulative rules. These are rules that control existing practices. Just as driving a car is an existing practice that is regulated by rules of the road, so there are many regulative rules that govern the practice of teaching: curriculum and assessment requirements, timetabled teaching hours, welfare matters and parent engagement. Authorities associated with career structures flowing from these two types of rules also go some way towards establishing an organizational structure on schools and school systems. We see these rules as part of the constraint set that shapes what leadership can accomplish.

The second broad consideration is the recognition that a social epistemology is required for a theory of problem-solving in organizational contexts. There are two main reasons for requiring a social epistemology. The first is that problem solving in organizational contexts cannot be separated from implementation. That is, one needs more than a theory or a decision for how the problem is to be solved. The theory or decision needs to be implemented with the result that the problem is actually solved, and implementation is nearly always a collective process. The second reason for a social epistemology is that our knowledge is fallible, particularly so when it comes to understanding social processes. Problem-solving strategies that rely heavily on getting the problem solved at a first attempt come to grief over the fallibility inherent in those strategies. In response, we propose a more piecemeal strategy that incorporates feedback from implementations into making improvements into the theories that inform those implementations. Problem-solving is thus theorized as a trajectory through time that embodies an epistemology of progressive trial and error correction. Feedback from a less than successful implementation is fed back into revising the theory that drove the implementation where the revisions are made through improving the coherence of the theory as it faces the next cycle of implementation.

These broad considerations concerning social contexts are elaborated in later chapters as having a number of consequences for understanding leadership. Leadership occurs within the constraints of our preferred social ontology – the informal features of collective intentionality together with those formal features arising out of constitutive and regulative rules – and the constraints imposed by the world described by natural science. As a result, it is an open question as to the extent to which individual agency is the author of organizational performance. A focus on what leadership can accomplish abstracted from the natural and social constraints in which it occurs results in methodological individualism as the default explanatory option. The extent to which an organization's functioning can be reduced without remainder to an account of what leaders do cannot be settled in advance of some specification of the constraints under which an organization functions. This kind of pragmatism reflects our stance on the balance we strike between the explanatory value of social structuralism on the one hand and the value of individualist accounts of human cognition on the other.

A further consideration against methodological individualism is the distributed nature of the social epistemology of problem-solving. Once implementation is built into the account, the epistemic unit engaged in practice is the group of people learning how to solve the problem. Locating epistemic authority in an individual leader often results in confirmation bias, or failure to learn from feedback that the leader does not expect.

In giving accounts of social phenomena, theorists make use of some distinctions or devices that help in simplifying matters, especially the relationships between the individual and the organization. One of these is a distinction between reasons and causes. Explanations in social science are said to be about reasons, while explanations in natural science are about causes. Since reasons are the result of causal processes in human brains, we see reasons as rational causes. When we deal with rational decision-making, our research program places this on the agenda of cognitive neuroscience. Another related device is the use of belief-desire theory. It can be extremely useful in predicting human behaviour if behaviour is theorized as the rational coordination of beliefs and desires. We accept the usefulness of this in instrumentalist terms but again place it on the naturalist's agenda of expecting an eventual cashing out of the propositional attitudes in terms of a more fundamental science from a neurocognitive perspective. This position is sometimes called eliminative materialism. Some simplifications can be made without recourse to the details of a naturalistic ontology. For example, in explaining why a range of containers can hold a litre of liquid, it can be sufficient for an explanation to make use of the level of geometry and topology without dealing with the physical constituents of the containers. We accept the value of adopting higher levels of explanation where useful in social science. Nevertheless, we make some explorations in the direction of naturalizing the study of social systems.

The third context that we consider is that of the individual. Just as leadership is constrained by the natural and the social world, it is also constrained by the scope for human agency. In addition to our naturalistic approach to how individuals learn, represent knowledge, and decide, our naturalism also considers the role of emotion in these processes. These factors function as constraints within the individual that must comport with other constraints. The result, again, is that we think the scope for individual agency is much limited, and without recognizing these limits, serious attribution errors can occur that lead to errors in attributing accountability, and in recognizing the true scope for such matters as school reform, improvement, and change. A critical focus on the individual can result in seeing the unit of leadership as extending well beyond individuals and into groups and organizations. The taxonomy of contexts given above has emerged slowly over a research program of many years.

Some key aspects of this developing research program have issued in book-length publications and include the following. Lakomski's *Managing Without Leadership: Towards a Theory of Organizational Functioning* (Elsevier 2005) is the locus classicus. Developments on distributed leadership and on the structural importance of organizational problems and their solution can be found in Katyal and Evers *Teacher Leadership: New Conceptions for Autonomous Student Learning in the Age of the Internet* (Routledge 2014). A sustained debate over the value of leadership as an explanatory resource is contained in Lakomski, Eacott, and Evers (Eds.) *Questioning Leadership: New Directions for Educational Organizations* (Routledge 2017). Philosophically oriented discussions of educational leadership are in Eacott and Evers (Eds.) *New Directions in Educational Leadership Theory* (Routledge 2016). Finally, a guide to the philosophy of social science we draw on in our work is given in Haig and Evers *Realist Inquiry in Social Science* (Sage 2016).

*Why Context Matters in Educational Leadership: A New Theoretical Understanding* is the first book-length treatment of context that explores this fundamental issue. We have structured the book in three parts following the three broad domains of our argument which, naturally, intersect and overlap. All three parts serve to explore and provide examples of the ways in which 'context' matters, where 'context' is broadly but importantly understood as a set of constraints under which leadership is exercised. Such a broad definition, as will be seen, has considerable ramifications for understanding, exercising and researching leadership.

In Part I, Philosophical Foundations, we lay out some of the theoretical tools of our naturalistic program and argue that leader centrism cannot be the default explanatory option because context determines what matters. We develop this argument by means of an examination of the doctrine of methodological individualism, the theoretical core of leader centrism, and by way of recent scientific insights into the nature of cognition. Part II, The Social Context of Leadership, is the methodological heart of the book. We begin by arguing that some prior tentative theory is essential for any empirical inquiry into leadership to be possible. We urge theories that cohere with natural science. Also, there are fundamental epistemological indeterminacies of inference in empirical research that can only be narrowed by theories that emerge as sustaining inference to the best explanation, a coherentist constraint. But this is still not enough, as the empirical particularities of context matter: the specification of problems as constraints, plus the demand that something be done, the feedback from implementation that guides epistemically progressive trajectories of inquiry. Part III, Individuals in Context – Reason, Emotion, Organization, makes a fundamental point almost entirely overlooked in the decision-making literature. Any thoroughly naturalistic account of decision-making must include an account of emotion as integral to a defensible account of rationality. Such accounts of emotion that exist in the educational administration and leadership literature are 'add-ons' to the standard story. In our book, emotion emerges as central for theoretical and empirical reasons. In addition, by extending the theory of distributed cognition, we offer a naturalized account of organization, including organizations such as schools, where the traditional organization/environment relation is recast as interconnected parts of a broader, culture-based, cognitive system.

Studies of leadership in education, including organizations such as schools, can only progress if the importance of context is understood. In this book, we offer something of a roadmap for a theory of context that demonstrates the poverty of leader-centrism and foreshadows a rich and exciting future for the study of leadership. In all things leadership, context matters.

*Colin Evers and Gabriele Lakomski*
*Sydney and Melbourne, August 2021*

# ACKNOWLEDGEMENTS

A central claim of this work is that knowledge grows through discussion, debate, and critical engagement with ideas. The development of our own ideas is no exception, and we have benefitted from the advice of many colleagues, collaborators, anonymous referees, journal and book editors, and conference organizers. Key arguments concerning leadership and research methodology have been discussed with Scott Eacott, Richard Niesche, and Stephen Marshall. We are most grateful for their feedback and support. Collaborations with Kokila Katyal and Stephanie Chitpin have prompted further advances in our thinking about leadership and learning as processes. A collaboration with Brian Haig lead to significant gains in our thinking about the scope of scientific realism in understanding social science. For advice on some statistical matters, our thanks go to Andrew Martin and Jihyun Lee.

Early work on the book was presented at three leadership theory conferences on two continents: two organized by Scott Eacott in Australia, and one by our colleague Paul Begley in Canada. These conferences proved crucial for extending our own ideas, and we wish to acknowledge the contributions of Robert Donmoyer and Chris Hodgkinson in particular whose 'friendly fire' made us rethink some issues. But also, the critical debates around central issues of our work led the other participants to question their own leadership assumptions. Further presentations, discussions and debates occurred during a number of sessions organized by the Educational Leadership Special Interest Group at some annual meetings of the *Australian Association for Research in Education*. We thank the organizers, other symposiasts, the various audiences, and in particular Fenwick English for his detailed attention to our work.

Some earlier work in progress has been submitted for publication, a process that resulted in further improvements thanks to referees' comments and suggestions. For permission to reprint previously published material, we are grateful to

Taylor & Francis, Springer, and Emerald Publishing. Full bibliographic details of previous publications we have drawn on are given below:

Evers, C.W. (2012). Organizational contexts for lifelong learning: Individual and collective learning configurations. In D.N. Aspin, J.D. Chapman, K.R. Evans, & R. Bagnall (Eds.), *Second international handbook of lifelong learning* (pp. 61–76). Dordrecht: Springer.

Evers, C.W. (2007). Lifelong learning and knowledge: Towards a general theory of professional inquiry. In D.N. Aspin (Ed.), *Philosophical perspectives on lifelong learning* (pp. 173–188). Dordrecht: Springer.

Evers, C.W., & Lakomski, G. (2013) Methodological individualism, educational administration, and leadership, *Journal of Educational Administration and History*, 45(2), 159–173. https://doi.org/10.1080/00220620.2013.768969

https://www.tandfonline.com/doi/full/10.1080/00220620.2013.768969

Evers, C.W., & Lakomski, G. (2015) Naturalism and educational administration: New directions, *Educational Philosophy and Theory*, 47(4), 402–419. https://doi.org/10.1080/00131857.2014.976932

https://www.tandfonline.com/doi/full/10.1080/00131857.2014.976932

Evers, C.W. (2007) Culture, cognitive pluralism and rationality, *Educational Philosophy and Theory*, 39(4), 364–382. https://doi.org/10.1111/j.1469-5812.2007.00345.x. https://www.tandfonline.com/doi/abs/10.1111/j.1469-5812.2007.00345.x

Lakomski, G., & Evers, C.W. (2010). Passionate rationalism: The role of emotion in decision-making. *Journal of Educational Administration*, 48(4), 438–450. https://doi.org/10.1108/09578231011054707

# PART I
Philosophical foundations

# 1
# NATURALISM, EDUCATIONAL ADMINISTRATION, AND LEADERSHIP

An overview

## Introduction

The new directions we present derive from a relatively mature research program, one that has been in development for some 25 years. The core ideas of this research program have been elaborated in three books and is characterized by three distinctive features (Evers and Lakomski 1991, 1996, 2000). First is an argument that epistemology shapes both the content and the structure of theories in educational administration. Second is a defence of our preferred epistemology which we call naturalistic coherentism. The coherentism part says that theories are justified by a range of considerations, notably, empirical adequacy, consistency, simplicity, comprehensiveness, fecundity, and coherence in the sense that all parts fit together. Taken together, justifying a theory by appeal to both its empirical and so-called super-empirical virtues is known as coherence justification. Naturalism refers to the demand that whatever account is given of the details of this epistemology, it must cohere with natural science, or with that part of science most relevant for the study of knowledge, its dynamics and its justification. And the third feature is to work out in some detail the consequences of the first two features for accounts of administrative theory and its various components such as views of organizations, leadership, decision-making, training, and social science research methodology, to name just a few.

This research program falls within the broad tradition of scientific realism. During the 1950s when attempts to develop a science of administration dominated the scene, the philosophical model of what constitutes science was some form of positivism or, more precisely, logical empiricism. A science of administration was therefore expected to exhibit key features flowing from that model. An administrative theory would be a hypothetico-deductive structure, justified by confirming empirical evidence, with all theoretical terms admitting of

**4** Philosophical foundations

operational definitions and reflecting the exclusion of ethics. That is, it should copy the structure and processes of natural science as these are interpreted by logical empiricism.

With the collapse of positivism and its variants as an account of science, the scene shifted to possible post-positivist accounts, of which there were many. Our research program is part of this post-positivist shift, but in a particular direction. For us, a science of administration is simply one that coheres with natural science and is justified by appeals to coherence criteria of justification.

In general terms, the 'naturalism' that we refer to in natural science is the doctrine that claims about whatever happens in the world are framed in terms, ultimately, as being the result of interactions between those entities posited by our best natural science. These entities, in whatever form they take, are currently supposed to be instantiations of mass/energy. Over time, this doctrine has had some notable successes in explaining phenomena. We no longer look to the beliefs, desires, or intentions of gods to explain and predict weather, relying instead on complex, computational intensive models of the atmosphere and its dynamics. And we no longer explain the difference between living and non-living things in terms of the former's possession of a posited 'vital force'.

Whether the explanatory resources of naturalism are sufficient to explain ethics, particularly the giving of ethical justifications, or to explain cognition, particularly the giving of reasons, is more controversial. There is a long tradition that says natural science is an entirely inappropriate model for application to social science (Weber 1947; Winch 1958). Unsurprisingly, some of this controversy has spilled over into discussions of our research program. Sustained critiques of ideas in our three books can be found in Special Issues of the following journals: *Educational Management, Administration and Leadership* (1993, 21, 3), *Educational Administration Quarterly* (1996, 32, 3), and *Journal of Educational Administration* (2001, 39, 6). As a result of these and other critiques, we have been forced to modify our position on some matters, and to strengthen our arguments on others. In what follows, we sketch a number of these new developments.

## Particularity versus generality

One feature of coherence justification is that it appears to favour the development of large-scale theories, or at least theories as large as those proposed by earlier logical empiricist attempts to engage in theory building. For example, a preferred theory of leadership might seem to be the outcome of an epistemological argument showing that it is the most coherent theory among alternative rival theories. This is an interpretation that could, with justification, be applied to our earlier work. In a searching critique of this work, however, Donmoyer (2001) raised an important objection. Here is how he puts it:

> A commitment to utilize a number of theories rather than an all-encompassing, single theory to symbolically formulate administrative experience

would at least minimize the degree of abstraction required and, hence, lessen the distance between experiential understanding and the symbolic formulations we construct to represent it.

*(Donmoyer 2001, p. 561)*

His argument highlights the following dilemma. Inasmuch as a theory is general, it fails to be sensitive to the particularities of administrative situations. But the particularities of context can be decisive in determining whether the advice a theory gives will work or not. On the other hand, inasmuch as a theory is sensitive to the particularities of context, and hence where it is most relevant or useful, it fails to be comprehensive in the sense required by coherentist justification.

This dilemma is serious and requires an answer. The sort of answer that has been developed involves two components. The first is to allow context to define the limits of comprehensiveness. The second is to focus on applying a coherentist epistemology thus modified to the process of building good theories. To see how it works, consider the case of defending a view of leadership that is most effective for promoting student learning. Perhaps the best known meta-analysis of research studies that captures the standard approach is that conducted by Robinson et al. (2008). The basic idea is to calculate from the research studies the effect sizes that different instantiations of leadership – in this case transformational leadership versus instructional leadership – have on measures of student learning. The result in that particular meta-analysis was that instructional leadership had the larger effect size.

But now consider the role of context by imagining two very different schools. The first is in an area of high socio-economic status (SES) and staffed predominantly by very experienced teachers, well trained and well versed in the learning needs of their particular cohorts of students. Under these conditions, the model of school leadership that works best for the promotion of student learning may well be distributed to a large number of teacher-leaders with the principal's role having very little instructional content. On the other hand, another type of school, say one in a low SES area staffed mostly by teachers with relatively modest experience, could well be greatly advantaged by having a principal whose major strength is instructional leadership. So, the question of what type of leadership most promotes student learning can only be answered when the context for exercising leadership is known or understood. What counts as the most coherent approach to leadership is therefore relative to the particularities of the schools.

Specifying the differences in contexts is one fairly broad way of arguing the particularities of leadership options. In addition, a more fine-grained, more nuanced view of leadership can be defended by looking at the details of what is required to improve student learning. In his book *Visible Learning* (2008), John Hattie summarizes a vast number of research studies – some 200 meta-analyses of 50,000 studies on a total of 200 million students – and gives the effect size of a range of factors in promoting student learning. So, to improve student learning, school leaders would want to target and strengthen a number of practices that have the largest effect sizes. The issues here are, first, not all schools are the same in their current practices, which means that the tasks of leaders, and possibly the types of leadership most appropriate will differ. Second, Donmoyer's dilemma breaks out again at the level of implementation because social science is too general to be relevant for the local particularities. (We take these issues up in more detail in Chapter 4.) Theories need to be developed tailored for particular contexts.

The solution we have adopted to deal with this issue is to focus on an epistemology of knowledge building. Research done by Chitpin and Evers (2005, 2012), Evers and Katyal (2007, 2008), and Evers (2007a, 2007b) supports the notion that theories in applied social science can be built up through a process of guided trial and error of the sort that Karl Popper (1979) proposed to explain the growth of scientific knowledge. We explain what we call 'Popper Cycles' in detail in Chapters 2 and 6, but in general terms, this problem-solving model begins with an initial problem to be solved, where 'problem' is to be understood as a set of constraints plus the demand that something be done. We start with an initial tentative theory for dealing with the problem and proceed with the process of error elimination that involves testing the theory to see if it meets the demands of problem-solving. The next problem to be solved arises out of the error elimination process, and the process continues over numerous cycles where each new tentative theory is the result of making coherent adjustments to earlier theories in the light of feedback evidence. Here is a simple example of how the model operates. At a school in a relatively low SES area with a large multicultural population, one factor that is thought to diminish student learning is a 20% student absentee rate on Fridays and Mondays. However, for the school's leaders it is not obvious what is to be done, especially in a time before text messaging was common as is the case in this example. There's no textbook answer. Instead, staff try out different ideas, measuring the effects of each. Table 1.1 captures this process.

Problems like these, and many others, are rarely solved by someone making a single correct decision. Administrative life is too messy and complex for that. Rather, the reality is more often captured by problems-solutions trajectories that are extended through time.

A school leader trying to improve student learning will therefore most likely have multiple trajectories of Popper Cycles all dealing with a range of proposals for solving the main learning problem. Under these conditions, there is value in having the different trajectories cohere, so that the solution for one issue does not impede the solving of another. Because of the additional nuances of multiple combinations of different sub-problems, all chosen subject to their relevance for context, what leaders do with the learning problem will be almost unique to context. The upshot is that a content-based approach to a theory of leadership does not make much sense, except as a starting point to knowledge building. A more useful approach is a process-based approach, one that sees leadership as centrally concerned with critical self-learning. The best theory of leadership

**TABLE 1.1** Decision-Making to Solve Absenteeism

| *Popper cycle 1* | *Popper cycle 2* | *Popper cycle 3* | *Popper cycle 4* |
| --- | --- | --- | --- |
| P1: Absenteeism among students peaks at 20% on Fridays and Mondays disrupting the pacing of classroom teaching. | P2: How can we communicate with parents of students who are absent on Fridays and Mondays? | P3: How can we arrange for letters to reach parents without being intercepted by students? | P4: How can the school communicate directly with parents of chronically absent students? |
| TT1: Mark the roll when school starts and then utilize all general staff to phone the home of all absent students. | TT2: Send a letter from the school to the address where students live, asking parents to contact the school to discuss the absenteeism problem in relation to their child. | TT3: Send letters to parents in unmarked envelopes. | TT4: Adopt a more piecemeal approach. Review all school functions where parents are able to attend, such as parent-teacher evenings, reporting meetings, etc. Attempt to adapt these so that there is more opportunity to raise the absentee problem for discussion. |
| EE1: There are very few parents at home to answer the calls. The strategy has very little impact on the level of absenteeism. | EE2: Very few parents make arrangements to discuss the problem, and data from roll calls still indicate high levels of absenteeism. This is puzzling, so further analysis and investigation was undertaken. It appeared that students who were almost always home before parents were intercepting the letters easily identified by their official school envelopes. | EE3: There is some improvement in the number of parents responding to the letter and a modest improvement in the absenteeism problem. But given the number of letters sent, the modest response rate is still puzzling. More follow-up produced the following likely explanation. The school's population is highly multicultural with some 36 different community languages spoken in homes. And the letters were in English. Evidently, it was common for students to translate the letters. | EE4: Progress is gradual, but parents are slowly made aware. School council and staff begin to explore other strategies for dealing with the problem. For example, student welfare policy, adjusting the timetable to reduce some of the bad effects of student absenteeism on Fridays and Mondays. |

**8** Philosophical foundations

will therefore be relativized to the context where the process of theory building resulted in the development of theories that solved the problems of practice. And this effectively deals with the dilemma that Donmoyer raised.

## Naturalism and ethics

Naturalism, as we use the term, has traditionally faced two major challenges. The first is over ethics. Simply put, naturalism appears to deal with claims about what the world is like; with giving an account of what is the case. Ethics, on the other hand, deals with matters of what ought or ought not to be done; with the goodness or badness of what obtains; its justice or injustice. Naturalism is about facts, whereas ethics is about values, and these two categories are thought to be logically distinct. Simon's classic *Administrative Behavior* (1947/1976) has an entire chapter devoted to defending this distinction and working out its consequences, and in the subsequent broad 'science of administration' tradition including the multiple editions of Hoy and Miskel's text *Educational Administration: Theory, Research, and Practice*, little mention is made of ethics, even in its latest, ninth, edition (2013). Our work opposes this omission and argues for the integration of ethics into administrative theory.

The second major challenge concerns naturalism's treatment of cognition and human subjectivity, especially its place in the explanation of social phenomena. We will take a little time to explain this before returning to ethics because there is a link. Later, we will also have more to say about the neuroscience of cognition. At its most fundamental level, this turns on a dispute at the foundations of modern sociology, that between reasons and causes. In general, while Durkheim (1895/1958) defended a science of sociology that looked for explanations in terms of causes, Weber (1947) argued for a method of understanding that appealed to reasons for human action. Without getting into too much detail, the sort of resolution that is often employed is to treat reasons as rational causes (Davidson 1963). Newell and Simon's (1976/1990) influential physical-symbol system hypothesis (PSSH) embodies this approach. The hypothesis states that "A physical-symbol system has the necessary and sufficient means for general intelligent action" (p. 111). Symbols are physical patterns subject to the laws of physics, with systems being physical entities that operate on the symbols. What makes the system describable as intelligent is "that in any real situation behaviours appropriate to the ends of the system and adaptive to the demands of the environment can occur …" (Newell and Simon 1976/1990, p. 111).

In our research program we have had two concerns with the PSSH. First, in being shaped quite conspicuously by the digital computer as a model for cognition, our response has been to argue that this is a poor model for human cognition. Instead, we have proposed, over the years, that models of human cognition should be based on models of how information is represented and processed in the human brain (see Evers 1990, 1994, 1998, 2000, 2003; Evers and Lakomski 2000). This central aspect of our research program is developed further in various chapters of this book. However, we here note and respond to one possible objection. Why can't we interpret the PSSH very generally so that it includes, for example, the kinds of representations and processes suggested by the various artificial neural network mathematical models of brain processes: vector representations of inputs, numerical values for weights representing synaptic junctions, weight adjustment algorithms for incremental learning, and so on? Well, either we can, or we can't. If we can, then the PSSH becomes a species of functionalism with the only major empirical constraint on cognitive architectures and processes being that desired outputs are produced from desired inputs by some physical mechanism. In abstracting itself away from any particular mechanisms, it robs itself of any useful contribution to understanding how leaders and other contributors can make good decisions, educational or otherwise. On the other hand, if it cannot be generalized beyond its original computer context, that of the digital von Neumann machine, the same conclusion follows.

The second main objection to the PSSH concerns the importance of emotion for rational decision-making (Lakomski and Evers 2010, 2012). There is empirical evidence for this from neuroscience. Damasio (1994) provides an early systematic marshalling of this evidence together with an account of the neural mechanisms involved. Basically, people who have suffered damage to those parts of the brain that are responsible for affect find that even though their intellect may remain intact, they end up making bad decisions. A simplifying analogy might help explain why this is plausible. Suppose you wish to decide from a menu, what meal to order subjects to the constraint that you have no sense of smell or taste. You might then choose on, say, grounds of nutritional value. But suppose that you don't care about nutritional value, or cost for that matter, or any other possible feature of the meals. Without some feeling of preference, the basis for deciding begins to become indistinguishable from coin tossing (Lakomski and Evers 2012, p. 654). In order to solve problems, or search for solutions, or play chess, computers need to have algorithms programmed into them in order to have the required preferences for these tasks. However, the generality/particularity problem with PSSH breaks out again.

Our dispute is not one of computer versus the brain, as should be clear from our championing of neural network models of cognition. Rather, we are objecting to the adoption of a favoured general characterization of the computer as a model for cognition. (For another, sustained attack on the PSSH, see Brooks 1990.) This is the reason why the approach we have used in our work is to see value in computer models of human cognition inasmuch as those models are able to represent important aspects of how information and its dynamics occur in the brain. Fortunately, since about the mid-1980s, much neural network software has become available, though of varying representational faithfulness. These are particulars, but in the right direction. Later, when we talk about the neuroscience of emotion in decision-making, we will make mention of some of the software that has been designed to simulate aspects of this.

**10** Philosophical foundations

## Naturalising ethics and its critics

Let us return to the first major challenge to naturalism: ethics. We will begin with a little background concerning our published position, and then move on to recent developments. (The original foundations of our position, and arguments for it, can be found in Evers and Lakomski 1991, pp. 166–191.) There have been two main arguments used to challenge the idea of a naturalistic ethics. The first is the well-known claim, originating with Hume, that you cannot derive an 'ought' from an 'is'. The reason this claim is important is because if you believe that all the evidence for a theory is empirical evidence, then our best theories about the way the natural world is will not contain any warranted ethical claims. Values simply cannot be derived from facts. In reply, we have argued that there is more to the justification of a theory than its empirical adequacy. Theories are also judged on their super-empirical virtues. Thus, theories need to be consistent, or free from contradictions. A theory is better than another if it is more comprehensive or explains more things; if it is simpler than another in the sense that it makes fewer assumptions to achieve its explanatory reach; if it coheres with other theories that enjoy these virtues. Such is the nature of coherence justification. However, this broadened view of justification now allows ethical claims to be justified. For example, different views of leadership require both the supposition of a certain amount of ethical infrastructure and its practice in order to be implemented successfully. Thus, the social arrangements required for being a good instructional leader arguably require that your expertise is both presumed and trusted; that you instruct with respect to your audience; that the audience values your knowledge as a way of advancing the value they place on certain educational goals; that these may be defended by the way they cohere with the empirical conditions for making a better society; and so on. Our model of leadership as involving critical self-learning (and the promotion of organizational learning) also comes with a preferred ethics, including: tolerance of different points of view; commitment to evidence and procedures for its assessment that are as impartial as we can manage; procedural fairness in the use of knowledge; the adoption of social practices that don't compromise future learning in leadership contexts.

Starratt (1998, pp. 248–249) makes a similar point when he talks about the ethics of scholarship. He argues that:

> Scholarship is meant to be trusted by the public, because the scholar is assumed to be committed to the fullest and clearest understanding of what he or she is studying, and to the honest and undistorted representation of that knowledge as circumstances allow. Scholars cannot report their findings in dishonest ways, bending their conclusions to fit a preconceived theory to which they have personally committed their reputation.
> 
> *(Starratt 1998, p. 148)*

In his massive, two volume, *The Open Society and Its Enemies* (1945/1995), Popper uses his fallibilist epistemology and its methodology for promoting the growth of knowledge, to argue for a view of liberal democracy against varieties of totalitarianism, with all the ethics that coheres with his position.

Churchland (2011) provides a congenial link between ethics, epistemology, and the naturalizing of both that draws on the most recent research in neuroscience. Her response to the use of Hume's claim about an is/ought bifurcation makes a point similar to ours: "In a much broader sense of 'infer' than *derive* you can infer (*figure out*) what you ought to do, drawing on knowledge, perception, emotions, and understanding, and balancing considerations against each other" (Churchland 2011, p. 6). Balancing considerations against each other is construed as constraint satisfaction, a notion congenial to us because we define problems, following Nickles (1981), as a set of constraints plus the demand that something be done. The tentative theories of our Popper Cycles are proposals for meeting these constraints and thus solving the problem. Another reason for favouring constraint satisfaction as an interpretation of coherence justification is because it permits, more readily, a naturalistic account of coherence. The person who has done most to develop constraint satisfaction neural network software for application to choosing theories using coherence epistemology is Paul Thagard, who developed the Computational Epistemology Laboratory at the University of Waterloo. (See http://cogsci.uwaterloo.ca/index.html, and also Thagard and Verbeurgt 1998.) Thagard's models permit the smooth integration of ethics into theories up for adjudication, and hence permit the justification of ethical claims (Thagard 1999).

The second major objection to naturalizing ethics comes from an argument developed by the philosopher G.E. Moore (1903/1988, pp. 5–15) who thinks that defining ethical terminology, such as 'good' or 'just' or 'right' in terms of natural features such as happiness, or growth of knowledge, commits what he calls the 'naturalistic fallacy'. His argument assumes some technical philosophical machinery. He first distinguishes between analytic statements and those that are synthetic. Analytic statements are supposed to be true by virtue of the meanings of terms, whereas synthetic statements are true by virtue of the way the world is. The next move is to claim that true definitions, that is, those that capture the nature of an object or idea, are always analytic. He then claims that "propositions about the good are all of them synthetic and never analytic; and that is plainly no trivial matter" (Moore 1903, p. 7). How does he know this? Answer: by the use of what he calls the 'open question argument'. Here is how it works. A statement that says, "a bachelor is an unmarried adult male" is thought to be analytic because it doesn't make sense to ask the question "Is a bachelor an unmarried adult male?". A statement such as "A bachelor is a sad and lonely person", is reckoned to be synthetic because we can always ask, "Is that really the case?". Every naturalistic account of good will fail the open question challenge because it will always make sense to ask, "Is good really (for example) the greatest happiness for the greatest number?".

Our response to this argument, early and late, has been to follow Quine (1951, 1960) in denying the analytic/synthetic distinction (Evers 1979, 1987, 1993).

What makes, say, Newton's second law of motion (F=ma) so good as a definition of force in non-relativistic contexts is because it is embedded in a good theory that enjoys the virtues of coherence. It is part of a wider, interlocking set of claims that mutually reinforce each other, both in terms of empirical adequacy and super-empirical virtues. And so it is with ethics. There is now a large body of research that seeks to understand how human brains come to acquire values. Churchland (2011) surveys much of this research when she comes to answer some fundamental questions:

> Where do values come from? How did brains come to care about others? If my genes organize my brain to attend to my survival, to reproduce and pass on those genes, how can they organize my brain to value others? *Some,* but only some, of the neurobiology of this is beginning to be understood. . . . What does it mean for a system of neurons to care about or to value something? On these questions, we do know quite a lot, and the answers will launch us into the more complex domain of social caring
> 
> *(Churchland 2011, pp. 12–13)*

So far, we have extended our treatment of ethics only a little beyond positing the most appropriate ethical infrastructure for maintaining a view of administrative ethics tied to an account of leadership as involving critical self-learning. However, we have looked at an important preliminary matter: the role of emotion in decision-making and its associated causal features as revealed by neuroscience.

## Cognition, educational administration, and neuroscience

Making decisions has always been a central, if not the central, part of the educational administrator's work and belongs within a broader cognitive perspective on organizational structure (Schwenk 1988; Evers and Lakomski 1996, Ch. 8). At the heart of much of the decision-making literature is the hope, as Hoy and Tarter (2010, p. 351) recently put it, that "... if leaders would only get the process right, they would make better decisions." However, it has long been recognized that there is no one best way to do so. Endemic uncertainty and cognitive limitations invest all human decision-making and making optimal decisions in the cognitive perspective requires 'cognitive simplification' (Schwenk 1988, p. 42). The most prominent attempt is the concept of 'bounded rationality' (Simon 1976, 1987), while another is known as the 'heuristics and biases' approach that proposes 'rules of thumb' to deal with complex problems and decision-maker bias (Kahneman 2002). However, as we have indicated, not only can cognition and emotion not be neatly separated in real biological brains (e.g. Panksepp 2003), but also for decision-making to be possible at all, emotion is essential. Recent scientific evidence that supports this claim is discussed especially in Chapters 8 and 9.

The emphasis on the biological brain's pattern recognition and decentralized processing abilities has not only undermined the distinction between emotion and reason, it has provided evidence that emotion is integral for rational, good decision-making to happen at all. The neurocognitive details of how precisely cognition interacts with emotion are the subject of ongoing research (and controversy) in affective and cognitive neuroscience. In general, the neural circuits of emotion are closely interconnected with those of cognition, and emotion circuits in turn consist of subcomponents. On the evidence available, it is no longer defensible to consider emotion as one single process. Furthermore, the traditional assumption held, *inter alia*, in (educational) psychology that emotions are *conscious* feeling states, has also been threatened. In recent discussions of emotion in the education literature (e.g. Schutz and Zembylas 2009; Special Issue of the *Journal of Educational Administration* 2010) emotions are treated as the discrete entities we know under the folk psychological labels of anger, fear, happiness, etc. To understand 'emotion', however, the level of analysis our naturalistic perspective engages is not at the level of commonsense understandings. Rather, we consider 'emotions' as multilevel, constructed phenomena that cannot be understood from one disciplinary vantage point alone. This is the focus of the discussion in Chapter 8 that presents the most recent scientific accounts of what emotions are.

It is one thing to say that cognition and emotion are neurally interconnected and that decision-making is therefore both 'emotional' and 'rational', thus, arguably, robbing the cognitive perspective of the point of the distinction. It is quite another to claim that rational decision-making, or choice, *depends* on emotion.

Here is the kind of clinical evidence that is relevant. 'Elliott', the name Damasio gave a patient who had a tumour removed from an area to do with affect, found that the surgery left him physically capable and with his mental abilities intact, but that it had fundamentally impaired his ability to make decisions in his social life (Damasio et al. 1991; Bechara and Damasio 2005; Naqvi et al. 2006). In healthy humans the cognitive-affective circuitry supporting decision-making does make choice possible, for reasons that may be initially opaque, as in hunches or gut reactions, but may become conscious on reflection. An initial gut reaction assigns a 'valence' before any *conscious deliberation* of future action takes place, and thus helps expedite rational decision-making while conserving computational energy by reducing the range of options to be processed. In this fundamental sense affect is integral to making good choices in ordinary life while its absence can lead to disaster (see Cisek 2012 for an interesting account of how the brain decides between actions).

In social life in general, and in school life in particular, decision-making more often than not happens in group contexts where people's emotions play an important role. But unlike the verbal exchanges of group members emotions get conveyed by *emotional contagion* (Hatfield et al. 1994; Barsade 2002; Lakomski and Evers 2012), a process that is fast, non-conscious, and automatic. As affect or emotion attaches to any decision, group decision-making is thus inherently 'emotional', as we saw above. This raises the problem of how to incorporate affect while making decisions that are the best possible for whatever issue or problem needs to be solved. The balance we need to strike is between 'preference' and 'impartiality'. This is particularly important where the outcome matters. Consider, for example, a school council that needs to find means that safeguard a school's long-term survival.

Every group member has an emotional stake in the outcome, and simple voting, for instance, may achieve consensus but leave many frustrated. If a consensus is reached quickly, it may not represent the best possible outcome. In other words, an emotional consensus may not equal a good decision. In this case, investigation of other possibilities that may both satisfy members' emotional commitments and present an objectively better solution has been short-circuited. A solution reached should be testable in light of evidence, that is, it should be epistemically progressive, and it should be one to which members commit emotionally. In the process, what needs to be warded against is that a group develops *confirmation bias,* the view that a favourite idea is kept no matter what (Hutchins 1995). As such bias prevents critical examination of any evidence, it stops learning, and in doing so it stops striving for agreement amongst differing views which is inimical to organizational growth.

The most promising way of learning more about how to account for and encompass the complexity of real-life group decision-making is the development of decision procedures that are able both to model large-group (rather than pair-wise, e.g. Thagard and Kroon 2006) decision-making and that include means to model emotional contagion. Such models do not yet exist, but we have made some suggestions on how to go about it by drawing on social network theory, and the notion of 'small worlds' (Watts and Strogatz 1998; Evers 2012). Furthermore, as it is necessary to avoid confirmation bias (or Groupthink, in an older terminology), a group decision model needs to be able to account for learning and the conditions under which social formations can accomplish this. This condition can be modelled under social epistemology which is a further application of social network models (for details, see Lakomski and Evers 2012, p. 666 onwards). There are interesting implications of such modelling, and we discuss some of these in Chapter 5.

To the extent that we have discussed emotion in relation to rational decision-making, we have contributed to its rehabilitation in what was believed to be a quintessentially non-emotional activity.

In the next section we explore further features of cognition as decentered, embodied, and embedded, and how such a broadening affects notions of leadership and organization.

## Leadership, distributed cognition, and organization

Implicit in all leadership theories is a view of cognition, or a theory of mind, as leaders have to learn how to become leaders. Both traditional and modern leadership theories, however, imply 'leader centrism', the view that it is the leader's skill set, particularly his/her cognitive abilities, that cause organizational outcomes, an assumption enshrined in the doctrine of *Methodological Individualism* (Evers and Lakomski 2013). But 'cognitive centrism' is not a feature of any brain, as we indicated earlier. Nor is it beholden to hierarchy. Cognition in organizations is *distributed* and leader cognition is just part of the bigger picture (Lakomski 2005). It is thus neither static nor simply distributed in the manner of the functional division of labour characteristic of modern economies. Cognition is 'distributed' in a more fundamental sense (e.g. Hollan et al. 2000; Clark and Chalmers 1998; Hutchins 2010; Barsalou 2010; Anderson et al. 2012; Pezzulo et al. 2013). Distributed cognition is an important research perspective that investigates the dynamic interactions between brain processes/mind, bodily interactions, and the environment that together propose "a unifying view of cognition" (Pezzulo et al. 2013, p. 1).

An important starting point is the fact that brains have limited computational powers that necessitate offloading intellectual (as well as physical) tasks. The results of such cognitive outsourcing are the very artefacts and systems agents invent that in turn engender new developments, thus extending cognitive grasp by creating new 'cognitive tools' (Wilson 2010). Such 'bootstrapping cycles' involve the body and the world, and in this way *supersize* the mind, as Clark (2008) put it.

The external environment on this view is not simply in a supply relationship to what happens in the brain. Summarized simply: goings-on in the brain and body and goings-on outside of it *together* constitute human cognition and mind and form a *cognitive system*. Cognitive phenomena thus expanded redraw traditional boundaries of what is considered the appropriate unit of analysis, raising the issue of "… what are the canonical instances of cognitive process and which are special cases of more general phenomena [?]" (Hutchins 2010, p. 712).

We know from everyday experience that the body plays a significant part in the cognitive system (e.g. Kirsh 2010). For example, there is evidence that manipulating objects can improve reading comprehension in school-age children (Glenberg et al. 2007), and while teachers of mathematics have known this for a long time, it is a novel observation in the teaching of reading comprehension.

Further support for, and extension of, distributed cognition has recently been offered in form of a new concept of brain organization: 'neural reuse' (Anderson 2010; Anderson et al. 2012). Neural reuse explains how biological brains acquire new abilities. Unlike neural plasticity (a kind of reuse), neural reuse claims that "neural circuits established for one purpose are exapted (exploited, recycled, redeployed) during evolution or normal development, and are put to different uses, often without losing their original functions" (Anderson 2010, pp. 245–246). This means that "the differences between cognitive domains are marked less by differences in the neural circuitry devoted to each, and more by the different patterns of cooperation between mostly shared circuitry" (Anderson et al. 2012, p. 721). Such a softening (if not outright elimination) of boundaries, if correct, has important, potentially radical, implications: (1) the traditional assumption of anatomical modularity is no longer plausible, as cognitive faculties are not located in specific brain areas; and (2) separate cognitive faculties are difficult to determine. The most far-reaching consequences of neural reuse is that if perception, action, and cognition are all supported by domain unrestricted components, "segregating the study of mind into those particular neighbourhoods is more likely gerrymandering than carving nature at its joints" (Anderson et al. 2012, p. 721). Also, the localization of cognitive faculties shows itself as critical and, for the time being, as indeterminate. (See Chapter 8 for more detail on recent accounts of brain functioning.)

The view that emerges from this research is that cognition is supported by softly assembled, temporary coalitions of entities engaged in collaborative tasks, exhibiting interaction dominant dynamics, or 'synergies' (Anderson et al. 2012, p. 719). The upshot of this is that it is near impossible to determine what causes what in the system. Synergies are just the kind of thing that characterize the flight patterns of birds in that these patterns are characteristic of emergent, dynamical, de-centralized (or distributed) systems that do not rely on a central organizer, or leader (Reynolds 1987; Lakomski 2005). Patterns or formations emerge in response to the ever-changing dynamics of the external system: every bird can be a 'leader', and, as Anderson et al. (2012, p. 719), muse, 'any old bird will do'. This example also demonstrates just how fundamentally implicated the environment is in determining cognition.

A further profound implication of neural reuse is that it breaks down the assumption of the individual agent as autonomous and bounded, the hallmark of Methodological Individualism, and thus accounts of leadership that depend on it (Evers and Lakomski 2013). It may now be more appropriate to speak of agents as forming cognitive systems, or synergies, as these were defined above. (For further examples of synergies, see Harrison and Richardson 2009; Riley et al. 2011.) As a consequence, the functional grouping of individual agents for a specific purpose and limited time, acting as one coherent unit, can be said to exhibit group cognition (Theiner et al. 2010).

Much of the detail of neural reuse theory is still speculative. Even so, it has considerable implications for leadership and organization. Most importantly, as causality in synergies is multi-directional, and perhaps even impossible to determine, any *a priori* attribution of causality is presumptuous. In the field of education and leadership, the *a priori* belief that leaders change organizations or determine outcomes is as eccentric as attributing the sound produced by clapping to the activity of just one hand. What any particular educational outcome is attributable to can only be determined after theoretical and causal analysis. On this view, the focus shifts from studying the individual teacher's/leader's inherent features as the relevant unit of analysis to units defined in terms of dynamic patterns of correlation across elements. That is, the study of leadership becomes part and parcel of the study of *the cognitive ecology of organizational functioning*. Yet another implication, only hinted at here, is that distributed cognition sanctions flexible organizational structures, where the nature of the appropriate structure may depend on the nature of purpose or task and is delimited by space and time. The task of coordination comes centre-stage.

## Conclusion

One of the advantages of working out an epistemological accommodation between a social science, such as administration and natural science is that we can help ourselves to the best natural science for understanding social phenomena. These understandings need not give the whole story – there are, after all, many contributions to be made by theories of culture, ethnicity, power and its distribution, and a range of hermeneutically relevant interpretations. Nevertheless, for a research program to cut itself off from knowledge that natural science can provide, for epistemic reasons, is to presume that such an epistemology is more warranted than the scientific knowledge it discounts. We find this presumption implausible. The penalty for finding it implausible is that our research program tends to be rather open-ended and changing in light of new science. But this is to be expected from our acceptance of fallibilism, naturalism, and coherentism.

## References

Anderson, M.L. (2010). Neural reuse: A fundamental organizational principle of the brain. *Behavioral and Brain Sciences*, 33(4), 245–313.
Anderson, M.L., Richardson, M.J., & Chemero, A. (2012). Eroding the boundaries of cognition: Implications of embodiment. *Topics in Cognitive Science*, 4(4), 717–730.
Barsade, S.G. (2002). The ripple effect: Emotional contagion and its influence on group behaviour. *Administrative Science Quarterly*, 47(4), 644–675.
Barsalou, L.W. (2010). Grounded cognition: Past, present, and future. *Topics in Cognitive Science*, 2(4), 716–724.
Bechara, A., & Damasio, A.R. (2005). The somatic marker hypothesis: A neural theory of economic decision. *Games and Economic Behavior*, 52(2), 336–372.
Brooks, R.A. (1990). Elephants don't play chess, *Robotics and Autonomous Systems*, 6, 3–15.
Churchland, P.S. (2011). *Braintrust*. Princeton: Princeton University Press.
Cisek, P. (2012). Making decisions through a distributed consensus. *Current Opinion in Neurobiology*, 22(6), 927–936.
Clark, A. (2008). *Supersizing the mind*. Oxford: Oxford University Press.
Clark, D., & Chalmers, D. (1998). The extended mind. *Analysis*, 58(1), 10–23.
Chitpin, S., & Evers, C.W. (2005). Teacher professional development as knowledge building: A popperian analysis. *Teachers and Teaching: Theory and Practice*, 11(4), 419–433.
Chitpin, S., & Evers, C.W. (2012). Using Popper's philosophy of science to build pre-service teachers' knowledge. *International Journal of Education*, 4(4), 144–156.
Damasio, A.R. (1994). *Descartes' error: Emotion, reason, and the human brain*. New York: Avon.
Damasio, A.R., Tranel, D., & Damasio, H. (1991). Somatic markers and the guidance of behavior: Theory and preliminary testing. In H.S. Levin, H.M. Eisenberg, & A.L. Benton (Eds.), *Frontal lobe function and dysfunction*, New York: Oxford University Press.
Davidson, D. (1963). Actions, reasons, and causes. *Journal of Philosophy*, 60(23), 685–700.

Donmoyer, R. (2001). Evers and Lakomski's search for leadership's Holy Grail (and the intriguing ideas they encountered along the way. *Journal of Educational Administration*, 39(6), 554–572.
Durkheim, E. (1895/1958). *The rules of sociological method* (trans: Solvay, S.A., & Mueller, J.H.). New York, NY: The Free Press.
Evers, C.W. (1979). Analytic philosophy of education: From a logical point of view. *Educational Philosophy and Theory*, 11(2), 1–16.
Evers, C.W. (1987). Naturalism and philosophy of education. *Educational Philosophy and Theory*, 19(2), 11–21.
Evers, C.W. (1990). Educating the brain. *Educational Philosophy and Theory*, 22(2), 65–80.
Evers, C.W. (1993). Analytic and post-analytic philosophy of education. *Discourse*, 13(2), 35–45.
Evers, C.W. (1994). Administrative decision-making as pattern processing. In F. Crowther et al. (Eds.), *The workplace in education* (pp. 266–275). Sydney: ACEA Yearbook 1994, Edward Arnold.
Evers, C.W. (1998). Decision-making, models of mind, and the new cognitive science. *Journal of School Leadership*, 8(2), 94–108.
Evers, C.W. (2000). Connectionist modelling and education. *Australian Journal of Education*, 44(3), 209–225.
Evers, C.W. (2003). Naturalizing ethical judgment: A neurocomputational perspective. In E. Samier (Ed.), *Ethical foundations for educational administration* (pp. 235–252). London: Routledge/Falmer.
Evers, C.W. (2007a). Culture, cognitive pluralism and rationality. *Educational Philosophy and Theory*, 39(4), 364–382.
Evers, C.W. (2007b). Lifelong learning and knowledge: Towards a general theory of professional inquiry. In D.N. Aspin (Ed.), *Philosophical perspectives on lifelong learning* (pp. 173–188). Dordrecht: Springer.
Evers, C.W. (2012). Organizational contexts for lifelong learning: Individual and collective learning configurations. In D.N. Aspin et al. (Eds.), *Second international handbook of lifelong learning* (pp. 61–76). Dordrecht: Springer.
Evers, C.W., & Katyal, K.R. (2007). Paradoxes of leadership: Contingencies and critical learning. *South African Journal of Education*, 27(3), 377–390.
Evers, C.W., & Katyal, K. (2008). Educational leadership in Hong Kong schools: Critical reflections on changing themes. *Journal of Educational Administration and History*, 40(3), 251–264.
Evers, C.W., & Lakomski, G. (1991). *Knowing educational administration*. Oxford: Pergamon Press.
Evers, C.W., & Lakomski, G. (1996). *Exploring educational administration*. Oxford: Pergamon Press.
Evers, C.W., & Lakomski, G. (2000). *Doing educational administration*. Oxford: Pergamon Press.
Evers, C.W., & Lakomski, G. (2013). Methodological individualism, educational administration, and leadership. *Journal of Educational Administration and History*, 45(2), 159–172.
Glenberg, A.M., Brown, M., & Levin, J.R. (2007). Enhancing comprehension in small reading groups using a manipulation strategy. *Contemporary Educational Psychology*, 32(3), 389–99.
Harrison, S.J., & Richardson, M.J. (2009). Horsing around: Spontaneous four-legged coordination. *Journal of Motor Behavior*, 41(6), 519–524.
Hatfield, E., Cacioppo, J., & Rapson, R.L. (1994). *Emotional contagion*. New York: Cambridge University Press.
Hattie, J. (2008). *Visible learning*. London: Routledge.

Hoy, W.K., & Miskel (2013). *Educational administration: Theory, research, and practice*. Boston: McGraw Hill.
Hoy, W.K., & Tarter, C.J. (2010). Swift and smart decision making: Heuristics that work. *Journal of Educational Administration*, 24(4), 351–358.
Hutchins, E. (1995). *Cognition in the wild*. Cambridge, MA: MIT Press.
Hutchins, E. (2010). Cognitive ecology. *Topics in Cognitive Science*, 2(4), 705–715.
Hollan, J., Hutchins, E., & Kirsh, D. (2000). Distributed cognition: Toward a new foundation for human–computer interaction research. *ACM Transactions on Computer-Human Interaction*, 7(2), 174–196.
Kahneman, D. (2002). *Maps of bounded rationality: A perspective on intuitive judgment and choice*. Nobel Prize Lecture, December 8, 2002.
Kirsh, D. (2010). Thinking with the body. In S. Ohlsson, & R. Catrambone (Eds.), *Proceedings of the 32nd annual conference of the cognitive science society* (pp. 2864–2869). Austin, TX: Cognitive Science Society.
Lakomski, G. (2005). *Managing without leadership*. London: Elsevier.
Lakomski, G., & Evers, C.W. (2010). Passionate rationalism: The role of emotion in decision–making. *Journal of Educational Administration*, 48(4), 438–450.
Lakomski, G., & Evers, C.W. (2012). Emotion and rationality in educational problem solving from individuals to groups. *Korean Journal of Educational Administration*, 30(1), 653–677.
Moore, G.E. (1903/1988). *Principia ethica*. New York: Prometheus Books.
Naqvi, N., Shiv, B., & Bechara, A. (2006). The role of emotion in decision making: A cognitive neuroscience perspective. *Current Directions in Psychological Science*, 15(5), 260–264.
Newell, A., & Simon, H.A. (1976/1990). Computer science as empirical enquiry: Symbols and search. *communications of the association for computing machinery*. In New York: Association for Computing Machinery. Cited as reprinted in M.A. Boden (Ed.), *The philosophy of artificial intelligence* (pp. 105–133). Oxford: Oxford University Press.
Nickles, T. (1981). What is a problem that we might solve it? *Synthese*, 47(1), 85–118.
Panksepp, J. (2003). At the interface of the affective, behavioral, and cognitive neurosciences: Decoding the emotional feelings of the brain. *Brain and Cognition*, 52(1), 4–14.
Pezzulo, G., Barsalou, L., Cangelosi, A., Fischer, M.H., McRae, K., & Spivey, M.J. (2013). Computational grounded cognition: A new Alliance between grounded cognition and computational modelling. *Frontiers in Psychology*, 3, 1–10.
Popper, K.R. (1945/1995). *The open society and its enemies*. London: Routledge.
Popper, K.R. (1979). *Objective knowledge: An evolutionary approach*. Oxford: Oxford University Press.
Quine, W.V.O. (1951). Two dogmas of empiricism. *Philosophical Review*, 60, 20–43.
Quine, W.V.O. (1960). *Word and object*. Cambridge, MA: MIT Press.
Reynolds, C. (1987). Flocks, herds and schools: A distributed behavioral model. *Computer Graphics*, 21, 25–34. Available from: http://www.red3d.com/cwr/boids/
Riley, M.A., Richardson, M.J., Shockley, K., & Ramenzoni, V.C. (2011). Interpersonal synergies. *Frontiers in Psychology*, 2, 1–7.
Robinson, V.M.J., Lloyd, C.A., & Rowe, K.J. (2008). The impact of leadership on student outcomes: An analysis of the differential effect of leadership types. *Educational Administration Quarterly*, 44(5), 635–674.
Schutz, P.A., & Zembylas, M.(Eds.) (2009). *Advances in teacher emotion research*. Dordrecht: Springer.
Schwenk, C.R. (1988). The cognitive perspective on strategic decision making. *Journal of Management Studies*, 25(1), 41–55.
Simon, H.A. (1947/1976). *Administrative behavior*. New York: The Free Press Macmillan.

Simon, H.A. (1987). Making management decisions: The role of intuition and emotion. *Academy of Management Executive*, 1(1), 57–64.

Starratt, R. (1998). Grounding moral educational leadership in the morality of teaching and learning. *Leading and Managing*, 4(4), 243–255.

Thagard, P. (1999). Ethical coherence. *Philosophical Psychology*, 11(4), 405–422.

Thagard, P., & Kroon, F.W. (2006). Emotional consensus in group decision making. *Mind and Society*, 5(1), 85–104.

Thagard, P., & Verbeurgt, K. (1998). Coherence as constraint satisfaction. *Cognitive Science*, 22, 1–24.

Theiner, G., Allen, C., & Goldstone, R.L. (2010). Recognizing group cognition. *Cognitive Systems Research*, 11(4), 378–395.

Watts, D.J., & Strogatz, S.H. (1998). Collective dynamics of 'small world' networks. *Nature*, 393(6684), 440–442.

Weber, M. (1947). *The theory of social and economic organization*. New York: The Free Press Macmillan.

Wilson, M. (2010). The re-tooled mind: How culture re-engineers cognition. *SCAN*, 5(2–3), 180–187.

Winch, P. (1958). *The idea of a social science and its relationship to philosophy*. London: Routledge and Kegan Paul.

# 2
# METHODOLOGICAL INDIVIDUALISM AND EDUCATIONAL LEADERSHIP

## Introduction

There are two major categories of explanation for organizational performance: structural and individual. With the shift away from systems-theoretic accounts that occurred in the 1980s, structural explanations have been replaced increasingly by the individualism of leadership and leader-centric explanations, especially when it comes to schools. In this chapter we argue that leader-centric accounts involve a commitment to methodological individualism and that there are four serious problems with this view. First, it is logically difficult to describe individual actions without recourse to structures. Second, methodological individualism fosters a centralized mindset inviting the attribution of leadership where none may exist. Third, evidence for distributed cognition compromises leader-centrism. And fourth, administrative tasks themselves are often highly structured. In response to these problems, we urge a more balanced approach to organizational functioning, one that involves both structures and individuals.

## The rise of leadership

Over the past 30 years or more, there has been a perceptible shift in the use of two major explanatory categories characteristically employed to account for certain organizational outcomes in schooling. In earlier times, roughly from 1950 to 1980 when systems theory provided the preferred model of organizational functioning, structural factors prevailed. That is, successes and failures were often attributed to the design of an organization or the way its component parts functioned dynamically. This is not to say that leadership, another major factor, was considered unimportant. However, from around 1980 onwards, leadership has been increasingly invoked as the dominant explanatory category.

DOI: 10.4324/9781003241577-3

One important reason for this shift is surely the rise of school-based management in many jurisdictions. Since this reform required change in the way schools operated, granted the assumption that schools would not spontaneously adapt, leadership in general, and transformational leadership in particular, were posited to be the main sources driving organizational change. As Caldwell and Spinks (1992, pp. 49–50) argued "a powerful capacity for transformational leadership is required for the successful transition to a system of self-managing schools".

The transition to leader-centric accounts of school functioning was reflected in a variety of changes in academia. The journal *Educational Management and Administration* was renamed *Educational Management, Administration and Leadership* in 2004. New journals began to proliferate, including *International Journal of Leadership in Education* (commencing 1998), *Leading and Managing* (commencing 1995), *Journal of School Leadership* (commencing 1991), and *School Leadership and Management* which nicely reflect the shift in explanatory emphasis by starting out life in 1981 as *School Organization* and then being renamed in 1997. Academic titles in the field also began changing: professors of educational administration became professors of educational leadership; new programs such as the Master of Educational Leadership flourished; handbooks on educational leadership appeared; many universities established centres for educational leadership, and some, such as England's National College for School Leadership, were government established with substantial resources and a significant national role in principal training.

One consequence of this broad pattern of change, though one in keeping with other market-oriented reforms underlying the new public sector management of the past and current period, was the rise of individualism, that is, explanations in terms of what individuals do, at the expense of structural accounts. Two examples can illustrate the difference. Suppose we want to explain an increase in a nation's level of unemployment. An individualist explanation might appeal to the fact that people do not have the right kind of education to get a job, or they lack motivation and are unwilling to try hard enough, or they are unwilling to work at the sort of jobs that are available, preferring instead to draw unemployment benefits. Paul Krugman (2012, p. 103) cites "real business cycle" theory as committed to these ideas where "the reduction in employment that takes place during a recession is a voluntary decision by workers to take time off until conditions improve". He adds immediately "if this sounds absurd, that's because it is". A structural account, on the other hand, may talk of a sharp fall in aggregate demand brought on by a government's aversion to deficit spending in the face of a collapsing housing market. In this case, the difference is significant, affecting the kinds of policies that should be adopted to deal with the problem.

Another example, much discussed in the literature (see Darling-Hammond 2010; Sahlberg and Hargreaves 2011), is why, since 2003, schools in Finland achieve such good student learning outcomes as shown by the OECD Program for International Student Assessment (PISA). A market-oriented individualism counsels that we formulate the issue in terms of what counts as rewards and penalties for teachers and students. Key elements of this story include testing all students on national standardized tests, publishing the results for schools, and linking teacher employment conditions, such as salary increments or retrenchments, to the learning outcomes they are thought to achieve. Interestingly, Finland has done none of these things. Its educational reforms are of a more structural kind, although not entirely so. Through the use of high salaries and high entry requirements, teaching is, culturally, a high status profession. Teachers, as individuals, enjoy a high level of professional autonomy. Almost all schools are government schools, and most importantly, Finland enjoys high levels of income equality. In their study of the effects of income inequality on a range of measures of human well-being, Wilkinson and Pickett (2010, pp. 103–117) plotted income inequality against educational achievement using the PISA 2003 country results for reading and mathematics. The outcome: a strong international relationship between educational achievement and equality of income. Such a conclusion raises questions about what practices can be borrowed from one country to improve education in another country. For it's one thing to borrow techniques for training teachers, but it's another matter entirely to borrow a country's income distribution.

The stance one adopts toward individualism or structuralism is therefore of some consequence when it comes to understanding the role of leaders in how schools function and achieve desired outcomes. But what determines an appropriate stance? The two examples above trade in fairly commonsense and informal versions of individual-like and structure-like explanations. However, if we wish to take seriously the current fashion for leader-centric accounts of school functioning and performance, then we need to examine the limits of such accounts. If, for example, all structural explanation is reducible without remainder to explanation in terms of the activity of individuals, which is the central thesis of methodological individualism, then the contrast in the given examples will merely be an artefact of inadequate analysis. Furthermore, it will disguise, or hide, the full scope of what can be achieved through the action of individuals. In what follows, we explore in some detail the scope of methodological individualism and what its limits mean for views of educational leadership.

## Individuals and structures

The issue we are exploring is an old one, going back to the classics in sociology. It is also a current issue which is mainly discussed in the field of the philosophy of social science. We consider ideas from both sets of literature.

Following Comte's positivism, Durkheim sought to develop a view of sociology that was both scientific – a science of society – and distinctive, that is, not reducible to some other discipline or set of disciplines. In the second chapter of *The Rules of Sociological Method* (1895/1958), he champions the importance of observable regularities in social explanation: "Every scientific investigation is directed towards a limited class of phenomena, included in the same definition

**24** Philosophical foundations

*... The subject matter of every sociological study should comprise a group of phenomena defined in advance by certain common external characteristics, and all phenomena so defined should be included in this group"* (pp. 34–35, emphasis in source). More importantly, the distinctiveness of sociology was expressed in the first chapter of *The Rules of Sociological Method* which is given over to defining social facts, concluding that *"A social fact is ... every way of acting which is general throughout a given society, while at the same time existing in its own right independent of its individual manifestations"* (p. 13, emphasis in source).

Part of the strategy in defining social facts this way is to prevent them from being reduced to psychology, or even physiology. They are independent of the individual. As Durkheim (1897/1951, p. 38) argues, "There can be no sociology unless societies exist and ... societies cannot exist if there are only individuals". Durkheim's holism is therefore a central aspect of his view of sociology.

Opposition to both Durkheim's view of the nature of a science of sociology and his holism can be found in the work of Weber. For Weber, social action is defined explicitly as being reducible to the actions, thoughts, and beliefs of individuals: "An action is social insofar as, by virtue of the subjective meaning attached to it by the acting individual (or individuals), it takes account of the behavior of others and is thereby oriented in its course" (Weber 1947/1964, p. 88). The basic model of action for Weber is rational action, with irrationality being seen as a deviation from this 'ideal type' (Weber 1947/1964, p. 96). Weber's view of a science of society depends on the interpretation of the meaning of actions. Even if we have high levels of regularity in social phenomena, that will not be sufficient for social explanation: "If adequacy in respect of meaning is lacking, then no matter how high the degree of uniformity and how precisely the probability can be numerically determined, it is still an incomprehensible statistical probability, whether dealing with overt or subjective processes" (Weber 1947/1964, p. 99). Explanations of social phenomena need to be cashed out in terms of the rational action of individuals.

Weber defines many contexts for rational action, including many that involve the economy, an approach that has been developed in considerable technical detail in defining the economic behaviour of individuals in markets. For example, under modest conditions of rationality, we have the striking result that rational actors maximize expected utility (Heap et al. 1992, pp. 9–11). This kind of instrumental rationality then feeds into a view of what motivates market participants, both sellers and buyers. In the context of education, buyers are supposed to be informed about a provider's (a school's) performance, in particular about its success in producing good educational outcomes. Rational producers (school leaders), seen as utility maximizers, will therefore attempt to meet this (and other) requirements important for attracting greater market share and its consequent rewards (see Power et al. 1997).

Most modern views of methodological individualism fit the pattern of linking it to rational choice theory, with Jon Elster being, for many years, its most prolific defender (see Elster 1978, 1983, and 1989). However, his later views contain an element of caution: "I now believe that rational-choice theory has less explanatory power than I used to think" (Elster 2007, p. 5). A more serious cautionary note has been voiced by the economist Kenneth Arrow. Thus, after noting that "it is a touchstone of accepted economics that all explanations must run in terms of the actions and reactions of individuals," Arrow (1994, p. 1) begs to differ. He claims that "… a close examination of even the most standard economic analysis shows that social categories are in fact used in economic analysis all the time and that they appear to be absolute necessities of the analysis not just figures of speech that can be eliminated if need be" (Arrow 1994, p. 1). One example he gives is prices at a competitive equilibrium, asking rhetorically: "What individual has chosen prices?" (Arrow 1994, p. 4). His principal example, however, is the case of social knowledge, particularly scientific and technological knowledge. This is not something held in the head of any one individual. Rather, it exists in dynamic aggregates, in processes, and in forms of storage such as books, computers, and other artefacts (Arrow 1994, pp. 6–8).

Arrow's point applies with equal force to rational leadership action, where decisions and behaviours occur within the context of knowledge of such social facts as organizational cultures, codified practices, normative standards, institutional goals, and distributed cognition. To see this more clearly, we begin by distinguishing two types of methodological individualism. The first type is ontological, claiming that the physical nature of an aggregate can be reduced to the physical nature of its component parts. In other words, the ontology of a society is no more than the ontology of all its individual parts. This is a relatively trivial thesis, though it has been contested (see, for example, Epstein 2009). The second type is explanatory individualism, which we have been considering so far. This is the more contentious thesis; although, in our view, the modern consensus is against it. (For explicit defences, see Elster 1982, and Tuomela 1990.)

## Against reduction in social explanation

Some of the arguments here are more pragmatic than principled, bending to the demands of complexity in organizations by taking advantage of the explanatory value of macro categories in the absence of detail about micro categories. An analogy will illustrate. Suppose we want to explain why a collection of different shaped containers made of different materials can all hold a litre of water. In giving an adequate explanation, it may be sufficient to go no further than an account of the geometry of the assorted containers. Although the geometry is sustained by the compositional micro-structure of the containers' material, that kind of information is not needed for the task at hand. A scientific realist ontology tells us to expect that a micro-structural account must eventually be possible, but an adequate explanation in this context can be satisfactory at the geometrical level. Explanation is also an epistemological enterprise, and it can only use the tools that are actually available at a given time. In his attack on methodological individualism, Kincaid observes:

> An ontological fact about composition (or other dependence relations) on its own entails nothing about our explanatory resources. Once it was realized that individualist claims about the inevitability of reduction are a version of the general fallacy that composition entails explanatory reducibility, such arguments for reductionist versions of individualism largely disappeared among philosophers. Unfortunately, social scientists have not fully gotten the message.
>
> *(Kincaid 2015, p. 1128)*

His point about explanation even applies when trying to account for individual behaviour. A good example of using what is epistemically accessible is the use of a dominant strand of folk psychology for explaining individual behaviour. A person is said to choose a course of action because they desire some goal and they believe that the chosen actions will achieve that goal. Behaviour, as explained by the rational coordination of beliefs and desires, does an enormous amount of explanatory, and predictive, work in our understanding of the social world. And in formalized individualist accounts of behaviour that appear in economics and in Elster's work, belief/desire theory is transformed into the mathematics of maximizing expected utility. But from an ontological perspective looking several levels down, we also know that these higher level conceptualized processes are driven by brain processes currently, but slowly and incompletely, being revealed by research in cognitive neuroscience (Lakomski and Evers 2017). Even here, however, these individualist explanations of behaviour are compromised.

In whatever way the pattern recognition capacities of our neural networks lock on to the salient regularities of the social world for purposes of epistemically bound explanation, the tools at our disposal lie in two directions. One appears to be ontologically reductive to individual brain process, the kinds of causes that ultimately account for the successes of belief/desire theory. But this is misleading for two reasons. First, the relevant descriptors of these salient features of the social world also describe social facts, thus taking us in the opposite direction from individualism. And second, much cognition in organizations is distributed, where the unit of cognition, including epistemically progressive problem-solving, is the group. We discuss this in a later part of this chapter and in subsequent chapters. Concerning the first, one influential argument propounded by Lukes (1968), provides a general account of why explanations in terms of individuals cannot avoid making use of structural concepts. Arguments like this work by showing that the explanatory demands faced by a model of explanation outrun its posited explanatory resources. A well-known example is the case of operational definition. Consider how to define 'length' operationally. We need to begin by defining a measurement procedure. Now this will make use of the concept 'rule'. But what makes a particular rule adequate? The answer is that it can be compared to a 'standard rule'. But now how is that defined? The current definition of a metre, as provided by the General Conference on Weights and Measures, "is the length of the path travelled by light in a vacuum during a time interval of 1/299,792,458 of a second" (CGPM 1983). Apart from containing the term 'length', a regress sets in with a number of terms in this definition clamouring for operational definitions.

Following Lukes (1968, pp. 124–127), we may consider how we describe what individuals do. If we are restricted to bodily movements, the descriptions will be insufficient for describing human actions (as opposed to happenings) which trade in reasons, intentions, and understandings. But if descriptions are broadened to sustain explanations in terms of Weber's method of understanding, then, ironically, individuals might engage in such social practices as voting, writing a cheque, or saluting. If we try to reduce these practices to the actions of individuals, a regress threatens. The reason is that these practices, along with a vast array of social practices based on institutional structures that include "money, marriage, governments, and property", are partly constituted by collective intentionality that sometimes must take the form of language for its expression (Searle 1995, pp. 59–78). And collective intentionality is not a property of individuals. Chapter 4 contains an elaboration.

In the case of school principals, their very existence as principals is constituted by social facts expressed in employment contracts and collective understandings, and their leadership role is partly constituted by contractual and conventional constraints on action, constraints whose specification includes the socially constituted definitions of teachers and other employees. Leader-centric accounts of organizational functioning are not ignorant of the structures that define and sustain leadership. The worry, rather, is that the emphasis on the leader as an individual can both bracket and discount the causal field in which organizational functioning occurs.

## The centralized mind, emergence, and self-organization

An extreme example of where this occurs is in the attribution of leadership under those conditions where it is, in fact, an epiphenomenon, an artefact of collective coordinated action that gives the appearance of leadership. It seems odd that despite all the recent knowledge we have gained about how our brains work, we seem to want to resist explanations that do not require the assumption of a central controller. In part, it may be that social reality appears to be too complex, and simplification of complexity might ease cognitive load. But we do not really know just yet why we persist with what Resnick (2000) calls the 'centralized mindset'. He means by that a feature that encapsulates the human propensity for and bias toward centralized thinking that attributes a single cause to an observed pattern, such as a flock of birds, or the operation of an organization. On this view, any pattern is presumed to be created by someone or something. Hence, birds flying in formation are 'led' by the bird that is flying at the head; ants are 'led' by the queen; God created the universe; or the Prime Minister leads the country. Leader-centric views of the behaviour of collectives possess such a hold over the imagination that it is worth going into some detail just to show what an alternative leader-less view might look like and how it might, under some conditions, be a better explanation of organizational functioning.

The apparent need to find a central controller enjoys some plausibility because many of the patterns and structures around us do appear to be controlled or led by a planner or designer. The movements of ballet dancers, individually and as an ensemble, are designed by a choreographer; orchestras are led by their conductors; a football team is controlled by its coach; and architects design buildings. Problems arise, however, when we assume that all observed patterns or regularities *must* have been created by a designer or central controller. We now have very good reasons and evidence for why this assumption is unwarranted. Regularities, patterns, as well as artefacts – whether arches built by termites or the Sydney Opera House – may be better understood as the result of initial, low level, context-bound, coordination and collaboration. In other words, they may be said to have 'emerged' rather than come about as a result of planning by a central controller. The human brain may just be the most spectacular example of de-centralization, and also of emergence in its most robust, 'strong' sense, as we will see shortly. (For historical treatments of emergence, see Baylis 1929; Ablowitz 1939; Johnson 2001; and Holland 1998 provide excellent contemporary discussions.)

The study of complex systems, both biological and artificial, much advanced through computer modelling and simulation, provides fascinating insights into how the world works. The concept of emergence plays a significant role here. Debated since the late 1900s, the concept of emergence is notoriously slippery. In Kim's (2006, p. 548) assessment, it is "very much a term of philosophical trade", and can mean "pretty much … whatever you want it to mean". Different theoreticians have ascribed different meanings to it in philosophy, the theory of mind, and the sciences both natural and social. Despite such latitude in interpretation, there seems to be some shared agreement in that emergent entities (properties or substances) 'arise' out of more fundamental entities and yet are 'novel' or 'irreducible' with respect to them (e.g. O'Connor and Wong 2006). But this is a broad characterization, and as always, the devil is in the detail. Consider the use of 'emergence' in sociological theory (e.g. Sawyer 2001), for example, whose central goal is the explanation of the relationship between micro and macro level social phenomena. In this view, macro phenomena, that is, social properties, arise from, or have emerged out of, individual action, as is claimed by Axelrod (1997). But while agreeing with the view that social phenomena have emerged out of individual action, methodological collectivists, or 'collectivist emergentists', reject the conclusion that collective phenomena are reducible to individual action. So different sociological perspectives employ the philosophical concept of emergence but draw opposite conclusions from it. This is just one example where lack of clarity regarding the meaning of emergence results in contradictory conclusions.

In the absence of space and time to provide a comprehensive account of emergence, we opt for the theoretically most progressive way to understand this intuitively appealing but analytically evasive concept as applied in cognitive science and the study of self-organizing systems. In the latter, it is aided by multi-agent modelling that addresses the issue of how collective behaviour emerges from, but is not reducible to, individual action. This gives us the best chance to figure out what emergence looks like. As Clark (2001, p. 113) points out, the fine line to walk here is, on one hand, to avoid a definition so broad as to sanction any development to count as emergent, and on the other, to make it so restrictive that no phenomenon could be included that is already amenable to scientific explanation. It is not overstating the case to say that this is a challenge of considerable difficulty. Holland's (1998, pp. 121–122) description of emergence of artificial and adaptive systems, enshrined in his genetic algorithm, seems an appropriate compromise. It depicts important features applicable to self-organizing systems, artificial and natural:

> Emergence is above all a product of coupled, context–dependent interactions. Technically these interactions, and the resulting system are *nonlinear*. The behaviour of the overall system *cannot* be obtained by *summing* the behaviors of its constituent parts. We can no more truly understand strategies in a board game by compiling statistics of the movements of its pieces than we can understand the behavior of an ant colony in terms of averages. Under these conditions, the whole is indeed more than the sum of its parts.

Importantly, the results of emergent behaviour are of a qualitatively different kind than the locally produced interactions that gave rise to it, sometimes also described as 'unpredictable novelty' (Goldspink and Kay 2010, p. 49). Chalmers' (2006) distinction between 'strong' and 'weak' emergence provides a helpful demarcation of how to think of emergence more productively by not confusing the two notions as they refer to different concepts. The designator 'strong' is applied to emergence when a "high level phenomenon arises from the low-level domain, but truths concerning that phenomenon are not *deducible* even in principle from truths in the low-level domain" (Chalmers 2006, p. 244). The suggestion of strong emergence is controversial, as is Chalmers' view (argued for in his 1996 book), that there is only one clear example: the phenomenon of consciousness, as consciousness cannot be deduced from any number of physical facts.

On the other hand, "a high-level phenomenon is *weakly* emergent with respect to a low-level domain when the high-level phenomenon arises from the low-level domain, but truths concerning that phenomenon are *unexpected* given the principles governing the low-level domain"; or more simply, "weak emergence is the phenomenon wherein complex, interesting high-level function is produced as a result of combining simple low-level mechanisms in simple ways" (Chalmers 2006, p. 254). It is this latter sense of emergence that applies in scientific discussions of self-organizing and complex systems. A couple of brief examples should suffice to indicate some of its basic features.

One of the best known is Reynolds's (1987) simulation of the flocking behaviour of birds, called boids. In keeping with the description of weak emergence above, Reynolds stipulated three simple rules: (1) avoid crowding local flock mates (Separation); (2) move towards the average heading of local flock mates (Alignment); and (3) move toward the average position of local flock mates (Cohesion). When these simple rules were followed, the patterns that emerged looked like real flocking behaviours of biological birds. What also emerged, unexpectedly, was that when faced with an obstacle, the flock of boids parted before it and re-assembled behind it! This behaviour was not programmed 'in the rules', and it appears that flocks maintain a kind of dynamic equilibrium that does not require any central control. There is no leader here.

Another intriguing example of emergent behaviour is represented by Sims's (1994) work of computer-generated creatures that evolve into life-like beings, a successor to Conway's earlier Game of Life. Sims created an artificial three-dimensional world that simulated Darwinian evolutions of virtual block creatures. Computer-generated, these organisms, amazingly, nevertheless evolved life-like behaviours and 'invented' realistic solutions to everyday problems that real life forms must solve. Again, some basic rules were needed, such as a way to define 'fitness' and how to measure it, some method for generating new variations, and some rules for making best use of adaptive improvements (Kennedy, Eberhart and Yuhui 2001, pp. 29–30).

While these are only two simplified examples of simulations of emergent, self-organizing systems, and regardless of many unresolved issues in simulating real-life behaviours, it seems clear that central control in the sense discussed here is not part of how high-level function came about as a result of combining some simple low-level rules or mechanisms. There is another important point to be made: in both cases, unexpected, novel behaviours emerged that could not have been predicted on the basis of the simple basic rules that first gave rise to them. This outcome gives us pause for thought especially when considering such non-linear complex systems as schools that are embedded in and responsive to social, political, economic, and other extraneous forces.

Insofar as multi-agent modelling and simulations accurately and surprisingly mimic or replicate real-life behaviours and patterns more explanatory mileage is to be had for complex social phenomena such as school activity (or any other organization function) if we concentrate on understanding de-centralized behaviours and emergence.

The point of this discussion on emergence is not to show that leader-centric accounts of organizational functioning are always wrong. Rather, it is to show that appearances can sometimes be misleading; that what looks like an example of leadership may in fact be nothing of the sort. It may be an epiphenomenon, the result of an emergent property of interacting individuals following organizational rules of interaction that require them to respond to certain aggregate features of the collective. The upshot is that appealing to leadership in accounting for organizational functioning should not be the default option.

## Distributed cognition

So far, we have examined two key arguments against explanatory methodological individualism. The first showed the difficulty in giving an account of what individuals do that does not make use of structural concepts. This means that accounts of what leaders do must also make reference to structures, thus invoking the relevance of a much wider causal field in the study of organizational performance. The second made two related points; firstly, that the behaviour of a collective of rule-following individuals can give the appearance that someone is in charge of the collective, but this appearance is misleading, and may be better described as an emergent property. And secondly, the formulation of these rules for individuals in a social, or organizational, collective will (in line with the conclusion of the first main argument) make use of structural terms – terms, as we saw in the case of the artificial boids, that refer to "the average heading of local flock mates" or "the average position of local flock mates".

In this section we consider a third argument against leader-centrism, one that draws on ideas about the distributed nature of cognition. The argument targets those views of leadership, such as transformational leadership, or instructional leadership, that posit as central the requirement that these leaders provide cognitive leadership, such as intellectual stimulation (one of the four 'I's of transformational leadership), special problem-solving skills, or knowledge leadership in instructional matters.

The knowledge that brains are not centralized in their processing function, that knowledge generation occurs beyond it by drawing on the artefacts and resources available in the external environment that act as cognitive 'scaffolding' (Clark's term) makes possible a much richer view of cognition that acknowledges our embeddedness in various contexts. Furthermore, it suggests a powerful explanation of what 'organization' (the collective or the social) is and how it might function. Later chapters provide extensive discussions of both cognition and organization. For present purposes, the central idea of what is known as the *theory of distributed cognition* and *the extended mind* (Clark 1997; Clark and Chalmers 1998; Hollan et al. 2000, 2008) is nicely illustrated by the use of a now common technological device, the iPhone:

The description David Chalmers (2008, ix) gives will resound with many users:

> The iPhone has already taken over some of the central functions of my brain. It has replaced part of my memory, storing phone numbers and addresses that I once would have taxed my brain with. It harbors my desires: I call up a memo with the names of my favourite dishes when I need to order at a local restaurant. I use it to calculate, when I need to figure out bills and tips. It is a tremendous resource in an argument, with Google ever present to help settle disputes. I make plans with it, using its calendar to help determine what I can and can't do in the coming months. I even daydream on the iPhone, idly calling up words and images when my concentration slips ... the iPhone is part of my mind already.

Just how intimate our relationship is with such a technological device becomes clear in our reactions when we have left our smart phone at home, lost or misplaced it, ranging from outright panic to feeling as if we had lost a limb. This reaction implicitly acknowledges that a non-biological, technological device has become a cognitive extension of our mind. But it is also fair to note that the theory of the extended mind in particular is controversial in terms of where to draw the boundary between the knowing 'self' and other external cognitive resources as one cognitive field, an issue examined in greater detail in Chapter 3.

Considered from this perspective though it becomes clear, at the very least, that the individual agent, be that a teacher or a school principal, in carrying out their daily tasks which involve their knowledge and skills, is not sealed off from other such agents but is in fact enmeshed with them in a vast cognitive field that comprises all the other agents in the school and all manner of resources, both material and non-material. In light of this, consider the common complaint that schools are underperforming in terms of student learning *because* of leaders' failures to exercise leadership and/or teachers to teach effectively. The explicit individualization of linear causality does not map on to the much more fluid and changing interrelationships, both cognitive and material, that are characteristic of cognition in context. The idea of the autonomous self that 'owns' its knowledge, a central assumption of methodological individualism, turns out to be more illusion than reality. Causality in teaching and learning, whatever else it might turn out to be, is multi-directional rather than linear and is thus much harder to determine. It follows from this that the solutions proposed to 'fix' underperforming schools – e.g. leadership training, leadership standards, professional teaching standards, performance pay – are less likely to solve the problem, no matter how beneficial they might be in individual cases, unless the unit of cognition is theorized in terms broader than the individual.

From the distributed cognition perspective, the distinction between the individual and the collective or social – between agency and structure – is not one of substantive difference but rather one of a difference in quality, dimension, and complexity. 'Organization' in this vein can thus be understood as a formation of extended minds in the way described, characterized by fluid boundaries and intimately bound to and formed by the contexts in which they operate. A view of leadership construed without acknowledgement of the extensive cognitive scaffolding that organizations, societies, cultures, and artefacts provide is seriously misleading.

## Structured problems

Individual cognition is not only scaffolded by artefacts and the social nature of the division of cognitive labour across other individuals, groups, and societies, but it is also scaffolded by the nature of cognitive tasks. Consider problem-solving. It is easy to theorize problem-solving in individualist terms, and there is a long tradition of doing so (Evers and Lakomski 2020). If a problem is defined by a set of constraints plus the demand that something be done, then a problem-solver is someone who figures out how to satisfy all the constraints. To illustrate: you have a bunch of keys and you need to open a locked door. For such a well-structured problem, the process of solving it can consist in merely trying out successive keys. It is solved when you find the key that opens the door. In this case, the cognitive properties of the individual problem-solver are relatively unimportant. Anyone can solve the problem by simply trying out keys.

Now consider decision-making. We note that the term 'decision-making' can be misleading if it suggests a one-off process of formulating a problem and then deciding how it is to be solved. Most decision-making takes the form of a problems-solutions trajectory. Even in the well-structured case of finding the right key, we have a trajectory that continues through successive trials until the right key is found. For successful decision-making in authentic school contexts where problems are rarely so well structured, we have a trajectory that is invariably more complex. Here we give an example.

In June 2013, the New South Wales government's Department of Education and Communities agreed to fund a research project to be conducted in three Sydney primary schools aimed at trialling a model for developing school leadership through promoting effective problem-solving. Each school identified four problems that they wanted to address, and team members who would work on each problem. The problems were expected to be relatively complex as the project was to run for a full year. We were the academic consultants for the project as it was employing some of our published ideas. There are two main issues. The first involves an analysis of the kind of constraints that impose structural boundaries that shape the scope of leader and team agency. The second involves pursuing the trajectories that result from successive attempts to solve the problem. Here we focus on the matter of constraints. In Chapter 6, we give a detailed account of an example requiring a succession of eight steps in the successful trajectory.

The problem we look at is that of implementing the use of iPads to facilitate student learning, eventually throughout the whole school. The school has an enrolment of 554 students organized into 23 classes K-6, a range of auxiliary staff including Italian and Learning Support, a non-teaching Deputy Principal, and Principal. It was located in a relatively high socio-economic area, with strong parent participation. Although all students would eventually be using iPads, they would first be introduced to Year 6 students. Almost every step along the way was shaped by constraints, beginning with costs. How much would the iPads cost? This was a hard constraint, the price being determined by Apple. How would the money be raised? This is usually the task of the school's Parents and Citizens Association (P&C), but its members had reservations, especially over the school's information technology (IT) expertise. This was a soft constraint, but it was only softened by a substantial commitment by teachers, at a staff meeting, to participate in fundraising. What else was needed before moving ahead? Contact with other schools suggested that an IT policy was required. The policy process revealed other constraints: security, access, departmental approval and support, and IT support and maintenance. The related issue of installing a WiFi system also emerged, along with costs, maintenance, and training. Storage, security, and access to the iPads also needed to be resolved, along with a cluster of issues around the selection and use of apps. Finally, there arose the matter of training staff to use the IT.

With the possible exception of fundraising, almost every step along the way to implementation was defined by agency-limiting hard constraints, the main choice being to meet the constraints or abandon the project. This was confirmed when teams from the other two schools met. One of the other schools was trying to solve the same problem but had started not with the issue of costs but with the issue of developing a policy. The resulting sets of constraints were almost identical. Agency-related features of leadership were diminished, if not to the point of irrelevance in the case of finding the right key, then certainly to a significant extent dictated by the nature of the task and the resources for getting it done.

## Conclusion

The current emphasis on leadership as an explanatory category in accounting for organizational functioning tends to understate the significance of a broader causal field of influences. This consequence is already partly recognized in the recent rise of models of distributed leadership (Hartley 2007; Gronn 2008). Leader-centrism has also partly transformed distributed leadership into influential models of teacher leadership where the same individualist assumptions are already feeding performance and accountability policies and practices. For an understanding of leadership that is both theoretically and practically adequate, we attempt to provide a more holistic approach to organizational functioning.

## References

Ablowitz, R. (1939). The theory of emergence. *Philosophy of Science,* 6(1), 1–16.
Axelrod, R. (1997). *The complexity of cooperation.* Princeton, NJ: Princeton University Press.
Arrow, K.J. (1994). Methodological individualism and social knowledge. *The American Economic Review,* 84(2), 1–9.
Baylis, C. (1929). The philosophic functions of emergence. *The Philosophical Review,* 38(4), 372–384.
Caldwell, B.J., & Spinks, J. (1992). *Leading the self-managing school.* London: Routledge/Falmer.
Chalmers, D. (1996). *The conscious mind: In search of a fundamental theory.* Oxford: Oxford University Press.
Chalmers, D. (2006). Strong and weak emergence. In P. Clayton, & P. Davies (Eds.), *The re-emergence of emergence* (pp. 244–257). Oxford: Oxford University Press.
Clark, A. (1997). *Being there: Putting brain, body, and world together again.* Cambridge, MA: MIT Press.
Clark, A. (2001). *Mindware.* Oxford: Oxford University Press.
Clark, A. (2008). *Supersizing the mind.* Oxford: Oxford University Press.
Clark, D., & Chalmers, D. (1998). The extended mind. *Analysis* 58, 10–23.

CGPM (1983). National institute of standards and technology reference on constants, units and uncertainty, Viewed 24 April 2012, http://physics.nist.gov/cuu/Units/meter.html
Darling-Hammond, L. (2010). *The flat world and education: How americas commitment to equity will determine our future*. New York, NY: Teachers College Press.
Durkheim, E. (1895/1958). *The rules of sociological method* (trans: Solvay, S.A. & Mueller, J.H.). New York: The Free Press.
Durkheim, E. (1897/1951). *Suicide: A study in sociology* (trans: Simpson, G.). New York, NY: The Free Press.
Elster, J. (1978). *Logic and society: Contradictions and possible worlds*. New York, NY: Wiley.
Elster, J. (1982). The case for methodological individualism. *Theory and Society*, 11(4), 153–182.
Elster, J. (1983). *Sour grapes: Studies in the subversion of rationality*. Cambridge: Cambridge University Press.
Elster, J. (1989). *The cement of society: A study of social order*. Cambridge: Cambridge University Press.
Elster, J. (2007). *Explaining social behavior: More nuts and bolts for the social sciences*. Cambridge: Cambridge University Press.
Epstein, B. (2009). Ontological individualism reconsidered. *Synthese*, 166, 187-213.
Evers, C.W., & Lakomski, G. (2020). Educational leadership in Hong Kong schools: Critical reflections on changing themes. *Journal of Educational Administration and History*, 40(3), 251–264.
Evers, C.W., & Lakomski, G. (2020). Cognitive science and educational administration. In R. Papa et.al. (Eds.), *The Oxford encyclopedia of educational administration*. Oxford: Oxford University Press.
Goldspink, C., & Kay, R. (2010). Emergence in organizations: The reflexive turn. *E:CO*, 12(3), 47–63.
Gronn, P. (2008). The future of distributed leadership. *Journal of Educational Leadership*, 46(2), 141–158.
Hartley, D. (2007). The emergence of distributed leadership in education: Why now? *British Journal of Educational Studies*, 55(2), 202–214.
Heap, S.A., Hollis, M., Lyons, B., Sugden, R., & Weale, A. (1992). *The theory of choice: A critical guide*. Oxford: Blackwell.
Holland, J. (1998). *Emergence*. Cambridge, MA: Perseus.
Hollan, J., Hutchins, E., & Kirsh, D. (2000). Distributed cognition: Toward a new foundation for human–computer interaction research. *ACM Transactions on Computer–Human Interaction*, 7(2), 174–196.
Johnson, S. (2001). *Emergence*. New York, NY: Simon and Schuster.
Kennedy, J., Eberhart, R., & Yuhui, S. (2001). *Swarm intelligence*. Amstrdam, Netherlands: Elsevier.
Kim, J. (2006). Emergence: Core ideas and issues. *Synthese*, 151(3), 547–559.
Kincaid, H. (2015). Open empirical and methodological issues in the individualism–holism debate. *Philosophy of Science*, 82, 1127–1138.
Krugman, P.R. (2012). *End this depression now*. New York, NY: WW Norton.
Lakomski, G., & Evers, C.W. (2017). Educational leadership and emotion. In D. Waite, & I. Bogotch (Eds.), *The international handbook of educational leadership* (pp. 45–62). Hoboken, NJ: Wiley-Blackwell.
Lukes, S. (1968). Methodological individualism reconsidered. *The British Journal of Sociology*, 19(2), 119–129.
O'Connor, T., & Wong, H.Y. (2006). Emergent properties. *Stanford encyclopedia of philosophy*. Stanford, CA: Stanford University.

OECD (2003). *Program for international student assessment*. Paris: OECD.
Power, S., Halpin, D., & Whitty, G. (1997). Managing the state and the market: "New" education management in five countries. *British Journal of Educational Studies*, 45(4), 342–362.
Resnick, M. (2000). *Turtles, termites, and traffic jams. Explorations in massively parallel microworlds*. Cambridge, MA: MIT Press.
Reynolds, C. (1987). Flocks, herds and schools: A distributed behavioral model. *Computer Graphics,* 21, 25–34. Available from: http://www.red3d.com/cwr/boids/
Sahlberg, P., & Hargreaves, A. (2011). *Finnish Lessons: What can the world learn from educational change in Finland?* Teachers College Press: Columbia University.
Sawyer, R.K. (2001). Emergence in sociology: Contemporary philosophy of mind and some implications for sociological theory. *American Journal of Sociology*, 107(3), 551–585.
Searle, J.R. (1995). *The construction of social reality*. New York, NY: The Free Press.
Sims, K. (1994). Evolving virtual creatures. *Computer Graphics*. Annual Conference Series, SIGGRAPH 94 Proceedings, July, 15–22.
Tuomela, R. (1990). Methodological individualism and explanation. *Philosophy of Science*, 57(1), 133–140.
Weber, M. (1947/1964). *The theory of social and economic organization (trans: Henderson, A.M., & Parsons, T.)*. New York, NY: The Free Press.
Wilkinson, R., & Pickett, K. (2010). *The spirit level: Why equality is better for everyone*. London: Penguin.

# 3
# LEADER COGNITION IN CONTEXT

## Introduction

It is a remarkable phenomenon that in light of the dearth of empirical evidence for leadership as causally connected to organizational performance, the importance of leader cognition has survived as an unchallenged assumption. In fact, the assumption that 'leader knows best' seems to have had something of a resurgence in the wake of large-scale restructuring and reform efforts in education in the 80s, especially in Western nations including Australia, where the school-based management movement (SBM) is the best known. (e.g., Caldwell and Spinks 1988; Caldwell and Spinks 1992; Caldwell 1992; Whitty et al. 1997, 2005). Closely connected is the successful school leadership movement (e.g., Leithwood and Day 2007) that supports the *International Successful School Principalship Project* (ISSPP) (e.g. Day 2005; Drysdale and Gurr 2011; Day and Gurr 2014). The core element of the ISSPP is the principal, who is seen as the key figure in accounting for a school's success (Drysdale and Gurr 2017) due to (usually) his personal qualities, skills, and competencies. Although the importance of contextual features is acknowledged, as well as the work of other organization members, it is the principal who manages context, although it is admitted that context might 'affect' leadership.

The relationship between (school) leader and context has been problematic throughout the history of leadership studies, with contingency theories (e.g. Vroom and Jago 2007) going furthest in considering the leader an integral part of the organizational web, and charismatic-transformational theories swinging the balance the other way in conceptualizing the transformational leader as independent and autonomous. (For review of leadership theories, see Lakomski and Evers 2020.) The current emphasis on leader centrism, as evidenced in the successful school movement, for one, is a variation of the latter. Importantly, the history of leadership theories shows that while leader centrism has always been a part of their core assumptions, the importance and influence of contextual factors has similarly been acknowledged, without leadership theorists ever resolving the tension between leader and context. This tension remains a central problem in leadership theory.

In this chapter we propose that this tension can be resolved in a much broadened, naturalistic, distributed theory of cognition that not only includes individual minds but also the contexts in which they operate. Several steps are involved in doing so.

We argue that the conception of cognition that shores up leader centrism is mistaken. The idea that cognition is a private property, located 'in the head', and primarily language based, is a central feature of empiricism's theory of mind and is indefensible. Second, just as the notion of cognition in leader centrism is mistaken, so is the view of an independent, autonomous self as the agent of leadership. Third, we defend a conception of cognition as fundamentally *distributed,* and argue that cognition is better understood as a dynamic system, characterized by reciprocal interactions between people, artefacts, and other environmental resources. Fourth, given such an expanded conception of cognition, we explore further the *how* of causal coupling between minds, tools, and artefacts. Finally, in Section five, we focus on the social-cultural world with particular emphasis on the notion of cultural practices or enculturated cognition (e.g. Hutchins 1996, 2006, 2008, 2010, 2011, 2014; Hutchins and Johnson 2009; Hutchins and Hazlehurst 1995; Menary 2007, 2010a, 2010b, 2012, 2015; Menary and Gillett 2016).

## Disembodied cognition

To the extent that the centrality of leader cognition continues to play a major part in contemporary school leadership approaches, the influence of its empiricist roots, especially its implicit theory of mind, are still visible and operational. As we have argued previously (especially in Evers and Lakomski 1991), a theory of knowledge always implies a view of what the mind is, because it is minds that do the knowledge constructing, a state of affairs commonly overlooked in education and leadership theorizing. This seemingly innocuous fact, however, turns out to be rather more powerful when we add the modest requirement that given the types of biological beings we are, a mind must be of a type that permits learning to take place, that is, it needs to be congruent with our biological nature.

As the philosophical difficulties regarding empiricism's theory of knowledge have been widely discussed (e.g. in Evers and Lakomski 1991; Sellars 1968, Ch. 5; Churchland 1988; Churchland 1989, especially Ch. 6), a few key points will suffice here to remind us of the origins, problems, and legacy of the theory of mind – what we have called the 'cognition in the head' view.

Underlying this view is a theory of the mind, that is, mental states and processes – 'mindstuff' – that is assumed to be radically different from 'bodystuff', meaning the physical body and the physical world generally. Dualism is the broad philosophical perspective that sanctions such different substances as 'mindstuff' and 'bodystuff' which has given rise to what is known as the 'mind-body' problem (see Churchland 1988, Chapter 2, on the various forms of dualism).

Although its roots go back a long way – Plato's Forms or Ideas are an early example – it has been discussed most frequently in relation to the work of René Decartes (1596–1650). For Descartes, to be human is to be a thinking thing, a *res cogitans*, and the most famous sentence in Western philosophy that expresses our human-ness is *cogito ergo sum* [I think therefore I am]. *Cartesian dualism* (Churchland 1988, p. 8) postulates that reality consists of two basic substances: the first is ordinary matter that extends in space and has spatial dimensions, while the second kind is *conscious reason* that is radically different from ordinary matter and has no position of any sort in space. The central characteristic of conscious reason is the activity of thinking, and it is this that constitutes our real essence, or selves, not our physical bodies. *Direct introspection*, Decartes believed, is the reliable and certain means of access to our inner self, the thinking substance that we are. In this way, any potential physical interaction or contamination of mind by matter is neatly bipassed. The ability to reason, Descartes maintained, is best exemplified in language use and mathematical reasoning. Based on his work in analytic geometry (which he founded), mathematics, because it is free of specific concrete content, became the quintessential model for thought. In also applying the mathematical calculation metaphor to his theory of ideas, Descartes was able to include ideas that arose through the senses as similar to mathematical ideas. Both could be treated formally. 'Reasoning' on this account, as Lakoff and Johnson (1999, p. 407) sum it up, "is akin to mathematical proof".

Descartes' position is more differentiated and complex than we can indicate in a short space, and he did realize the difficulty of needing to explain how mind can have any causal influence on physical matter, such as the body, or in contemporary scientific language, "to explain how brains and minds could interact" (Bechtel et al. 2001, p. 13). His solution was to postulate 'animal spirits', which are fine fluids said to act as a kind of mediating substance that flow through the nerves and thus affect behaviour (Bechtel et al. 2001, p. 14). Needless to say, this postulate did not solve the problem, as it does not explain how something entirely physical can interact with something entirely non-physical. Without going into the various critiques of the more radical form of dualism, *substance dualism* (e.g. Churchland P.M. 1988; Churchland P.S. 1980, 1989; Evers and Lakomski 1991; Lakomski 2007), the plausibility of the (substance) dualist view is seriously undermined by "the *neural dependence* of all known phenomena" (Churchland 1988, p. 20; emphasis in source). For if mindstuff were indeed a separate substance, it should not be affected at all by trauma suffered to the physical brain as the two are said to constitute essentially separate substances. Yet, we have overwhelming evidence that the opposite is true. Trauma to the brain (the physical stuff) seriously affects, and in some cases, destroys, the ability for rational thought (the mental stuff), which is not supposed to be possible on

Descartes' more radical view. In other words, the quintessentially human capacity for rational thought is causally dependent on a well-functioning brain. The knock-out blow for all dualisms, however, is to be found in our evolutionary history, some of which will be discussed in later sections.

On this very brief account of Cartesian dualism, we can see why mind and cognition are reckoned to be *dis-embodied*. The human capacity for rational thought is what makes us human, where the exemplar of rational thought is language and mathematical calculation; rational thought has nothing to do with the physical body. It is important to note here that Descartes' model of thought has in fact created a theory of mental representation, a theory that formed the foundation for first generation of cognitive science. According to Lakoff and Johnson (1999, pp. 407–408):

> In this theory, you can separate the problem of how we think with ideas from the problem of what the ideas are supposed to designate. Even if the second problem is only solvable for restricted special cases, the first problem at least can have a general, mathematically precise solution. That was the attraction of a representational theory of mind for first-generation cognitive science.

The metaphor of the 'brain as computer' so prominently developed in Newell and Simon's (e.g. 1963) work is the result of this philosophical tradition. (For a discussion of cognitive science in educational administration, see Evers and Lakomski 2020).

The idea that minds are separate from brains is still deeply engrained in commonsense understandings of what a mind is and is implied in current leader-centric accounts. But the form of contemporary dualism is less radical than Descartes' initial substance dualism. What Churchland (1988, p. 9) calls *popular dualism* accepts that minds have spatial properties and are located "*inside* the bodies they control: Inside the head, on most views, in intimate contact with the brain". Again, the determination of what is meant by "intimate contact with the brain" is left unspecified and this view suffers the same consequences in the end as its more radical ancestor. Nevertheless, this has not stopped the philosopher Karl Popper and the neuroscientist John Eccles to provide a dualist account of self, reminiscent of Descartes, in their famous book *The Self and its Brain: An Argument for Interactionism*, published in 1985. Perhaps Bechtel et al. (2001, p. 14) have it right when they note that "The attraction of dualism is that it seems to enable the mind to be the creative agent outside the ordinary causal nexus …". It is not hard to see why this reading might be attractive especially to those leaders who believe themselves to be 'transformational'.

Closely related to the idea of a disembodied mind is the view that we have a self, a central core that makes us different from anyone else. In the following section, we take a closer look at what a self is.

## Self as constructed

The preoccupation with understanding self has a long and complex history but has not led to a unified conception. (For discussions, see the collection of essays in the Lakoff and Johnson 1999; Gallagher 2000; Strawson 2000; *Annals NY Academy of Sciences* 2003; Gillihan and Farah 2005; Baumeister 2011, Ch. 13). Rather than rehearsing this history here, and in keeping with our naturalistic perspective, we approach this issue by asking, with Damasio (2010, p. 5): "How does the brain *do* mind?" And secondly, how does the brain make the mind conscious? (Damasio 2010, p. 5). Consciousness research is of immense complexity and there are no definitive answers yet. But there are working hypotheses, such as those advanced by Damasio (2010), Gazzaniga (2011), LeDoux (1996) and Prinz (2015).

Damasio (2010, p. 8) characterizes the self as a process and not a thing. Self-as-process is present at all times when we are conscious. There are two senses in which we talk about the self, from the point of an *observer* who can assess a dynamic object, and the point of view of self as a *knower* that makes possible the organizing and further assessing of our experiences (Baumeister 2011). This dual perspective has already been recognized by James (1890, Ch. X). Furthermore, James's description of the forms of self as (1) the material self; (2) the social self; and (3) the spiritual self has laid the foundations for contemporary naturalistic inquiries of self, including those of Damasio's, as will be shown in the following.

The self as 'I', the knower and subject, is "the key reference in the process of consciousness. The self endows us with a subjective experience" (Damasio 2003, p. 254). And it is the arrival of the subjective perspective that denotes an important stage in biological evolution, in that it builds on the self as object by adding a new layer of neural processing that facilitates yet another layer of mental processing (Damasio 2010, pp. 9–10). It is important to emphasize that the self is assembled through neurobiological processes, from the ground up, so to speak, and that to understand what a self is one has to understand it from the perspective of "the representation of the continuity of the organism ... [and this] is the neural system responsible for the representation of our own bodies" (Damasio 2003, p. 254). Quite clearly, Damasio supports the *embodiment of mind* thesis that rejects the dualistic view of mind as discussed in the previous section that considered the "mental realm [as] *merely correlated with* physical states" (Legrand 2005, p. 413; Gallagher 2000). For Damasio (2003, p. 255): "[T]he backbone of the self as we know it ... is an ongoing, composite representation of a host of body activities, which occurs in a host of brain structures, as many as a dozen, and it is based upon signals coming from the body to the brain, some purely chemical, and some neural, that is, neurochemical". And furthermore, "There is a sameness to this representation, a stability, which contrasts with the variety and discontinuity of external sensory representations" (Damasio 2003, p. 255). Although there can be variations of the organism to maintain homeostasis, the most important goal for any living organism, these are narrowly constrained, and for good reason: too much variation and the organism gets sick or dies.

Thus, self is a process that emerges from the coordinated efforts of the body and through many distributed brain structures over three evolutionary stages, as postulated by Damasio (2010). The unconscious mind, or *protoself*, which is merely an awake 'felt me', which evolved into the *core self*, when the relationship between organism and object comes into existence, and issued in the *autobiographical self*, defined in terms of biographical knowledge of the past and linking it with events in the future. It is the latter, *social self*, that is of most relevance here.

The *social self* can be both overt and covert, working below consciousness where refashioning of one's memory takes place which in turn leads to a subtle rewriting of our history over time. Although we cannot recall all memories, relying on some key episodes instead to make sense of a new episode, constructing the autobiographical self is a coordination problem of immense dimensions. Not only are those brain structures involved that generate the core self – brain stem, thalamus, and cerebral cortex – but also those structures involved in the coordination mechanisms (for details see Damasio 2010, especially pp. 215–225; also, Northoff et al. 2006). At heart, so to speak, the autobiographical self is *the synaptic self* (LeDoux 2002).

A second important result of the evolved self is that there is no central controller, homunculus, or "center of narrative gravity" (Dennett 1992) that coordinates mental activity; third, it follows that self is not a metaphysical entity but is grounded in our biology; fourth, there is no one brain centre or location that produces the self. One might say that self in the brain (= self-representational apparatus) is everywhere and nowhere simultaneously (e.g. Vogeley and Gallagher 2011). It is in this sense that we can speak both of having a self and of describing it as 'distributed'. (For detail on what happens when a brain breaks down, see Damasio 2010, pp. 231–241; LeDoux 2002, Ch. 10 on synaptic sickness.) Given this brief discussion, a notion of self emerges that is "something like a squadron of capacities flying in loose formation ... [or more precisely] a loosely connected set of representational capacities" (Churchland 2002, p. 63, 64) where 'representation' means neural patterns of activity that stretch across populations of neurons that carry information.

## From extended mind to cognitive ecologies

As we argued in the first section, the idea of a theory of mind and of cognition as disembodied is highly implausible when compared with what we know about how our biological brains function and what can happen to our ability to reason when the brain suffers trauma. The explanatory power and scope of the latter trumps the poverty of explanation of the former. A disembodied, dualist account of the mind is unable to explain what the causal processes are that are involved in human thinking and acting, and how biological beings learn. For conceptions of leadership, especially those that advocate transformational leadership, this implausible theory of cognition comes with a high price: it is unable to explain how the very features that are asserted to 'make' leadership, such as good judgment, influencing people, and orchestrating change, can be acquired. Furthermore, as discussed in the previous section, the idea of an autonomous self, so central to leader-centric views of leadership, turns out to be just as implausible when examined through the lens of neuroscience.

Furthermore, the recognition that brains do not resemble serial computers in their operations, and the subsequent switch from the brain-as-computer metaphor to a focus on real, biological brains constituted an important move "outwards into the environment and downwards into the brain" (Bechtel et al. 1999, p. 77; Bechtel and Herschbach 2010). A clearer idea of the details of neural activity had emerged through improved neural net modelling (Evers 2000), while Gibson's (1979) original work on visual perception, *the ecological approach to perception*, demonstrated the importance of the 'outside', that is, the active role the environment plays in human perception whose purpose it is to guide action. Thus, the focus has shifted to the study of perceptual systems, to the "brain, sensory surfaces, and the moving body of the animal – as surrounded by the information-rich environment" (Hutchins 2010; Anderson and Chemero 2017, p. 8).

The softening, if not dissolution, of the inside/outside boundary of cognition, that is, the view that cognition is embodied and embedded, and that the boundary of cognition is therefore much wider than previously drawn, is at the centre of two prominent theories of cognition that despite shared theoretical commitments draw the boundaries of cognition in diverging ways. Our purpose here is not to ascertain which is true, but to see which theory "gives us the best scientific leverage" (Hutchins 2010, p. 707).

The *Extended Mind* or cognition thesis (EM/C) originally advanced by Clark and Chalmers (1998) and defended by Clark (2008), and the *theory of distributed cognition* (DC), initially proposed from the perspective of human-computer-interaction (HCI) (Hollan et al. 2000) both share the assumption that the unit of analysis for cognition comprises the interconnected, reciprocally active relationships between brain, body and social world: cognition is no longer 'in the head' (although the skull-skin distinction remains important for EM) (Clark 2008, 2010, 2011; Wilson and Foglia 2017). As a consequence, culture, context, and history, excluded on the classical cognitive science view, are now included as integral to understanding how humans think. (See Hutchins 1996, Ch. 9, for discussion.) Both perspectives share this fundamental theoretical commitment but take different views on what is the principal focus of study, and particularly on what is the role of brain-bound cognition within a distributed, dynamic system.

An important reason for the expansion of cognition is the view that biological brains, though powerful, are computationally limited and need to offload both memory and computation in order to solve complex problems. Hence, as argued by Clark, non-neural resources such as iPhones, for example, or pen and paper and the abacus in earlier times, amplify or extend our minds, and therefore our cognitive grasp. It is this kind of cognitive bootstrapping that, on a larger scale, has led to the development of social organization and culture which Clark describes as the manifestations of the externalized mind. It is in this broad sense that cognition is extended and is therefore more appropriately seen as a *cognitive system* that comprises the dynamic interaction between all its components.

But EM claims more than that we need to 'lean' on extra-neural and extra-body resources, the 'external scaffolding' (Clark 2015, p. 3758), to accomplish tasks and solve problems. Rather, "when parts of the environment are coupled to the brain *in the right way*, they become parts of the mind" (Chalmers 2008, x; emphases added; Clark 2015, p. 3758). Specifically, evidence for the 'right coupling' is a circumstance "when internal and external resources become fluently tuned and integrated so as to enable the larger system – the biological agent plus specific items of cognitive scaffolding – to engage in new forms of intelligent problem solving" (Wilson and Clark 2009, p. 64). Take Otto, a person with memory impairment, who extensively uses his notebook so that he can successfully negotiate his environment and get to his destination. His constant use of the extra-biological (reliable) artefact of the notebook augments his biological capacities and is therefore an example of extended mind. While 'Otto' was a thought experiment, Clark (2008) provides many examples from a vast array of the sciences to support this claim. It is the postulated parity between external resources (Otto's notebook) and the brain/mind (Otto's 'augmented' brain/mind) that has given rise to much controversy, fuelled by a certain vagueness, *inter alia*, about what exactly Clark meant by 'extended', and what constitutes 'the right way'. (For discussions see Menary 2010a; Special Issue on Extended Cognition, *Philosophical Psychology*, 27, 1, 2014; Special Issue on Socializing the Extended Mind, *Cognitive Systems Research,* 25–26, 2013; Wilson 2002; Shapiro and Spaulding 2009; Walter 2010; Shapiro 2010; Michaelian and Sutton 2013; Cash 2013; Osbeck and Nersessian 2014.) Importantly, in this mashing of external resources with the internal resources of the biological agent plus cognitive scaffolding, the brain remains the central player, "recruiting some complex, non-linear combination of contributions from various types of onboard neural circuit and resources, and doing so in a way expressly tailored to accommodate and exploit the additional and computational potentials introduced …" (Wilson and Clark 2009, p. 65).

For the theory of *distributed cognition* (DC), the primary unit of analysis is at the *systems level,* and this is the first significant difference with EM/C. The causal flow in EM/C is generally from the inside out, from brain to environment, although external resources flow back in ('loop') and therefore shape cognitive processes in turn (Wilson and Clark 2009). For DC, individuals as well as the informational artefacts they use to solve problems, are integral parts of the unit of analysis, the cognitive system, or, as Hutchins (2014) calls it, the *cultural ecosystem of human cognition*. What matters for DC is to understand the *organization* of the cultural-cognitive ecosystems. Here, it is not assumed that the mind 'leaks' into the world but that the world, always and already, contains cognitive processes constituted by functional relationships made up by dynamic patterns of correlation across elements that can be identified. Although EM/C pays attention to the "distributed and extended nature of [soft] assembled cognitive systems", it is the biological brain that does the assembling, the position Clark (2008) adopts with some ambivalence (see Hutchins 2011, for detail; also, Shapiro and Spaulding 2009). DC in contrast focusses on sociotechnical systems such as Hutchins' (1995) study of an airline cockpit, or Hutchins' (1996) famous cognitive ethnography of ship navigation. They exemplify DC's fundamental assumption that "all instances of cognition can be seen as emerging from distributed processes". (Hutchins 2014, p. 36). The navigation example stands in for the general point that complex problem-solving depends on the collective, coordinated efforts of many brains, hands, and artefacts and is beyond the resources of a single individual mind. Problem-solving in social organizations such as schools and universities is no different. Consider such socially and culturally distributed systems as educational curriculum designs, sorting algorithms, critical thinking courses, research funding policies (Cash 2013, p. 64), and the like. The social organization of education, the cognitive abilities and activities of educators, and the communication systems operating between them is thus an important partner because it is social organization that largely determines how information flows through a group, so *the social organization itself is a form of cognitive architecture* (Hollan et al. 2000, p. 177; emphasis added). This, Hollan et al. (2000, p. 177) note, has the odd consequence of being able to 'use the concepts, constructs and explanatory models of social groups to describe what is happening in a mind'.

The brain/mind is not considered as the instigator or source from which extension proceeds into the world. Indeed, for DC, there is no extension. This is not to say, however, that the brain is unimportant. Rather, Hutchins (2011, p. 445; emphases added) explains, the brain "appears as a super-flexible medium that can form functional subsystems that establish and maintain dynamic coordination among constraints imposed by the world of cultural activity, by the body, and by the brain's own prior organization. *The brain has causal powers, but when it comes to human cognition, most of the causal powers of the human brain derive from previous experience in cultural practices"*. Describing the brain's causal powers in this way is a radical departure from the extended mind/cognition perspective.

As to the question of whether or not there is a centre to a cognitive system, where the boundary is of any such system, or whether there is a skull or skin boundary, are matters for empirical investigation. Furthermore, unlike EM/C, distributed cognition operates at different spatial and temporal scales while the former "operate[s] on a spatial scale somewhat larger than an individual person" (Hutchins 2014, p. 37). As Hutchins (2014, p. 36; 2006) emphasizes, 'cognition' in distributed cognition "is a perspective on all of cognition."

A further and significant difference between distributed cognition and EM/C is that Clark (2008, p. 13) is ambiguous about how he understands 'assembly', that is, the 'on the spot' recruitment of relevant mix of problem-solving resources, as either a process or the product. Here, Hutchins suggests, the recruitment process can be better understood if we took note of "the role of cultural practices in the orchestration of soft-assembly of extended systems" (Hutchins 2011, p. 440), a point Clark (2011, p. 460) concedes. This is an important point because, although brains are excellent at pattern recognition and anticipating what to do next (Churchland and Sejnowski 1994), this, according to Hutchins (2008, p. 2017) says little about "What determines which patterns are found in experience? The nature of sensory apparatus and gestalt principles provide biases that make some possible patterns more salient than others. Beyond that, however, we are in the realm of cultural practices. Both the techniques of perceiving patterns and the organization of the system of patterns that are perceived are matters of cultural practice".

Focusing on the (empirical) study of *cultural practices* has the consequence that the idea of the mind/brain as the essential core element drops out – a step too far for Clark (2011). In light of the question raised earlier regarding which theory gets us further by way of empirical investigation, Clark (2011, p. 460) has, for all intents and purposes, ruled out EM/C: "I am now fairly convinced that … that there will be no straightforward empirical resolution to the questions concerning cognitive extension".

While the extended mind/cognition hypothesis brings mind, body, and world together by way of something like cognitive bootstrapping, it is the study of cultural practices that operate in, and are constrained by a cognitive ecology, that is, *encultured cognition* (Hutchins 2011, p. 445), that helps us understand cognitive phenomena in social-cultural contexts, including school leadership.

## Cognitive practices and enculturated cognition

Given the emphasis on cognitive cultural practices in distributed cognition, it is important to understand more clearly what cultural practices are, and how cognition is enculturated through their use. (For discussion see Tollefsen 2006; Vogeley and Roepstorff 2009; Cash 2010; Wilson 2010; Gallagher 2013.)

In Hutchins' (2011, p. 440; 1996; 2008) cognitive anthropological perspective, a practice is *cultural* "if it exists in a cognitive ecology such that it is constrained by or coordinated with the practices of other persons. Above all else, *cultural practices are the things people do in interaction with one another*" Such practices are also *patterned* in certain ways in that they display regularities that come about through everyday activities, which in turn shape them (Roepstorff et al. 2010, p. 1051). Practically all external representations are the result of cultural practices, including all forms of language. They are "emergent products of dynamic distributed networks of constraints" (Hutchins 2011, p. 441) where constraints may arise from many different sources, either internal and mental or external, including social others. Language (and language-like behaviours, such as speaking, Roepstorff et al., 2010), are prime examples of collective cognitive activity (Hutchins and Johnson 2009, p. 523).

Unlike Cartesian assumptions, language is something that evolved through shared, collective activity over time and is not something any one person has invented. Just as there was no first teacher of mathematics (Sloman 2010), there was no first teacher of language, both cognitive achievements being the result of evolutionary pressures. So, if there was no 'central controller', what are the kinds of processes that have led to the development of shared lexicons and grammars? Since we cannot go back in evolutionary time, the best way to find out is by means of computational modelling that simulates the emergence of language. Hutchins and Hazlehurst (1995) have developed and run connectionist networks that successfully created a lexicon 'from scratch' on the assumption of embodiment, the emergence of language in the context of inter-agent communication, and incremental change resulting from series of interactions between pairs of agents in a community (Hutchins and Johnson 2009, p. 525). The model thus represents a theory of cognition where symbols are the outcome of inter- and intra-individual organizations of behaviour, that is, the result of cultural process (Hutchins and Hazlehurst 1995, p. 158).

The other core example of encultured cognition is mathematical cognition, discussed by Menary and Kirchhoff 2013; Menary 2015; Menary and Gillett 2016. Although Menary (2007, 2012) assumes an integrationist theoretical framework, *Cognitive Integration* (CI), he shares the fundamental assumptions of DC, and the view of cognition as a dynamical system (Menary 2010b). Proceeding from a broad evolutionary perspective with particular reference to the developmental case for the plasticity of the brain and cultural learning, enculturated cognition is constituted through *normative patterned practices* (NPPs) (for detail see Menary and Gillett 2016, p. 78).

The cultural capital thus inherited contains not only physical artefacts but also representational systems such as writing and number systems, together with the skills and methods for training and teaching new skills (e.g. Menary and Kirchhoff 2013). The fact that we have acquired/learnt higher cognitive functions such as writing and number systems in a relatively short period of time required more than the basic neural circuitry evolution has endowed us with. This must be the case because, according to Dehaene (2005, p. 133), reading was "invented about 5400 years ago, and symbolic arithmetic is even more recent: Arabic notation and most of its associated algorithms were not available even a thousand year ago".

What we have inherited are basic cortical functions for what Dehaene called 'number sense' (Dehaene 1997, 2005, 2007; Ansari 2008), by which is meant an approximate, non-linguistic, number system (ANS) for "discriminating non-symbolic numerosities greater than 4" (Menary 2015, p. 12), an early evolved ability we share with other animals. The explanation of how we managed to get from ancient number sense to a second, discrete numerical system such as arithmetic in a much shorter time scale than is possible for biological evolution, Menary (2015) suggests, is through *cultural learning*. (Some of the complexities involved in this shift are outlined in Sloman 2010, who provides many examples of empirical discovery learning in young children and toddlers that leads to non-empirical discoveries, his 'toddler theorems'.)

Cultural learning, as indicated above, is made possible by behavioural and neural plasticity, facilitated by 'neuronal recycling', which is "a process of pre-empting or recycling preexisting brain circuitry" (Dehaene 2005, p. 134).

(For a similar proposal, *neural reuse*, see Anderson 2010, and his discussion of Dehaene's theory, in Anderson 2010, pp. 262–263.) So, as a result of neural plasticity and subsequent cultural learning, humans have acquired a digital model of mathematical cognition which overlaps with the older model and cannot be mapped directly onto the older one (Menary 2015, p. 13, Menary and Gillett 2016, pp. 80–83). As Dehaene and Cohen (2007, cited in Menary 2015, p. 13) describe the development, "The arithmetic intuition that we inherit through evolution is continuous and approximate. The learning of words and numbers makes it digital and precise. Symbols give us access to sequential algorithms for exact calculations".

Not only is the learning of modern mathematics an example of enculturation par excellence, the mathematical practices thus acquired have transformed human cognition in immeasurable ways. In terms of evidence for their transformative effects on the brain, Tang et al. (2006), for example, demonstrated the effects of culture on the neural correlates of number processing of native English and Chinese speakers. (For other cross-cultural differences in the brain mechanisms that underlie a range of other cognitive functions, see Ansari 2008; Dehaene and Cohen 2007; Menary and Gillett 2016, pp. 80–81.) There is still much debate and lack of detailed understanding how culture and learning show up in the brain's architecture, so to speak. But the point to be made here is a broader one.

The perspective of distributed or enculturated embodied cognition with its focus on cultural practices constrained and defined by their cultural niches upends traditional ways of understanding cognition and thus social behaviour. Rather than assuming that a small neural change somewhere in our early evolutionary history was the trigger for the development of our modern cognitive abilities (e.g. Clark 2001), it may equally well be a series of small changes in cultural practices that were responsible. As Hutchins (2008, p. 2018) notes, "there is no reason to favour changes in the brain over innovations in cultural practices as drivers of primate cognitive development".

As our brains are not isolated from the body and the social-cultural world, it follows that social practices such as teaching, learning, and leading cannot be understood by studying just one of their components. Therefore, the customary attribution of, say, school success to the cognitive abilities of the principal is a misattribution as it ignores the wider cognitive web of which the principal's cognition is but a part. The result of such cognitive tunnel vision is to miss out on determining which social-cultural factors contribute to whatever school success was defined to be.

## Conclusion

As a consequence of the broadening of cognition from skull-bound to distributed in the sense we discussed it here, the tension between leader cognition and context can be considered resolved. The unit of analysis is the cognitive *system*, whatever system is the purpose of study at any given time. This makes the explanatory task more complex and requires a different approach.

The most important consequence of the argument we developed is that leaders can no longer be assumed to be the (cognitive) centres *a priori* for all contexts and purposes, the central assumption of leader-centric views. As most organizational tasks and solutions in schools are distributed, they tend to draw on different cognitive centres. Such cognitive collaboration and coordination are always shaped by structural constraints, and these are beyond the control of any one individual. But we should not conclude from this that now no one is responsible. Determining the causes that account for, say, increased student performance, or, alternatively, declining student numbers, requires careful investigation, not jumping to conclusions that traditionally held the principal responsible.

Given that the traditional notion of autonomy and the autonomous self are mere fictions, the issue that needs resolving now is to work out how individual agents, such as principals, "can make autonomous decisions while acting in ways that are dependent upon and shaped by ... socially distributed systems" (Cash 2013, p. 66). Being autonomous and responsible as an agent means that autonomy and responsibility are 'relational' in the sense of being shaped and constrained by relationships, legal and ethical institutions, and the norms and practices that obtain in the culture. So, as Cash (2013, p. 67) suggests, the question of responsibility begins not with the individual, but with the distributed practices, and the issue then is that we need to provide reasons for *"whether I can reasonably be said to be responsible* for the actions and ideas that result from the ways I am embedded in this socially distributed milieu of relations, norms, practices, institutions, and the tools and resources they provide me" Cash (2013, p. 67) suggests that a distributed cognitive process *"counts as mine if it is appropriate to hold me responsible – to blame me or praise me, punish me or credit me – for the ideas or actions produced by this process"*. Giving and asking for reasons is a shared social practice which has its own norms, and it is this practice that constitutes when someone can be fairly held responsible for an action, and to what degree. Like all socially distributed practices, this normative practice too changes over time.

## References

*Annals NY Academy of Sciences* (2003). 1001.
Anderson, M.L. (2010). Neural reuse: A fundamental organizational principle of the brain. *Behavioral and Brain Sciences*, 33, 245–264.
Anderson, M.L., & Chemero, A. (2017). The brain evolved to guide action. In S.V. Shepherd (Ed.), *The Wiley handbook of evolutionary neuroscience* (pp. 1–20). Oxford: John Wiley & Sons.
Ansari, D. (2008). Effects of development and enculturation on number representation in the brain. *Nature Reviews Neuroscience*, 9, 278–291.
Baumeister, R.F. (2011). The unity of self at the interface of the animal body and the cultural system. *Psychological Studies*, 56(1), 5–11.

Bechtel, W., & Herschbach, M. (2010). Philosophy of the cognitive sciences. In F. Althoff (Ed.), *Philosophy of the special sciences*, Albany, NY: SUNY Press.

Bechtel, W., Mandik, P., & Mundale, J. (2001). Philosophy meets the neurosciences. In W. Bechtel, P. Mandik, J. Mundale, & R. Stufflebeam (Eds.), *Philosophy and the neurosciences: A reader*, Oxford: Basil Blackwell.

Bechtel, W., Abrahamsen, A., & Graham, G. (1999). Part 1: The life of cognitive science. In A. Bechtel, & G. Graham (Eds.), *A companion to cognitive science* (pp. 1–107). Oxford: Blackwell.

Caldwell, B.J. (2005). School-based management. *The international institute for educational planning (IIEP) and the international academy of education (IAE)*, Paris and Brussels: UNESCO 2005.

Caldwell, B.J. (1992). The principal as leader of the self-managing school in Australia. *Journal of Educational Administration*, 30(3), 6–20.

Caldwell, B.J., & Spinks, J. (1988). *The self-managing school*. London: Falmer.

Caldwell, B.J., & Spinks, J. (1992). *Leading the self-managing school*. London: Routledge/Falmer.

Cash, M. (2013). Cognition without borders: "Third wave" socially distributed cognition and relational autonomy. *Cognitive Systems Research*, 25–26 61–71.

Cash, M. (2010). Extended cognition, personal responsibility, and relational autonomy. *Phenomenology and the Cognitive sciences*, 9(4), 645–671. http://dx.doi.org/10.1007/s11097-010-9177-8.

Chalmers, D. (2008). Foreword. In A. Clark (Ed.), (2008). *Supersizing the mind*, X. Oxford: Oxford University Press.

Churchland, P.M. (1988). *Matter and consciousness*. Revised edition. Cambridge, MA: MIT Press.

Churchland, P.S. (1980). Language, thought, and information processing, *Nous,* 14, pp. 147–170.

Churchland, P.S. (1989). *Neurophilosophy*. Cambridge, MA: MIT Press.

Churchland, P.S. (2002). *Brain-wise*. Cambridge, MA: MIT Press.

Churchland, P.S., & Sejnowski, T.J. (1994). *The computational brain*. Cambridge, MA: MIT Press.

Clark, A. (2015). What 'extended me' knows, *Synthese*, 192, 3757–3775.

Clark, A. (2011). Finding the mind. Book symposium on supersizing the mind: embodiment, action, and cognitive extension. *Philosophical Studies*, 152, 447–461.

Clark, A. (2010). Memento's revenge: The extended mind, extended. In R. Menary (Ed.), *The extended mind* (pp. 43–66). Cambridge, MA: MIT Press.

Clark, A. (2008). *Supersizing the mind: Embodiment, action, and cognitive extension*. Oxford: Oxford University Press.

Clark, A. (2001). *Mindware: An introduction to the philosophy of cognitive science*. Oxford: Oxford University Press.

Clark, A., & Chalmers, D. (1998). The extended mind. *Analysis*, 58, 7–19.

Damasio, A.R. (2010). *Self comes to mind: Constructing the conscious brain*. New York, NY: Pantheon Books.

Damasio, A.R. (2003). Feelings of emotion and the self. *Annals of the NY Academy of Sciences*, 1001, 253–261.

Day, C. (2005). Introduction to ISSPP. *Journal of Educational Leadership*, 43(6), 533–538.

Day, C., & Gurr, D. (Eds.) 2014). *Leading schools successfully: Stories from the field*. London: Routledge.

Dehaene, S. (2007). Symbols and quantities in parietal cortex: Elements of a mathematical theory of number representation and manipulation. In P. Haggard, Y. Rossetti, & M. Kawato (Eds.), *Attention & performance xxii. Sensori-motor foundations of higher cognition* (pp. 527–574). Cambridge, MA: Harvard University Press.

Dehaene, S. (2005). Evolution of human cortical circuits for reading and arithmetic: The "neuronal recycling" hypothesis. In S. Dehaene, J.R. Duhamel, M. Hauser, & G. Rizzolatti (Eds.), *From monkey brain to human brain* (pp. 133–157). Cambridge, MA: MIT Press.

Dehaene, S. (1997). *The number sense – How the mind creates mathematics.* London: Penguin.

Dehaene, S., & Cohen, L. (2007). Cultural recycling of cortical maps. *Neuron*, 56, 384–398.

Dennett, D.C. (1992). The self as a center of narrative gravity. In F.S. Kessel, P.M. Cole, & D.L. Johnson (Eds.), *Self and consciousness: Multiple perspectives* (pp. 103–115). Hillsdale, NJ: Lawrence Erlbaum Associates.

Drysdale, L., & Gurr, D. (2017). Reflections on successful school leadership from the international successful school principalship project. In G. Lakomski, S. Eacott, & C.W. Evers (Eds.), *Questioning leadership: New directions for educational organisations* (pp. 164–178). London and New York: Routledge.

Drysdale, L., & Gurr, D. (2011). The theory and practice of successful school leadership in Australia. *School Leadership and Management*, 31(4), 355–368.

Evers, C.W. (2000). Connectionist modeling and education. *Australian Journal of Education*, 44(3), 209–225.

Evers, C.W., & Lakomski, G. (1991). *Knowing educational administration.* Oxford: Elsevier.

Evers, C.W., & Lakomski, G. (2020). Cognitive science and educational administration. In R. Papa et al. (Eds.), *The Oxford encyclopedia of educational administration.* Oxford: Oxford University Press.

Gallagher, S. (2013). The socially extended mind. *Cognitive Systems Research*, 25–26 pp. 4–12.

Gallagher, S. (2000). Philosophical conceptions of the self: Implications for cognitive science. *Trends in Cognitive Sciences*, 4(1), 14–21.

Gazzaniga, M.S. (2011). *Who's in charge? Free will and the science of the brain.* New York, NY: Ecco *(imprint of HarperCollins).*

Gibson, J.J. (1979). *The ecological approach to visual perception.* Boston: Houghton Mifflin.

Gillihan, S.J., & Farah, M.J. (2005). Is self special? A critical review of evidence from experimental psychology and cognitive neuroscience. *Psychological Bulletin*, 131(1), 76–97.

Hollan, J., Hutchins, E., & Kirsh, D. (2000). Distributed cognition: Toward a new foundation for human–computer interaction research. *ACM transactions on computer–human interaction*, 7(2), 174–196.

Hutchins, E. (1995). How a cockpit remembers its speeds. *Cognitive Science*, 19, 265–288.

Hutchins, E. (1996). *Cognition in the wild.* Cambridge, MA: MIT Press.

Hutchins, E. (2006). The distributed cognition perspective on human interaction. In N.J. Enfield, & S.C. Levinson (Eds.), *Roots of human sociality: Culture, cognition and interaction* (pp. 375–398). Oxford: Berg.

Hutchins, E. (2008). The role of cultural practices in the emergence of modern human intelligence. *Philosophical Transactions of the Royal Society B: Biological Sciences*, 363, 2011–2019.

Hutchins, E. (2010). Cognitive ecology. *Topics in Cognitive Science*, 2, 705–715.

Hutchins, E. (2011). Enculturating the supersized mind. *Philosophical Studies*, 152, 437–446.

Hutchins, E. (2014). The cultural ecosystem of human cognition. *Philosophical Psychology*, 27(1), 34–49.

Hutchins, E., & Hazlehurst, B. (1995). How to invent a lexicon: The development of shared symbols in interaction. In N. Gilbert, & R. Conte (Eds.), *Artificial societies: The computer simulation of social life* (pp. 157–189). London: UCL Press.

Hutchins, E., & Johnson, C.M. (2009). Modeling the emergence of language as an embodied collective cognitive activity. *Topics in Cognitive Science*, 1, 523–546.

James, W. (1890). *The principles of psychology.* New York, NY: Henry Holt.

Lakoff, G., & Johnson, M. (1999). *Philosophy in the flesh.* New York, NY: Basic Books.

Lakomski, G. (2007). Renewing the mind or bringing the knowledge age to the schoolhouse. *Australian Journal of Education*, 51(3), 315–327.
Lakomski, G., & Evers, C.W. (2020). Theories of educational leadership. In R. Papa et al., LeDoux, J. (2002) (Eds.). *The synaptic self*. New York, NY: Penguin Books.
LeDoux, J. (1996). *The emotional brain*. New York, NY: Simon & Schuster Paperbacks.
Legrand, D. (2005). Being a body. *Trends in Cognitive Sciences*, 9(9), 413–414.
Leithwood, K., & Day, C. (2007). Starting with what we know. In C. Day, & K. Leithwood (Eds.), *Successful school leadership in times of change* (pp. 1–16). Dordrecht, The Netherlands: Springer.
Menary, R. (2015). Mathematical cognition – A case of enculturation. In T. Metzinger, & J.M. Windt (Eds.), *Open MIND*, 25, 1–20. Frankfurt am Main: MIND Group.
Menary, R. (2012). Cognitive practices and cognitive character. *Philosophical Explorations*, 15(2), 147–164.
Menary, R.(Ed.) (2010a). *The extended mind*. Cambridge, MA: MIT Press.
Menary, R. (2010b). Cognitive integration and the extended mind. In R. Menary (Ed.), *The extended mind* (pp. 227–243). Cambridge, MA: MIT Press.
Menary, R. (2007). *Cognitive integration: Mind and cognition unbounded*. Basingstoke: Palgrave Macmillan.
Menary, R., & Gillett, A.J. (2016). *Embodying culture*. In J. Kiverstein (Ed.), *The routledge handbook of philosophy of the social mind* (pp. 72–87). London: Routledge.
Menary, R., & Kirchhoff, M. (2013). Cognitive transformations and extended expertise. *Educational Philosophy and Theory*, 46(6), 610–623.
Michaelian, K., & Sutton, J. (2013). Distributed cognition and memory research: History and future directions. *Review of Philosophy and Psychology*, 4, 1–24.
Newell, A., & Simon, H.A. (1963). GPS: A program that simulates human thought. In E.A. Feigenbaum, & J. Feldman (Eds.), *Computers and thought* (pp. 279–296). New York, NY: McGraw-Hill.
Northoff, G., Heinzel, A., de Greck, M., Bermpohl, F., Dobrowolny, H., & Panksepp, J. (2006). Self-referential processing in our brain – A meta–analysis of imaging studies on the self. *NeuroImage*, 31, 440–457.
Osbeck, L.M., & Nersessian, N.J. (2014). Situating distributed cognition. *Philosophical Psychology*, 27(1), 82–97, DOI: 10.1080/09515089.2013.829384
Popper, K.R., & Eccles, J.C. (1985). *The self and its brain: An argument for interactionism*. New York, NY: Springer International.
Prinz, J. (2015). *The conscious brain*. New York: Oxford University Press.
Sloman, A. (2010). If learning maths requires a teacher, where did the first teachers come from? Slide presentation, *Symposium on Mathematical Cognition AISB2010*. Learning Sciences Research Institute, University of Nottingham 2nd Feb 2010. Revised May 6, 2010.
Strawson, G. (2000). The phenomenology and ontology of the self. In D. Zahavi (Ed.), *Exploring the self: Philosophical and psychopathological perspectives on self-experience* (vol. 23, pp. 39–54). Amsterdam: John Benjamins.
Vroom, V.H., & Jago, A.G. (2007). The role of the situation in leadership. *American Psychologist*, 61(1), 17–34.
Roepstorff, A., Niewöhner, J., & Beck, S. (2010). Enculturing brains through patterned practices. *Neural Networks*, 23, 1051–1059.
Sellars, W.F. (1968). *Science, perception, and reality*. London: Routledge & Kegan Paul. Third impression.
Shapiro, L. (2010). James bond and the Barking dog: Evolution and extended cognition, *Philosophy of Science*, 77, 400–418.

Shapiro, L., & Spaulding, S. (2009). Supersizing the mind: Embodiment, action, and cognitive extension. *Notre Dame Philosophical Reviews*, 1–3.

Tang, Y., Zhang, W., Kewel, C., Feng, S., Ji, Y., Shen, J., Reiman, E.M., & Llu, Y. (2006). Arithmetic processing in the brain shaped by cultures. *Proceedings of the National Academy of Sciences*, 103(28), 10775–10780.

Tollefsen, D.P. (2006). From extended mind to collective mind. *Cognitive Systems Research*, 7(2–3), 140–150. http://dx.doi.org/10.1016/ j.cogsys.2006.01.001.

Vogeley, K., & Gallagher, S. (2011). Self in the brain. In S. Gallagher (Ed.), *The Oxford handbook of the self* (pp. 111–36). Oxford: Oxford University Press.

Vogeley, K., & Roepstorff, A. (2009). Contextualising culture and social cognition. *Trends in Cognitive Sciences*, 13, 511–516.

Walter, S. (2010). Cognitive extension, the parity argument, functionalism, and the mark of the cognitive. *Synthese*, 177, 285–300.

Whitty, G., Power, S., & Haplin, D. (1997). *Devolution and choice: The school, The state and The market*. Buckingham: Open University.

Wilson, M. (2010). The re-tooled mind: How culture re-engineers cognition. *Social Cognitive & Affective Neuroscience*, 5, 180–187.

Wilson, M. (2002). Six views of embodied cognition. *Psychonomic Bulletin and Review*, 94, 625-636.

Wilson, R.A., & Clark, A. (2009). How to situate cognition. In P. Robbins, & M. Aydede (Eds.), *The Cambridge handbook of situated cognition* (pp. 55–78). New York, NY: Cambridge University Press.

Wilson, R.A., & Foglia, L. (2017). Embodied cognition. In E.N. Zalta (Ed.), *The stanford encyclopedia of philosophy* (pp. 1–41). Stanford, CA: Metaphysics Research Lab, Stanford University.

# PART II
# The social context of leadership

# 4
# LEADERSHIP, EVIDENCE, AND INFERENCE

## Introduction

We begin with an analogy that may be a useful orientation to the arguments that follow. In Newtonian celestial mechanics, the central focus of what happens in the world is the behaviour of matter and energy in the broad context of Euclidean space. But importantly, this space is causally inert, playing no role in the behaviour of this material world. In Einstein's general relativity, however, the context of non-Euclidean space is an active causal participant in the behaviour of matter and energy. The geometry of space causes matter to move in certain ways. Our view is that much educational research draws too sharp a boundary between the behaviour of people while understating the broader causally active contexts in which they act. Part of the reason for this is epistemological. While no one believes that regularities in social science data can ever enjoy the status of law-like generalizations, there is nevertheless a need to compress data by omitting what seem to be less relevant causal influences. How to achieve this compression is a feature of many statistical devices employed in quantitative leadership research. We argue that the mechanism involved operates by bringing prior theory to bear on the design of such research, the creation of data categories, and the analysis of data.

If limiting consideration of contexts lends support to making (albeit modest restricted) generalizations, attending closely to the details of context that qualitative research permits, can have the opposite effect. For example, the leadership Churchill demonstrated during World War II may be so embedded in those circumstances that very little of it may have been applicable beyond that context. Indeed, Churchill was voted out of office after the war. We do not mean to say that lessons can never be learned from particular examples. Rather, the conditions for such learning need to be closely circumscribed, in our view having most to do with the commonalities that go into the type of constraints that are found in the examples and their intended application by way of inference. We explore these issues in what follows.

## Learning from other leaders

In his book *Educational Leadership: The Moral Art*, Hodgkinson (1991) regards leadership in organizations as occurring at four levels of organization each involving four different aspects of morality. At the lowest level, Type III values reflect individual affect. At the next level, Type IIB values reflect considerations of group solidarity. At the next level, Type IIA values are about the rational coordination of means and ends. However, at the top of the organizational hierarchy where leaders are responsible for setting the organization's vision and moral purpose, leaders need to be guided by trans-rational Type I values, those that involve a capacity for understanding and discerning higher moral demands. Hodgkinson helps to distinguish the higher values by considering what kind of training is most appropriate. For Type IIA values, he associates training with what might be found in a typical MBA curriculum, with a focus on rationality, logic, efficiency, effectiveness, and the like (Hodgkinson 1991, p. 157). For Type I values, he suggests something entirely different, including the Oxford University PPE program (Philosophy, Politics, and Economics), psycho-biography, protégéship, dramaturgy, and adventures (Hodgkinson 1991, p. 157). As biographical accounts of 'great men' have been rather popular in the leadership literature, we here single out biography to illustrate a point about the logic of inference from the particular. For some, it is supposed there is much to be learned from such studies.

At a time when scepticism abounded (and still does) in belief in some essence that all leaders have in common, Gardner, in *Leading Minds: An Anatomy Of Leadership* (1995) sought to find some common factors among eleven leaders ranging from Margaret Mead and J. Robert Oppenheimer, to Margaret Thatcher and Mahatma Gandhi. By incorporating common contextual factors, he made the task more plausible. Nevertheless, the contexts in which the most influential leaders have acted in history have been very different. Yet, adherents of religious and cultural traditions with fealty to Jesus, or Mohammad, or Confucius, or Buddha readily draw inspiration and lessons on how to act today. Education also has its leaders who have left behind a body of ideas and inspired the creation of school systems: Steiner, Montessori, Dewey, and A.S. Neill's experimental school Summerhill. Gronn's monumental biography *Just as I Am: A Life of J.R. Darling* (2017) is another example thought to contain lessons in leadership beyond Darling's time at Geelong Grammar.

Making inferences about what a school leader might do today based on evidence from what they did in another time and place involves reasoning about counterfactuals, or contrary-to-fact conditionals. Here is an example. During the Korean War, there was some speculation over whether the commander of the US forces, General Douglas MacArthur, wanted to use the atom bomb. To illustrate the problems of counterfactual reasoning, Quine (1960, p. 222) constructed the following example concerning advice that Julius Caesar might have given.

If Caesar were in command, he would use the atom bomb,
If Caesar were in command, he would use catapults.

Everything we know about Caesar from his *War Commentaries* shows that he used catapults in his military campaigns. Yet, this would be plainly nonsense in the context of the Korean War. So, the issue seems to be one of finding some common description of two very dissimilar contexts in a way that allows a choice. Suppose we try the following: Caesar made use of the most powerful weapons available in order to win a battle; the atom bomb is the most powerful weapon available in that context; therefore, Caesar would have used it. But now further contextual wrinkles emerge. For example, the Russians also had the atomic bomb, and there was a chance they would have intervened if the United States had used it. Some of Caesar's opposing armies also had catapults, but the consequences of both sides using them are qualitatively different to both sides using atomic bombs. The more the relevant features of the two contexts diverge, the less plausible it becomes to sustain an inference from what is done in one context to be applicable to another context.

The reason the pair of sentences above are counterfactuals is because their antecedent clause 'If Caesar were in command' is false, or contrary to the facts. In the standard logic of sentences – the propositional calculus – the expression 'p implies q' is read as 'if p, then q' and is true for all truth values of p and q except where p is true and q is false. But when p is false, the inference is true regardless of whether q is true or false. Since there are many examples beyond the Caesar example where we can make perfect sense of counterfactuals, the standard logic of the propositional calculus is not sufficient for determining their truth value. Providing an adequate semantics for understanding the truth conditions of counterfactuals is something of a cottage industry in philosophy of science and philosophical logic. (For a detailed look, see Starr 2019.) We take sides on this, but without getting too involved in the machinery. As an approximation, consider the counterfactual: if the battery were flat, the car would not start. The reason this is fairly straightforward is because we have a plausible understanding of the causal role the battery plays in starting that particular car. Counterfactuals work because they are sustained by causal regularities, not regular coincidences. Moreover, because of the similarity of the causal role of batteries in most cars, we can plausibly generalize to other vehicles.

## Similarity in classification

Counterfactuals don't just turn up in studies purporting to learn lessons from individual leaders. They also turn up in ex post facto studies, that is, studies that seek to find patterns in the natural social order as it pertains to certain types of schools, and then infer what can be applied to other schools. A good example of this is the International Successful School Principalship Project. (See Drysdale and Gurr

2017, for an overview.) Given that not all principals manifest successful leadership, the logic is to apply the patterns as found in successful principal leadership and recommend their use in counterfactual contexts. The hidden assumption is that there is enough causal similarity for these lessons to be applicable. Counterfactuals can also turn up in experimental studies. For example, the kind of rigorous experimental designs employed in cognitive load theory (Sweller et al. 2019) may only produce findings that are applicable to those experimental conditions rather than the counterfactual circumstances of the regular classroom where variables are not controlled. We begin to tackle this issue with a discussion of similarity.

In his book *Knowing and Guessing*, Watanabe (1969, pp. 362–377) proved a remarkable theorem which he called "the theorem of the ugly duckling" after the Hans Christian Andersen story. The theorem states that in the absence of any bias in choosing properties, there are as many similarities, or properties in common, between two swans as there are between a swan and a duck. Watanabe's formal proof is technical, covering an arbitrarily large number of objects and properties, and was not much noticed at the time of publication (although a number of philosophers who worked in logic and set theory had earlier reached the same conclusion). These days, when practical applications of pattern recognition and extraction are prominent in computer science, much work acknowledges the theorem by focusing on finding task specific efficient biases or weights in assigning to presumed properties. (Wang et al. 2008, deals with this problem in neural networks. An introductory account of neural networks can be found in Evers 2000.) There are also now many simplified proofs of the theorem available. (An abbreviated presentation of the proof and its relevance to competing claims about human nature in educational theory can be found in Evers 1982, pp. 271–274.)

Here is a commonly used illustration of the proof by way of an example. Suppose we have in a row, three objects, a swan (S), then another swan (S), and then a duck (D). We consider all logically possible combinations of two features, First in the line-up and White in colour, that can be possessed by the three objects. Where the logically possible combinations we can call 'properties' apply to an object we signal this by a '1'. Where they don't apply we write a '0'. Here is what a complete table would look like:

## Swans, a duck, and property possession

| S, S, D | Swan, Swan, Duck |
|---|---|
| 1, 0, 0 | First and White |
| 1, 1, 0 | First or White |
| 1, 0, 1 | First or Not-White (exclusive "or") |
| 0, 1, 1 | Not-First or White |
| 0, 0, 1 | Not-First and Not-White |
| 0, 1, 0 | Not-First and White |
| 0, 0, 0 | First and Not-White |
| 1, 1, 1 | Not-First or White |

By looking down the columns beneath each of S, S, and D, we can see that they each have four properties in common with each other (the same number of '1' entries), though not the same properties. That is, the duck has as many properties in common with either swan as each swan has to the other swan. More generally, without some biasing or weighting of properties, there is no such thing as a class of similar objects (Wikipedia contributors, 2021, July 1).

This problem was known to Quine who used the absence of a similarity class without prior bias to develop a theory of epistemically progressive bias acquisition required to sustain an account of 'natural kinds' used in many branches of science (Quine 1969, pp. 114–138. For other attempts to construct useful biases or weightings see Wilkins and Ebach 2014). One of the most systematic uses of this result can be found in the work of Popper (1959, 1963). Popper developed his own argument, published ten years before Watanabe's proof. The argument was more of a sketch than a formal proof. Instead of swans and ducks, Popper (1959, pp. 420–441) used a series of geometric shapes, circle, triangle, square, and rectangle, with a variety of features, size, shading, and dots. He says "these diagrams show that things may be similar in *different respects,* and that any two things which are from one point of view similar may be dissimilar from another point of view. Generally, similarity, and with it repetition, always presuppose the adoption of *a point of view*", (Popper 1959, p. 421). The argument is that the task of searching for patterns among data is necessarily, logically, preceded by some classification scheme, or prior set of biases that, with sophistication, can be regarded as a theory. (Technical note: it may be thought that this result is an artifact of an extensional system of logic, the predicate calculus, and that if an intensional system is used similarity could be saved. But this move just shifts the identification of similarities to the semantics for an intensional logic and is thus question-begging.)

The upshot is that the biases, initially innate for first learning to occur in infancy, need some epistemic mechanism to improve over time to produce the vastly sophisticated points of view we recognize as modern science, and for us to navigate through the social and material world having "better than random or coin tossing chances of coming out right…" (Quine 1969, p. 127). Popper was sceptical of using a prior theory developed from empirical evidence based on its own classifications of evidence to improve itself through accumulating more confirming evidence of its epistemic merits. A theory that leads a charmed empirical life, abetted by a built-in confirmation bias that hunts for confirming instances, garners no reasons for making changes. Popper's suggestion was that the growth of knowledge is driven by efforts to falsify theories. Revisions are prompted when theoretically motivated expectations are disappointed by experience. His claim was that knowledge grows by a process of making conjectures, preferably bold ones, and then engaging in a concerted effort to refute those conjectures (Popper 1963). The required narrowing is that conjectures are best seen as tentative theories designed to address problems, thus leading to the 'Popper Cycle' model discussed in Chapter 1, and that will be elaborated in Chapter 6.

In examining research into educational leadership, our central claim is that the prior viewpoints we bring to the task of specifying similarities among our observations are to do with prior theories of leadership and prior methods of inquiry used to identify data that can function in inferences usually to do with answering research questions.

## Theory-ladenness

The meanings of the words we use are given primarily through two sources. The first, most relevant at infancy, is via ostensive definition. A word is associated with a particular range of sensory input. The second, and most common beyond initial language learning, is via the conceptual role a word plays in a wider linguistic context. An example is the meaning of the word 'force'. Within the network of claims comprising Newtonian mechanics, it means mass times acceleration: F=ma. Within special relativity, adjustments need to be made, for example, that the mass of an object increases as its velocity increases. Within general relativity, when it comes to the force of gravity, it is given a geometrical meaning. Something like this also applies in social science, but with the initial meaning of words being given by theories embedded in various usages in ordinary language. The Thesaurus for Microsoft Word provides a list that includes "control, guidance, direction, and headship" as its suggestions for 'leadership'.

Where the meaning of a term like 'leadership' is significantly due to its conceptual role within some theory, there arises a question as to how empirical evidence might be relevant to such an account of leadership. Some words, such as 'bachelor', can be bound so tightly to a conceptual role that empirical evidence is of no consequence. Thus, a social scientist would not bother to survey what proportion of the population of bachelors are married because the very definition of 'bachelor' includes being unmarried. The sentence 'a bachelor is an unmarried adult male' is thus thought to be analytic, or true by virtue of the meaning of its terms. This is an extreme example of the presumed epistemic authority of meanings as given by conceptual role. In reality, the sentences comprising claims about leadership are neither analytically black, nor empirically white, but rather a mixture of the two and are in any case only as warranted as the theory that embeds them. And we have a continuum, based largely on the centrality of a claim within the embedding theory.

The reason this matters in conducting ostensibly empirical research into educational leadership is because what looks like empirical support for claims may merely be a reproduction of the prior semantic relations among terms that went into the research design beforehand. A good example of this is research into leadership traits. This research most commonly involves the investigation of two classification tasks. The first is how the cognitive architecture for classifying leadership behaviours as traits gets built up or elaborated through the process of encoding. Our prior folk-theories of leadership are augmented through experience or training to build a cognitive prototype of leadership traits. The second classification task is a "recall and prototype matching" exercise (Scott and Brown 2006, pp. 231–232). This second task might involve classifying a behaviour such as working back late as an example of the trait of dedication. One consequence of this distinction is that where leadership traits are encoded into prototypes for one population of leaders, the recall and prototype matching, when applied to a different population, may deny leadership traits to that new population. This is claimed to be the case when encoding for male leaders creates mismatches when applied to females (Scott and Brown 2006). This difference is said to reflect a difference between individualistic agentic prototypes and communal prototypes. These prototypes, which are the source of conceptual links between leadership and lexical items for traits can empirically reproduce biased conceptions of leadership through the role of leader traits being used in the selection of leaders. The antecedent conceptual framework thus shapes the empirical evidence for leadership.

Antecedent semantic webs are ubiquitous in all educational research on leadership where evidence is in the form of participant perceptions. For example, with the International Successful School Principalship Project mentioned earlier, what counts as 'success' is actually driven by perceptions of success (Drysdale and Gurr 2017, p. 166). In an influential study of differences in student learning effect sizes between transformational school leaders and instructional school leaders, the distinction between these types of leaders was based on teacher perceptions of leadership (Robinson et al. 2008). And more widely in educational research, such as research on good teaching, that too depends in many cases on prior semantic webs being used to code for data, and the use of perceptions for assessing some outcomes (Loughland 2019).

## Falsification and theory choice

There are two important methodological checks on what are essentially closed confirmation loops of semantic links. The first is to shift evidential focus onto conditions and evidence that might falsify the theory in which theoretical terms and coding categories derive their meaning. A lot of scientists follow this practice, for example, Stephen Hawking (1988, p. 11): "As philosopher of science Karl Popper has emphasized, a good theory is characterized by the fact that it makes a number of predictions that could in principle be disproved or falsified by observation". It is a first step in breaking out of the methodology of confirmation in which a theory is supported by data selection categories defined in terms of the theory under investigation. A second step is to have alternative data categories, meaning that it is important to make use of the claims of rival theories and their evidence in testing a theory. In educational leadership research, there are many rival theories that can be used. Approaches that make use of critical perspectives employ data categories that make use of views of social justice, feminist theory, relational sociology, political science, institutional theory, to name a few. (A comprehensive number of these perspectives can be found in Courtney et al. 2020. See also Niesche and Gowlett 2019.) To counter prevailing views of leadership in this book, we make use of data categories drawn from theories of cognitive neuroscience, distributed cognition, information theory, neuroscience of emotion, philosophy of science and language, and epistemology. In drawing on rival theories to test theories under investigation, we are taking a third step, that of explicit theory competition and its adjudication. The epistemology of this is that our candidate for a provisional best theory is one that is empirically adequate in meeting confirmation requirements, survives tough tests that aim to disconfirm it, and enjoys the super-empirical virtues of consistency, comprehensiveness, simplicity, and both internal coherence and coherence with other well-justified theories. For us, this latter point means coherence with the best theories in natural science: hence our naturalistic coherentism. (For a sustained attempt to show how this works in educational administration and leadership, see Evers and Lakomski 1991, 1996, 2000; Lakomski 2005; Lakomski et al. 2017; Lakomski and Evers 2017; Lakomski and Evers 2020.)

In qualitative case study research, a rough approximation to this epistemology would take the following form. Begin with a well-worked-out theory of the case, including the regulative and constitutive rules that govern organizational arrangements. The Theorem of the Ugly Duckling shows that researchers must already possess a prior theory of the case, however rudimentary, in order for any data categories to exist. That is, there is no such thing as approaching a case with the mind as a blank slate. Awareness of biases, as opposed to ignorance of them, permits the possibility of bias testing through seeking disconfirming evidence driven by data categories drawn from alternative theories. This is the solution to the threat of confirmation bias assumed to attend the well-furnished mind. Since logically, biases cannot be removed, the task is to replace bad biases with good biases, that is, those that are more conducive to promoting the growth of knowledge. As the divergent data come in and are evaluated in the field, or subsequently, an alternative theory may come to be seen as enjoying more epistemic advantages than the one with which a researcher began. Such are the dynamics of knowledge growth. This approach is antithetical to the practice of researchers conducting their different research programs in silos, those metaphorical edifices wherein researchers talk only to the like-minded. A research epistemology of theory competition and adjudication through broad coherence criteria requires silos to engage each others' ideas in debate (Haig and Evers 2016, pp. 115–139).

## Theory and the search for patterns

Much educational research into leadership is motivated by a search for patterns among data. Some of these patterns may, as we have suggested, merely reflect semantic relations among widely shared folk theories of leadership. Assuming this can be dealt with, we can explore a more complex role for theory in data definition, collection, and analysis. We begin with a definition of 'pattern'. Roughly speaking, patterned data can be compressed. Consider a set of data points that express a relation between two variables x and y. These can be expressed as points in the following way: $(x_1, y_1), (x_2, y_2), (x_3, y_3), \ldots, (x_n, y_n)$, where n is, say, 1000. Now if all of these points lie on a straight line, say, $y = mx + b$, then the line expresses the data using fewer bits than the representation of points as pairs of x and y, a bit map of the data. Thus, the set of 1000 points is highly patterned because it can be compressed into an expression, $y = mx + b$, that uses fewer bits than a bit map for the data points. Data are said to be random, or not patterned, if they cannot be compressed. This is known as the Kolmogorov/Chaitin definition of pattern (or conversely, randomness). An elaboration is given in what is known as algorithmic information theory as developed by Chaitin. On randomness, Chaitin says: "A series of numbers is random if the smallest algorithm capable of specifying it to a computer has about the same number of bits of information as the series itself" (Chaitin 1975, p. 48).

Let us suppose that in the above abstract characterization, we are exploring a data set where 'y' is equated to some measure of success, and 'x' is equated to some measure of 'capacity building'. The task of finding whether there is a patterned relationship between the two amounts to finding a suitable compression of the data, perhaps in the form of an equation accompanied with some estimate of the extent to which the points lie on the proposed equation. The standard way of doing this is to use the method of least squares. The method attempts to specify an equation that meets the condition that the sum of the squares of perpendicular distances from all the points to the equation is a minimum. This method was invented by Gauss as part of the mathematical machinery he needed to plot the orbit of the minor planet (or very large asteroid) Ceres, in the asteroid belt between Mars and Jupiter. Observations of Ceres were very difficult to come by, with Gauss having only a modest number of agreed points to work with. Unfortunately, these points greatly underdetermine the task, with many curves (including lines) meeting the least squares criterion. Fortunately, Gauss had a theory that determined the shape of the curve. Newton's law of gravitation said that Ceres' trajectory would be an ellipse. Using this theoretical assumption, Gauss was able to successfully determine the orbit of Ceres.

The problem in applying this method, widely used in educational research, is that in our leadership example we don't have prior knowledge of the shape of the curve. In statistical packages the default assumption is that the relationship is linear. Where data sets are complex, more sophisticated analyses, such as structural equation modelling, make use of multiple concatenated linear relationships. Just as prior theory has an ineliminable role in defining and selecting data categories, so it also figures in how data are to be analysed in the quest for patterns. To be sure, if we put linearity into our analytic assumptions, the least squares method will grind out equations that meet this criterion. But it will do that even if the data are non-linear. For example, if we plot children's language learning of the past tense of English verbs, plotting correct usage against time, we find that improvements are initially steady. But then children over-generalize by adding '-ed' to irregular verbs: go-ed instead of went, run-ed instead of ran. The error rate begins to climb. But then over time the over-generalizing diminishes and the irregular verbs are treated correctly as exceptions. There exist other examples of non-linearity in educational research. Piaget's theory of cognitive development posits non-linear transitions between his posited stages. The learning of science construed as acquiring alternative conceptions posits sharp transitions between children's science and scientists' science. Critical events in learning, including experiences in leadership, can result in what appear to be discontinuous jumps in leader behaviour.

In providing tools for analysis amid uncertainty about prior theory, the methodological challenge is to find an equation that combines goodness of fit with data compression. Here is how the process might begin for the data points (x, y) where these represent data for (capacity building, leadership success). Let's assume that all the points lie within an ellipse with a rough difference between a major axis and a minor axis, suggesting there is some kind of pattern. A linear relationship is further assumed because it offers the greatest opportunity for data compression. The least squares method (LSM) will produce values for m and b in the equation y = mx + b, although possible symmetries in the data might not guarantee uniqueness. With the line defined, we then need to know how good a fit it is to the data. This will be given by a correlation coefficient, r, calculated by a formula that takes into account results for LSM. More formally:

$r^2$ = 1 − LSM/(Sum of the squares of success scores minus the mean of success scores).

Where all the points lie on the line, LSM = 0, $r^2$ = 1, and so r = +1 or -1. Where LSM is the same as the above denominator, $r^2$ = 1 − 1 = 0, and there is no correlation.

Suppose there is some correlation but that we think we can do better on goodness of fit by using a quadratic equation. This costs us some compression since the quadratic will likely have more bits, and three constants now need to be determined rather than two. But let us suppose we achieve greater fit. How much further can we improve goodness of fit? In the limit, using Fourier analysis, we can devise an elaborate concatenation of sine functions into an equation that passes through every data point. However, there is now no compression at all as the resulting equation will contain about as many bits as the bit map of the original data. What this means is that, under these conditions, the equation is not projectible. Given a new value for 'capacity building', the resulting output for 'leadership success' will have no epistemic value. Using the equation will be like using a look-up table. If the new data value is not in the table, there will be a nil result.

The upshot is that there is a trade-off between goodness of fit and compression, a trade-off signifying that the matter is not decided by empirical adequacy. It is underdetermined by data. Note that the same underdetermination arises when using exploratory factor analysis to find patterns by the compression of possible causes of variability among variables into a smaller number of explanatory causes. "Although typically ignored by factor analytic researchers, factor indeterminacy is an epistemic fact of life that continues to challenge factor analytic methodologists" (Haig and Evers 2016, p. 104).

We have a suggestion for dealing with this problem, but as in most matters to do with growing knowledge, it is procedural. Consider the case of physics, where high levels of compressibility of data are the normal expectation. And take the example of ballistics. Where an object is moving under the influence of gravity, its trajectory takes the form of an inverted parabola. But not quite. Air resistance, and even air turbulence, can act on the projectile in ways that are also dependent on the shape of the projectile. The resulting challenge is not so much to treat divergence from the parabola as just a certain amount of error, but rather to try to explain the divergence as though points falling off the curve are falsifying what might be an incorrect idealization. Under this epistemic regime, even one anomalous data point that resists explanation can prompt a major investigation and substantial theoretical revisions. In doing large clinical trials on a potential vaccine, one unexplained bad reaction among 10,000 otherwise safe cases can prompt a halting of the trial until the anomaly is satisfactorily explained within our best theories of viral medicine.

In social science, where expectations of data compression are lower, and in cases where we have no theoretical reason to suspect non-linearity in data, attempting to fit data to a straight line, or multiple concatenated straight lines, has the advantage of projectability that comes with greater data compression, subject to reasonable correlation. But again, there needs to be a focus on falsification, on why data are off the line rather than a confirmatory focus on goodness of fit. There are two advantages of this epistemic strategy. The first is that explaining anomalies forces one to look to theory revision, or other theories, as a way of seeing more pattern in data. Using critical perspectives is a good example of this, although in educational leadership there are many other theoretical lenses. The second is to look for more pattern by significantly expanding the amount of data being considered. Our own version of this approach is to require leadership theory (and even social science) to cohere with natural science. Here is how it works methodologically.

In explaining leadership behaviour, we make overwhelming use of folk psychology, particularly belief/desire theory. That is, we explain or predict leadership behaviour by supposing it is the result of a rational coordination of beliefs and desires. The behaviour is the believed means for bringing about a desired end. And the patterns in individual and organizational life revealed by this theory greatly simplify navigation through the social world of organizational life. But if the social world is part of the natural world, then social world data will also need to cohere with a vast amount of theorized natural world data and their explanation. This means that patterns described in terms of belief/desire theory are more likely to require eventual articulation with the causal theories of cognitive neuroscience than the behaviour of neuronal assemblies being more likely to be incorporated into belief/desire theory. Causal theories of human cognitive functioning, including distributed cognition at the organizational level, can fail to compete for compression in the limited domain in which folk theory operates, but they do much better as a research program when drawing on the concepts of natural science over the vast domain of data from the wider natural world. The obvious strategy is to treat useful folk theory, from an ontological perspective, instrumentally and to treat natural science accounts realistically. Less obvious is how to deal with the folk-theoretic expressions of social facts that we used to criticise methodological individualism in Chapter 2. However, these are best seen as lexical proxies standing for shared cognitive patterns in organized distributed cognition. In this context, the pattern elements needed to sustain collective intentionality behind regulative and constitutive rules would be given by a naturalistic relational sociology. (Eacott 2017 provides some theoretical tools for this project.)

It is worth pointing out, as an aside, that these conceptual options affect what counts as validity when it comes to measures of leadership. Ambitiously, we can say that a measure such as success, or student learning outcomes, or moral excellence, is valid if it measures what leadership really is. Unfortunately, what leadership really is contested, and will be the outcome of an epistemic contest among rival theories. Less ambitiously, we might retreat to validity as the measure accurately measuring what it purports to measure. But this is arbitrary unless some constraints are placed on what can be reasonably purported. Again, this is arbitrary unless the notion of reasonableness draws on epistemology, and the epistemic virtues that make one theory better than the other.

## Theory and effect size

Another much-used quantitative approach to leadership that seeks to discover patterns in the data about leadership is that which makes use of effect sizes. Hattie's work contains the most sustained attempt to provide empirical research data to determine the effect size of various categories of causes, including leadership, on student learning outcomes. (Hattie 2008, 2012; Hattie et al. 2015.) Since having a positive effect on student learning outcomes has been seen as an important way of determining the advantages of instructional leadership over transformational leadership (Robinson et al. 2008), the methodology of effect size bears closer investigation. Consider an experimental set-up designed to determine whether a new method of teaching reading is better than what has been done previously. One group of students, the experimental group, is taught by the new method, while the other (matched) group, the control group, is taught by the old method. On the simplest definition of effect size (ES), we measure the ES of the new method as the difference between the means of the learning performances of the two groups divided by the pooled standard deviations of the two groups. If the experimental group performs at a full standard deviation above the control group then, niceties aside, we can say that $ES = 1$ for the new method. ESs are basically proportions of standard deviations. Hattie (2008) has used about 800 meta-analyses of over 50,000 research studies with a total of over 200 million students to calculate aggregate effect sizes on dozens of different potential causes of student learning, and has placed all of these ESs on a scale with the average ES = 0.4. The normative point of this research is that if you want to improve student learning outcomes, adopt practices or interventions that have an ES > 0.4, and preferably those towards the top of the scale.

There are several problems with this research. The first is that it conflates two types of common research designs. The first type is experimental, where we can construct a test for some hypothesis by controlling for variables and then implementing the test or design. The second type is ex post facto. Here, researchers are conducting a pattern search on events that have actually happened. Typical of this research is to look at a group of schools that have exceptional learning (or some other) outcomes and then study the statistical structure of the situation to see the contribution of those factors, such as leadership, deemed relevant to producing such outcomes. What we wish to observe is that research design itself has an effect on effect size. Take the example of determining the effect of carbon dioxide ($CO_2$) on plant growth. An ex post facto design would look at a wide range of factors thought relevant, such as water, altitude, climate and seasons, temperature, sunlight, soil nutrients, and, of course, $CO_2$. But while the other factors might vary in nature, the proportion of $CO_2$ in the atmosphere is much the same everywhere. In correlating the variability of these other factors with variation in plant growth, we might expect some positive or negative correlation. But since $CO_2$ does not vary, it would account for none of the variability in plant growth. Converting correlation to effect size, it would yield an effect size of zero. Now change the research design and conduct an experiment. Haul the plants into the lab and turn up the $CO_2$. The experimental design permits the manipulation of a variable that is relatively constant in the natural ecosystem. And so, in this case, we can achieve a larger effect size simply by switching to a different research design.

The reason this matters is because the methodology for determining the effect size of possible factors on learning outcomes varies according to the type of factor under investigation. Some factors, for example those associated with different teaching methods, lend themselves to more experimental designs. However, in studying leadership effects, most designs are ex post facto. It is just hard to do experimental testing on leadership. With research design itself as a variable that affects effect size, putting all effect sizes on the same scale is like putting apples and oranges on the same scale. It doesn't make for an acceptable basis of comparison. The two additional difficulties we raise concern the application of effect size research to applications in practice.

A central feature of sound experimental research is control of variables. The classic error of this is the experiments on worker productivity at the Hawthorne Western Electric plant, conducted in the 1920s. Despite various configurations of worker activity in the relay assembly room, productivity rose steadily, even when the configuration was reset to its original format. The uncontrolled variable turned out to be the workers' desire to please the experimenters. In applying rigorous experimental research findings to natural environments such as classrooms or schools, we are moving to an environment of less rigorous control of variables, and hence a corresponding loss of confidence that the experimental findings will work. On our process view of leadership where leadership knowledge is grown through epistemically progressive practices in context, the best experimental research should be merely a starting point, its application being the beginning of such progressive epistemic practices. This is discussed in detail in Chapter 6 where we elaborate on the use of Popper Cycles.

In the case of ex post facto research on leadership, we focus on the comparison with $CO_2$. Educational leadership usually has an effect size on student learning outcomes of about 0.4, with a recent meta-analysis giving it about 0.32 (Kardag 2020 p. 57). Nevertheless, even on leader-centric variables that focus on leader autonomy, there are significant factors that diminish variability among these variables. These are mostly to do with training, experience, selection, and the constitutive and regulative rules that filter who gets to become an educational leader, particularly a school principal, and what they can do in that role. Add to this a jurisdictional philosophy of defining and promoting standards for leaders and we have a broadly administrative suppression of variability among leaders and leadership groups that functions not unlike the way the laws of thermodynamics function to diffuse $CO_2$ uniformly. The more effective the administrative press for excellence is, the more the case can be made for the compatibility of good leadership with small effect size. Furthermore, as regards outcome variability, a stronger case can be mounted that variability is due to non-leadership contextual factors such as demographics, economics, cultural, and linguistic factors.

Using evidence from ex post facto studies for justifying improvement interventions faces the challenge of making counterfactual inferences. The assumption that the statistical structure of leadership in successful schools bears a close relationship to that of unsuccessful schools requires considerable justification, if for no other reason than it would be hard to explain the difference in school outcomes. Unsuccessful schools simply cannot apply the lessons of successful schools without some further attention to the context of application. Again, we would recommend a process approach. Use the research as a starting point for initiating an epistemically progressive trajectory of context-driven application. It might be thought that if ex post facto research contained lessons from research on school trajectories for going from unsuccessful to successful, it might solve this problem. However, as will be obvious from the example in Chapter 6, many more factors come into play over a trajectory. Even similarity of starting point will not be sufficient after a few iterations of interventions for projecting the same path to a successful outcome.

In general, as Meehl (1970) argued, interventions based on ex post facto research invite one to make inferences counterfactually, arguing for making changes that undermine the purported causal structure that produced the data that was used to provide evidence for the patterns that the intervention is undermining. Once an intervention undermines the purported causal basis of evidence for its original support, it can hardly provide guidance for how the intervention will turn out. We say 'purported' because we need more than statistical structure to get to causal structure.

Ex post facto studies can be useful, but only when harnessed with good theorizing. We can see this in relation to the distinction between coincidental regularities and causal regularities. Bertrand Russell's example of the former is good enough. When the factory hooter goes off in London, the workers in Birmingham always knock off work. But if the factory hooter in London failed to go off, the workers in Birmingham would still knock off. There is no causal relation between the two events. On the other hand, when there is a flash of lightning, it is always followed by thunder. We know this is a causal regularity because it sustains the counterfactual that if there was no flash of lightening there would be no thunder. As statistical evidence yielding identified patterns in data does not distinguish accidental from causal regularities, we need stronger sources of evidence for causation. The appropriate combination is to test hypothesized causal theories through falsification of inferred predictions, and to test for predictions in counterfactual situations. Although the former can be extremely helpful for theory building, the latter can also be useful in avoiding distraction by coincidence. Mostly, however, we rely as we mentioned earlier in the case of the car battery, on the presumption of possessing a good theory to sustain belief in causality. This may sound circular if it is assumed that we use statistical regularity to infer causal structure. But in fact, since some initial theory must be presumed for research that produces statistical structure to begin, it is best to see the statistics as part of the feedback required to improve our initial provisional causal theory. Ultimately, the most powerful epistemic strategy is to require leadership theories to cohere with the kind of large-scale causal theories typical of natural science.

## Conclusion

There are many ways of conducting research into leadership. We have focussed on pattern detection, with a conception of pattern as deriving from algorithmic information theory. A key lesson to emerge from this approach is epistemic modesty. Empirical adequacy is insufficient for theory choice. Indeterminacy prevails. The discovery of patterns that can effectively compress research data even further requires an openness to rival theories and a willingness to explore these both for defining alternative coding categories and for focusing on falsification strategies. Theory choice can be further strengthened by appeal to other epistemic criteria, such as simplicity, consistency, comprehensiveness, and both internal coherence and coherence with wider established theories, preferably those of natural science. In the end, theory is not an outcome of research. It is present from the beginning and is improved by the kind of research practices that we recommend as context constrained knowledge building processes for educational leadership. To limit further the indeterminacy of inference that results from theory driven research, the addition of contextual details is essential. This will be elaborated in the subsequent three chapters of Part II.

## References

Chaitin, G. (1975). Randomness and mathematical proof. *Scientific American*, 232(5), 47–52.
Courtney, S.J., Gunter, H.M., Niesche, R., & Trujillo, T. (Eds.) (2020). *Understanding educational leadership: Critical perspectives and approaches*. London: Bloomsbury.
Drysdale, L., & Gurr, D. (2017). Reflections on successful school leadership from the international successful school principalship project. In G. Lakomski, S. Eacott, & C.W. Evers (Eds.), *Questioning leadership: New directions for educational organizations* (pp. 164–177). Oxford: Routledge.
Eacott, S. (2017). *Beyond leadership: A relational approach to organizational theory*. Singapore: Springer.
Evers, C.W. (1982). *Logical structure and justification in educational theory*. (Unpublished PhD thesis). University of Sydney, Australia.
Evers, C.W. (2000). Connectionist modelling and education. *Australian Journal of Education*, 44(3), 209–225.
Evers, C.W., & Lakomski, G. (1991). *Knowing educational administration: Contemporary methodological controversies in educational administration research*. Oxford: Pergamon Press.
Evers, C.W., & Lakomski, G. (1996). *Exploring educational administration: Coherentist applications and critical debates*. Oxford: Pergamon Press.
Evers, C.W., & Lakomski, G. (2000). *Doing educational administration: Coherentist naturalism into administrative practice*. Oxford: Pergamon/Elsevier.
Gardner, H. (1995). *Leading minds: An anatomy of leadership*. New York: Basic Books.
Gronn, P. (2017). *Just as I am: A life of J.R. Darling*. Melbourne: Hardie Grant Books.
Haig, B.D., & Evers, C.W. (2016). *Realist inquiry in social science*. London: Sage.
Hattie, J. (2008). *Visible learning: A synthesis of over 800 meta-analyses relating to achievement*. London: Routledge.
Hattie, J. (2012). *Visible learning for teachers: Maximizing impact on learning*. London: Routledge.
Hattie, J., Masters, D., & Birch, K. (2015). *Visible learning in action: International case studies of impact*. London: Routledge.
Hawking, S. (1988). *A brief history of time*. London: Bantam Books.
Hodgkinson, C. (1991). *Educational leadership: The moral art*. New York: SUNY Press.
Kardag, E. (2020). The effect of educational leadership on students' achievement: A cross-cultural meta-analysis research on studies between 2008 and 2018. *Asia Pacific Education Review*, 21, 49–64.
Lakomski, G. (2005). *Managing without leadership: Towards a theory of organizational functioning*. Oxford: Elsevier.
Lakomski, G., & Evers, C.W. (2017). Educational leadership and emotion. In D. Waite, & I. Bogotch (Eds.), *The international handbook of educational leadership* (pp. 45–62). Hoboken, NJ: Wiley-Blackwell.
Lakomski, G., & Evers, C.W. (2020). Theories of educational leadership. In R. Papa (Ed.), *The Oxford encyclopedia of educational administration*. Oxford: Oxford University Press. DOI: 10.1093/acrefore/9780190264093.013.603
Lakomski, G., Eacott, S., & Evers, C.W. (2017). *Questioning leadership*. Abingdon, UK: Routledge.

Loughland, T. (2019). *Teacher adaptive practices: Extending teacher adaptability into classroom practice*. Singapore: Springer.

Meehl, P. (1970). Nuisance variables and the ex post facto design. In M. Radner, & S. Winokur (Eds.), *Minnesota Studies in the philosophy of science: Volume IV* (pp. 373–402). Minneapolis: University of Minnesota Press.

Niesche, R., & Gowlett, C. (2019). *Social, critical and political theories for educational leadership*. Singapore: Springer.

Popper, K.R. (1959). *The logic of scientific discovery*. London: Hutchinson & Co.

Popper, K.R. (1963). *Conjectures and refutations: The growth of scientific knowledge*. London: Routledge.

Quine, W.V. (1960). *Word and object*. Cambridge, MA: MIT Press.

Quine, W.V. (1969). *Ontological relativity and other essays*. New York: Columbia University Press.

Robinson, V.M.J., Lloyd, C.A., & Rowe, K.J. (2008). The impact of leadership on student outcomes: An analysis of the differential effects of leadership types. *Educational Administration Quarterly*, 44(5), 635–674.

Scott, K.A. & Brown, D.J. (2006). Female first, leader second? Gender bias in the encoding of leadership behavior. *Organizational Behavior and Human Decision Processes*, 101(2), 230-242.

Starr, W. (2019). Counterfactuals. *The Stanford Encyclopedia of Philosophy* (Fall 2019 Edition), Edward N. Zalta (ed.), URL = <https://plato.stanford.edu/archives/fall2019/entries/counterfactuals/>.

Sweller, J., van Merrienboer, J.J.G., & Paas, F. (2019). Cognitive architecture and instructional design: 20 years later. *Educational Psychological Review*, 31, 261–292.

Wang, Z., Chen, S., Liu, J., & Zhang, D. (2008). Pattern representation in feature extraction and classifier design: Matrix versus vector. *IEEE Transactions on Neural Networks and Learning Systems*, 19(5), 758–769.

Watanabe, S. (1969). *Knowing and guessing*. New York: John Wiley & Sons.

Wikipedia contributors. (2021, July 1). Ugly duckling theorem. In *Wikipedia, The Free Encyclopedia*. Retrieved 08:28, July 31, 2021, from https://en.wikipedia.org/w/index.php?title=Ugly_duckling_theorem&oldid=1031480179

Wilkins, J.S., & Ebach, C. (2014). *The nature of classification: Relationships and kinds in the natural sciences*. London: Palgrave Macmillan.

# 5
# DEVELOPING LEADERSHIP – FROM UNCERTAINTY TO SOCIAL EPISTEMOLOGY

## Introduction

In the previous chapter, we looked at how limits to some standard research methodologies and associated patterns of inference implied limits to the kind of knowledge leaders and groups could acquire, suggesting instead that knowledge needs to be supplemented by epistemic processes of leadership self-learning. In this chapter we develop more general arguments about the limits of knowledge and explore some options from social epistemology for how groups may grow knowledge, recognizing those aspects of leadership knowledge building that are group processes. The two arguments we discuss concern theoretical limits to knowledge, the first arguing for a principled uncertainty that invests social prediction, and the second suggesting the possibility of a system's chaotic behaviour. The options for social epistemology include the ideas of Dewey, Kitcher, Popper, and some mathematical modelling of organizational learning. We also consider individual learning within the context of learning organizations. Popper's views on individual and social epistemology are discussed further in Chapter 6.

## Uncertainty and social prediction: Popper's argument

If, in the thirteenth century, someone had speculated on what kind of learning would be appropriate for alchemists in a more advanced age, it would be unlikely that they would have come up with the correct answer: none. Unlikely, because the theoretical framework informing this social forecast would have included a belief in the possibility of transforming base metals into gold. Of course, if there were some way of predicting the future growth of scientific knowledge, the forecast could have been made more accurate. Unfortunately, no such prediction is possible.

It is a well-known fact that social forecasting is fraught with hazards, accepted even among its most eminent practitioners. In his classic book *The Coming of Post-Industrial Society: A Venture in Social Forecasting* (1974), Daniel Bell offered a view of what a society would be like with over 50 percent of its employees as knowledge workers:

> The concept of a "post-industrial society" emphasizes the centrality of theoretical knowledge as the axis around which new technology, economic growth and the stratification of society will be organized.
> *(Bell 1974, p. 112)*

On reading it now, for all its merits, the results of the venture are mixed. For example, the large proportion of space given over to engaging Marx, and Marxist ideas, will strike today's reader as odd. But then not many people in the early 1970s were predicting the collapse of the Soviet Union. Equating the power of scientists and 'Research men' in a post-industrial society with the power of businessmen and landowners in industrial and pre-industrial societies respectively, fares better – spectacularly so in the cases of Microsoft and Apple – though misses, among other factors, changes in education that produced a ready supply of highly specialized knowledge workers who fitted into the familiar roles associated with being employees, and changes in knowledge diffusion, such as the Internet, that made knowledge relatively inexpensive.

There are two theoretical arguments that we want to consider for why social forecasting has its limits. The first is due to Karl Popper, which he sets out in summary form over five points in the Preface to his *The Poverty of Historicism* (1957). The key steps in the argument can be reduced to three essential claims:

1. The course of human history is strongly influenced by growth of human knowledge (....).
2. We cannot predict, by rational or scientific methods, the future growth of scientific knowledge (....).
3. We cannot, therefore, predict the future course of human history.

*(Popper 1957, pp. xi–xii.)*

The first premise Popper takes to be obviously true. To be sure, there are many other factors that have influenced the course of human history, for example, climate change, pandemics, population growth, and resource demands (Diamond 2011), but the growth of human knowledge, particularly scientific knowledge and its social application in the form of engineering and technology, is certainly of profound importance. We are happy to endorse this premise.

It is the second premise that requires some argument, and Popper had done so in another quite technical publication (Popper 1950), which he further amended (see Popper 1982). Here we can sketch some of the details of his strategy. Let us suppose that human knowledge (which includes scientific knowledge) does indeed shape social life in important ways. Suppose further that we have a body of such knowledge formulated as rigorously as we please, together with complete knowledge of all relevant current states of affairs. Then, in its most precise form, a prediction concerning what will be future knowledge is a deduction made from all of that prior knowledge – a deduction about what will be known in the future. Unfortunately, as Popper (1950) argues, not all new knowledge can be derived from what is currently known. His argument is not that the calculation is too difficult or complex, but rather that the task is theoretically impossible. Deductions from our current knowledge will always incompletely capture future knowledge for the same reason that we cannot derive every true claim in mathematics from a set of true axioms, no matter how we axiomatize mathematics. The incompleteness of axiomatized systems of mathematics, that is, their failure to capture every true mathematical statement, was first proved by Gödel (1931). According to Popper, we now know that the same consequence applies to scientific knowledge, and in fact, the broader network of knowledge in which science coheres.

When applied to the future course of history, using Gödel's incompleteness theorem, Popper (1950) went on to argue that a society cannot predict all of its own future states, no matter how comprehensive its knowledge is, of both a society's initial configuration, and the laws that govern the causal evolution of that society. There will always be a true statement about a society's future that cannot be derived from complete knowledge of its current state and the laws that operate on that current state if those future states depend on the growth of scientific knowledge. (For more detail, see Evers and Lakomski 1991, pp. 206–209. For a discussion of other versions of this argument and a defence of it see Lagerspetz 2004.)

Of course, no social forecaster ever pretends to have anything like comprehensive knowledge of even an aspect of the present. Instead, the talk is, quite properly, about discerning trends. But if comprehensive theory can miss significant future developments in knowledge that have society-changing consequences, then surely a resource that can sustain no better than an analysis of trends will miss even more. The upshot is that predicting the nature of something like the future knowledge requirements of the workforce, the nature of jobs, the dynamics of a population's interests, or any of a multitude of knowledge requirements for further learning in a society one of whose hypothesized forces for social change is the growth of scientific knowledge especially, would seem, on first consideration, to be risky at best and unachievable at worst. And this principled unpredictability will apply to organizations' life in those future social systems. Popper used this argument for the principled unpredictability of social life to apply his model of the growth of scientific knowledge to social science. He also used it as the basis for his views on social epistemology. The constraints that define this version of the problem of uncertainty are thus embedded in the structure of all mathematical systems whose axioms are strong enough to yield elementary arithmetic.

## Uncertainty and social prediction: Chaos

One problem with learning about the social that has increasingly attracted the attention of theorists has been the issue of chaos. The worry is that even relatively tiny epistemic interventions of the sort favoured in piecemeal social change can set in train quite significant changes. This is our second theoretical argument for placing restrictions on social forecasting. Sometimes referred to as the butterfly effect, the idea is that a butterfly flapping its wings in Tokyo can trigger a chain of events that leads to a hurricane striking North America. To see how this idea works, consider a simple n-step process where the next state of a system, $X_1$, (say, part of a wider social system) is some function, f, of the previous, initial state of the system, $X_0$. Thus:

$$X_1 = f(X_0)$$

Now, since the process specified above is iterative, we have

$$X_2 = f(X_1) = f(f(X_0)) = f^2(X_0)$$

And for the general case we have

$$X_n = f(X_{n-1}) = f^n(X_0)$$

It's easy to see how sensitivity to initial conditions can arise with even simple functions. Let f be a function that squares initial values for X. Thus

$$X_1 = X_0^2.$$

But iterating this n times gives

$$X_n = X_0^{2^n}.$$

These iterations would result in an extraordinary magnification of even the smallest error in $X_0$, although the function is not equally sensitive for all chosen initial conditions, and so is therefore not technically chaotic (Banks et al. 2003, pp. 150–153). A simple non-linear logistic function that does have chaotic behaviour is

$$X_{n+1} = 4X_n(1-X_n)$$

since all succeeding iterates change quite sharply over very small variations in earlier values of X. It also meets two other technical conditions for chaotic behaviour: transitivity and density (see Banks et al. 2003, pp. 157–177, for details). Systems obeying this formula are unpredictable in the presence of even tiny errors.

These considerations still leave open the question of whether some social phenomena are really the result of chaotic system behaviour, or at least to sensitivity at certain points in the system's dynamics, for we need to know how to model the system with appropriate formulas. Unfortunately, even if it were theoretically possible to do so, social systems are too complex to lend themselves to this sort of modelling. Some writers have used the above formalism of iterated functions to try to establish general conditions for social stability and instability, and hence predictability. (See Saperstein 1999, on predicting the outbreak of wars.) Why, for example, did the "murder of Archduke Franz Ferdinand in the Balkans in 1914" lead to the mass slaughter of World War I, but 'the downing of a Korean Boeing 747 by Soviet warplanes did not escalate into a major armed conflict'? (Geeraerts 1998, pp. 5–6). Such examples of tipping points suggest the plausibility of supposing some system sensitivity even if there is insufficient modelling to prove it formally.

Whether unpredictability due to chaos is known or unknown, the hedge against it is the familiar one of attending to feedback and adjusting theoretically motivated expectations. As Wilkinson (1999, p. 116.) notes:

> As odd as it may seem, the presence of chaos may be an advantage in control systems, if rapid responses are required. Chaotic systems would seem to be utterly unreliable, given their extreme sensitivity to initial conditions. Yet … That same sensitivity allows a control mechanism to control the system with very small corrective signals, provided the developing chaos can be analyzed rapidly, i.e. proper feedback is available.

What this means in the case of social science is that outcomes of iterated previous states of affairs need to fall within certain measurable boundaries linked to the goals of the system. A school, for example, however sensitive to a particular configuration of conditions that it passes through, will have its goals mediated by the parameter settings of its main variables: budgets, staffing levels, job requirements, student performance, and the like. And as these will most likely be both internally and externally monitored, our knowledge of the operation of the school will be procedurally incremental. We know that even incremental change can nevertheless result in sudden, large-scale school change. For example, after suffering incremental declines in enrolments a school crosses a threshold where it is forced to close down.

Again, a more appropriate approach to doing better than chance in dealing with uncertainty in a complex, changing, social world is to engage in continuous learning from experience. All experience is, of course, interpreted from the vantage point of knowledge built up from a variety of sources. But the need for a continuous taking stock of the passing show of experience seems an imperative when it comes to social knowledge. The constraints that impose change in systems that are ultimately chaotic are embedded in the mathematical models of dynamical systems theory that might accurately describe them.

## Social epistemology: Dewey, Kitcher, and Popper

Broadly speaking, social epistemology is the study of those social arrangements of individuals that engage in the acquisition of knowledge. It examines the conditions under which knowledge is acquired by those arrangements and the various circumstances that make it possible, or make it more or less efficient. A more specific account is provided by Kitcher (1993, p. 303):

> The general problem of social epistemology, as I conceive it, is to identify the properties of well-designed social systems, that is, to specify the conditions under which a group of individuals, operating according to various rules for modifying their individual practices, succeed, through their interactions, in generating a progressive sequence of consensus practices.

There are many examples of social epistemology, and we highlight the conceptions of three prominent advocates: John Dewey, especially as espoused in the context of his work about the nature of education; Philip Kitcher, whose conception emphasizes the learning organization; and Karl Popper, whose primary focus is the nature and growth of scientific knowledge.

Dewey held a praxis view of knowledge, which may best be understood by contrasting it with more traditional empiricist views. For classical empiricists, such as Hume or Locke, learning occurred in individuals through a build-up of sensory impressions concatenated by virtue of the thin resources of logic. One serious limitation of this approach was that there seemed to be no way out of solipsism, the notion that a learner's knowledge was restricted to just their inventory of sensory impressions. Construed as a representational structure, knowledge was thus of the contents of their own sensory experiences, not some world that might have given rise to these sensory impressions. Dewey's theory of knowledge avoided this, and other, problems of classical empiricism. For him, epistemology was a method: the experimental method. Construed in terms of individual learners, this method had two dimensions:

> On the one hand, it means that we have no right to call anything knowledge except where our activity has actually produced certain physical changes in things, which agree with and confirm the conception entertained. ... On the other hand, the experimental method of thinking signifies that thinking is of avail; that it is of avail in just the degree in which the anticipation of future consequences is made on the basis of thorough observation of present conditions.
>
> *(Dewey 1916, p. 338)*

In this method, our knowledge drives expectations of the consequences of actions that in turn validate such knowledge through confirmation by experience. The method of knowing is itself initiated by the perception of problems and the need to reach a solution, or the resolution of the tensions to which they give rise. The issue of solipsism cannot arise because it is the natural, external world that is an essential ingredient in shaping the growth of knowledge. In this sense, Dewey is a realist (Godfrey-Smith 2009).

Framed in terms of individual resource development for the solution of problems, this epistemology is quite narrow. However, Dewey addresses the issue by considering the wider social context in which individuals act, particularly in his formulation of a democratic conception of education. Here, human association can function as an epistemic resource in two distinct but complementary ways. Dewey aims to produce an account of an epistemically progressive form of human association that is both realistic in the sense of being grounded in actual practices and normative in the sense that it can embody realizable suggested improvements. The first of the two elements to his social epistemology "signifies not only more numerous and more varied points of shared common interest, but greater reliance upon the recognition of mutual interests as a factor in social control" (Dewey 1916, p. 86.). This is the 'within group' dynamic without which individuals see fewer ways of strengthening and developing their own viewpoints as a partially shared enterprise that builds on their interactions with interest-relative peers in that group. The second element concerns how groups in a social formation interact. It "means not only freer interaction between social groups (once isolated so far as intention could keep up a separation) but change in social habit – its continuous readjustment through meeting the new situations produced by varied intercourse" (Dewey 1916, pp. 86–87). Herein lies the principal source of diversity of viewpoint, with the society as a whole benefiting epistemically by this dual structure of within group focus and between group diversity. Dewey regards these two features of human association as constituting a democratic society.

Although an organization could be construed in this social epistemology as just one group in a larger social formation, it is easy to see how the epistemology could be applied within an organization by making certain structural adjustments. For example, a research-oriented organization, specifically in the business of promoting the growth of knowledge, might be partitioned into a number of competing research teams. An individual's knowledge is extended both through collaboration within the team and by exchanges of information between teams, and the organization's knowledge grows when any team is successful in solving the problem. Once the problem is solved, individuals grow in knowledge through the sharing of this success across teams. This broadly Deweyan approach sees individual learning occurring within the context of the whole democratic society advancing its knowledge. Part of Dewey's constraint set for his social epistemology is the constitutive and regulative constraints that define his view of democracy and, derivatively, education.

Kitcher (1990) imagines a similar example, though with an emphasis on the learning organization, in a paper that explores possible differences between individual and collective rationality when it comes to specifying the division of cognitive labour within a community of scientists located among different research teams. The difference he examines is the community advantage of having a range of competing research teams working on possible solutions to a problem versus the notion that some individual scientist will be obliged to work in research teams exploring what they believe to be less plausible theories, or lines of attack. His key issue is that "only if we situate the individual in a society of other epistemic agents ... does it begin to appear rational for someone to assign herself to the working out of ideas that she (and her colleagues) view as epistemically inferior" (Kitcher 1990, p. 8.). But how, exactly? This is the nub of the problem. How may we reconcile a community optimum (CO) distribution of cognitive labour, requiring a spread of research teams with an individual rationality (IR) based distribution of cognitive labour where everyone works on the research team that is the most promising? Kitcher considers both altruistic and non-altruistic IR alternatives. The problem is easily resolved in an altruistic model by simply defining an IR agent as one who would prefer to work in a community that maximizes CO, where this is assumed to maximize "the chances of discovering the correct answer" (Kitcher 1990, p. 14.). However, Kitcher also shows how a convergence of CO and IR distributions is possible in the case of non-altruistic IR agents where these are posited to be 'ruthless egotists'. The trick is to set a very high non-epistemic reward for success – say a Nobel prize – divided by the number of researchers in the team. The utility of combining a low probability of success with a high pay-off research program will be sufficient to attract a modest number of IR ruthless egotists to work on it, as might be expected under a CO distribution of cognitive labour.

The pursuit of lifelong learning under these organizational arrangements is therefore tied to a mixture of both epistemic rewards, getting the right answer, and non-epistemic rewards, a chance of fame and money. (See Kitcher 1990, p. 17. For critical discussion of Kitcher's work, see Weisberg and Muldoon 2009.) In Kitcher's model, the extent of individual learning will therefore be stratified, at least initially, being more likely to take place among those individuals working on the research team with the highest probability of success. Members of other teams then will acquire this knowledge through dissemination. Kitcher's bifurcated constraint set is basically driven by an assumption of altruism for one class of cases and a maximization of expected utility for agents in non-altruistic circumstances. Leadership at both the individual and the social levels would thus diverge in these two social arrangements.

Broadly supportive of a conception of democracy as an epistemic ideal, the primary focus of Popper's epistemology was on the nature and growth of scientific knowledge. Contrary to many writers on epistemology (see Boole 1854/1958) who maintained a standard bifurcation in relation to understanding the nature and growth of scientific knowledge – justification as a matter of logic and discovery as involving psychology – Popper challenged this bifurcation in his great work, *The Logic of Scientific Discovery* (1959). Psychology, he argued, had no important place in discovery either (see Popper 1959, pp. 30–31). Although the idea of exploring conditions under which knowledge grows, while ignoring the contribution of psychology, may seem strange, remember that we are working not with a transmission view of knowledge growth but with a view of learning things that were previously unknown.

Popper spells out the nature of the testing process and its associated logic in great detail in *The Logic of Scientific Discovery*. How the basic ideas lead to both a social epistemology and a powerful tool for theorizing organizational learning and the role of individuals within learning organizations, is easy enough to describe. Roughly speaking, scientific knowledge is said to grow by a process of conjecture and refutation, as we noted briefly at the end of Chapter 2 and Chapter 4. Problems prompt tentative theories that are hypothesized to provide solutions and then these theories are rigorously tested in a process that hopefully leads to the elimination of errors, a process we have called 'Popper Cycles' in Chapter 1 (see Popper 1979, pp. 164–165 for detail).

Now regardless of the schema's status as a logic of knowledge, for it to be applied in real knowledge building situations, it needs to be instantiated in some kind of social configuration. As it turns out, something like this schema is ubiquitous in models of organizational learning, once it is recognized that the process of theory testing amounts to adjudicating the outcome of theory-driven feed-forward expectations against the feedback from experience in testing the theory. Argyris and Schön's (1978) single and double loop learning models are arguably the most famous examples of this process.

Under what conditions might an efficient social epistemology for organizations be compatible with the enhancement of individual learning? To get some purchase on this issue, we need to take a closer look at the matter of theory testing. The first point to be made is that testing theories is a complex matter, owing to both the complexity of test situations and the complexity of theories. The problem becomes acute when large-scale social theories are up for testing as the growth of knowledge in Popper's view depends on the possibility of being able to falsify theories. There are so many possible causes operating and so many hypotheses within a social theory that are simultaneously being tested that it is difficult to know what claim is being falsified by what condition. Much of *The Poverty of Historicism* (1957, especially p. 67) is devoted to working out the implications that social complexity and unpredictability have for the growth of social knowledge. Maintaining the social conditions for the growth of knowledge, inter alia, requires incremental reform and engaging in criticism, notably those practices that permit theories to face the tribunal of evidence. Like Dewey, Popper's social epistemology also requires a democratic form of human association (Popper 1957, p. 155).

Popper's anti-psychologism notwithstanding, it is reasonable to characterize this epistemology in the language of individual and collective learning. For real social processes requiring individual actors are the means for instantiating its operation. As this is so, we can now ask how much of this can be used to underwrite recommendations for organizational structures that make for both organizational and individual learning? In the case of a society, 'the vast majority' of its institutions, rather than being consciously planned, have just grown (Popper 1957, p. 65). But when it comes to the design of particular organizations we have much latitude. One organizational design that assists to reduce both organizational complexity and the problem of theory holism is modularity, a conclusion also reached by Herbert Simon (1976, especially p. 294). Where organizational functioning is highly partitioned by a suitable division of organizational labour, the conditions that make for successful learning from experience may likewise be partitioned. So, whenever conditions exist for learning through Popper Cycles, it can occur at all levels, from individuals to large social configurations. For Popper, the relevant constraint sets are both the broader social context of a problem and its more specific features that are a function of its positionality.

Much traditional work in social epistemology relied on intuitions of social functioning in order to draw conclusions, often under counterfactual circumstances, concerning how particular social relations of learning would actually operate. But in the last 30 years or so, powerful modelling techniques have been developed to simulate these processes on computers. To explore assumptions about relations between individual learners and learning organizations in a more detailed way it is useful to look at this research on artificial organizations.

## Modelling learning organizations and individuals in context

The most general mathematical tool for modelling social learning is graph theory, where a graph is a collection of nodes (or points) connected in various ways by paths (or lines). Hutchins (1995, pp. 243–262) offers an account of learning in a small artificial organization comprised of four individuals. The individuals, in turn, are represented as containing two sets of nodes representing the hypotheses that are connected by paths in such a way as to define two different theories. These individuals are then connected by paths that link the hypothesis-representing nodes. The paths among the individuals are thus said to represent communication about hypotheses. The whole network also has an input signal signifying evidence. In this model, the issue under investigation was the role of leadership (as represented by strong signals coming from one of the individuals to the others) in shaping the organization's decision-making capacity and its learning capacity. The key finding was that there was a trade-off between the two. Leadership tended to hasten decision-making, but it also increased confirmation bias with the leader's view possessing a higher chance of prevailing in the face of evidence to the contrary (see also Evers 2007; Evers and Lakomski 2020). Conversely, to improve learning in this organization, less leadership reduced confirmation bias, although it also reduced decision-making capacity.

In a very small artificial network, this result on the propagation of influence may have been an artefact of the network's design. However, more detailed modelling using the resources of social network theory has produced similar results. Hutchins's (1995) network architecture and its dynamics was based on neural network modelling. But social network models are also graphs, although in that case, the nodes represent people rather than hypotheses. A considerable impetus for the mathematical study of social networks arose out of the discovery by Watts and Strogatz (1998) of 'small worlds', networks that had very interesting properties concerning the propagation and diffusion of information.

Imagine a network consisting of an array of nodes variously connected to each other by paths. This network can be described, in part, with reference to two important properties. The first is distance. This is the number of paths one can travel along to get from one node to another. The average path length expresses this for the whole network. The second is the clustering coefficient. It comes in two varieties. The local clustering coefficient for a node in an undirected network (one where the direction of the path does not matter) is the number of paths that connect it to its nearest neighbours divided by the total number of paths that could exist between these neighbours. The average clustering coefficient for a network is therefore the average of all these local clustering coefficients. A small world network is one that has the properties of a low average distance and a high average clustering coefficient (Evers 2012).

In a network characterized by relations of friendship, it is a small world if "on average a person's friends are more likely to know each other than two people chosen at random" (Watts 2004, p. 77) – an effect of the large clustering coefficient – and "it should be possible to connect two people chosen at random via a chain of only a few intermediaries" (Watts 2004, p. 77) – an effect of low average distance. So how does the relationship between leadership and learning play out in various network designs, including small world designs?

Zollman (2007) has undertaken a variety of computer simulations of network learning for a number of different network architectures. We consider two sets of his findings, the first being for three of these architectures, each containing the same number of individuals. The first network is a cycle, with each node joined by a path to only its two adjoining neighbours. The second is a wheel which is like a cycle except that there is one node at the centre connected to all other nodes. The third is a complete graph, where every node of a cycle is connected to every other node. In doing the simulations, a trade-off similar to the one noticed by Hutchins was observed. The cycle was the most efficient learning configuration, followed by the wheel and then the complete graph, and this held up for networks of many different sizes. However, the speed with which the networks reached their results was the reverse. The complete graph was the fastest, followed by the wheel and then the cycle. In general, "the trend seems to be that increased connectivity corresponds to faster but less reliable convergence" (Zollman 2007, p. 580). In terms of confirmation bias, it looks like the greater the amount of connectivity, the greater is the capacity for a strong leader or, as it is sometimes called, a Royal Family, to exert its influence. This interpretation seems to be borne out by the second set of simulations.

These simulations examined a variety of network architectures that differed primarily on degree of connectivity: five that were minimally connected and five that were strongly connected. (Zollman 2007, p. 583). Again, the basic trade-off was one of accuracy versus speed. The most sparsely connected networks performed most robustly against error, or the effects of getting locked into a false view. The comparison with Dewey's social epistemology is useful, as Zollman (2007, p. 586) concludes that where accuracy of learning is important, the sort of architecture that works best is one where there are groups of highly connected individuals, but the groups themselves are relatively sparsely connected. This is exactly the architecture of Watts' and Strogatz's (1998) small worlds. (See also Lakomski and Evers 2012.)

In these simulations, the distinction between what the individual learns and what the organization learns is collapsed by virtue of the way organizational learning is defined. For, roughly speaking, an organization is said to have learned to take some action (or accept some proposition or theory) if every individual meets that condition (Zollman 2007, p. 579). Part of the justification for this is a focus on the problem of confirmation bias which arises if we posit, as important, the learning of an elite within the organization. However, the situation is more complex than this focus suggests. In general, the main lesson we learn from modelling is that where evidence is more ambiguous and goals are subject to contestation, it is better to have less influential leadership in order to avoid confirmation bias that attends the 'Royal Family' effect. Much decision-making in schools is sensitive to the interpretation of data and can thus benefit from a more distributed version of decision-making. Some complexities are discussed below.

## Organizational and institutional constraints on learning

In general, we think that the structures that support a learning organization will vary according to the nature of the theories under test and the nature of the evidence that figures in these tests. For example, an organization that is solving highly constrained or very well-structured problems can be very efficient in its learning while being hierarchical with little support for individual learning beyond the top of the hierarchy. This is especially the case where evidence is unambiguous in the sense of being interpretable in the same way by all relevant organizational actors. Single loop learning can work. The sorts of issues that shaped Dewey's or Popper's social epistemologies will rarely go over into the design of organizations. Deweyan democratic societies have no overarching set of purposes or goals beyond providing the social infrastructure enabling citizens successfully to work out their own life plans in socially compatible ways. Most organizations have quite definite goals and purposes that extend beyond the enabling conditions of their members.

These considerations suggest a broad initial division for classifying relations between individual learning and the learning organization: namely, those organizations whose purposes and operations are partly constituted by the exercise of judgment requiring high levels of professional autonomy, and those that are not. Consider now, for illustrative purposes, the example of a school as an organization of the former kind. A central goal, such as providing a good education, can be not only contested by teachers as to what it means, but also subject to further debate and difference over how it is achieved, and what should count as evidence for its achievement. Moreover, this kind of debate is highly theoretical, invoking recourse not just to knowledge of techniques of teaching, that is, knowledge relevant only to the classroom, but knowledge that expresses an extended view of teacher professionalism, drawing on accounts of the nature of education, good educational outcomes, worthwhile knowledge, student autonomy, the social relations of learning, and a host of other matters. (For an overview of issues and their relevance to conceptions of good education, see Biesta 2010.) Under these conditions of ambiguity and recourse to professional judgment, the most appropriate structure for promoting learning in this school would be more like a 'small world' organization with a good distribution of leadership among teachers, high levels of individual learning, and good communication and shared decision-making between the various clusters of teachers in the organization. (See Silins and Mulford 2002, 2004, for a view of schools as learning organizations.)

However, schools (and other organizations) exist in an institutional framework that has implications for how they operate. One motivation for the development of institutional theory was because organizations did not seem to fit the model of a rational system, that is, one that selected the best means for achieving desired goals. Organizations also seemed to function as natural systems, expressed as behaviours concerned with flourishing in the prevailing wider environment. (For more in institutional theory, see Hanson 2001, and Burch 2007.) A simple example of this conflict can be seen among organizations that manufacture computer keyboards. For historical reasons entirely unconnected to today's technology, the QWERTY keyboard, which is the least efficient design, dominates English language versions. But to deviate from this design given prevailing skills and practices would cost market share. The manufacturer would fail to flourish in the wider institutional setting.

Now consider a common institutional framework in which our hypothesized school operates. At system level we may suppose that there are accountability requirements, perhaps concerning student achievements, and, where schools are hypothesized to operate in an educational market, these accountability measures may be public. In stepping outside the discourse of teachers' extended professionalism, the major casualties are, first, a nuanced understanding of the learning and teaching environment of the school, and second, a detailed understanding of each student's achievements that are educationally important as the professionals see matters. One of the tensions that can arise when the work of a small world community of teachers is being evaluated on outcomes that have been formulated to meet institutional requirements where data have been de-professionalized and simplified for the wider market audience, is that between relatively flat organizational structures of autonomously operating professionals, on the one hand, and the more hierarchical structures made possible by the informational currency of disambiguated, a-professional data, on the other. In this way, institutional pressures for accountability can, perversely, narrow the scope of individual learning and increase recourse to leadership control into previously autonomous domains of individual judgment.

There has been much analysis of this kind of shifting emphasis in institutional constraints on organizations and its effects on individual organizational actors. Wider analyses, such as critiques of neoliberal reforms of public sector management, clearly apply to more than schools. (For an overview, see Fusarelli and Johnson 2004.) And for analyses that both include and extend beyond the public sector, a four-fold taxonomy based on two organizational and two institutional factors can be employed. This 'New Institutionalism' partitions organizational environments into those that are technically weak and technically strong, and institutional environments into those that demand weak or strong conformity (Rowan and Miskel 1999, pp. 364–365). The matter of degree of conformity is clear enough. Examples of weak institutional conformity would be the many cases of businesses producing commodities, such as supermarket items, or services, such as hairdressing, for a competitive market. Hospitals, on the other hand, operate in a strong conformity institutional environment. When it comes to the matter of technicality, however, the issue is more complex. The idea seems to be that technical strength is a matter of being able to closely specify criteria for efficient (and effective) job performance and, ultimately, organizational performance. Thus hospitals, and some businesses, are classified as technically strong, whereas schools, because of their 'uncertain technologies' are deemed to be technically weak (Rowan and Miskel 1999, pp. 364–365).

Now if we overlay this modestly specified sense of technicality with an epistemic reading, there will be some organizations whose weak technicality is due to the highly context-sensitive nature of what counts as good individual performance, and a heavy reliance on excellence in professional judgment, rather than some useful algorithm, for how to act appropriately in those contexts. With this reading in mind, we can use the four-fold taxonomy of this version of institutional theory to extend our exploration of the various relations between individual learning and the learning organization and the kind of structures that support the latter. For three of the four possibilities, one can readily construct coherent relations between the individual and the organization when it comes to the dynamics of learning. The fourth possibility is the example under discussion where institutional strong conformity fails to cohere with the epistemic openness of weak organizational technicality.

## Organizational scaffolding of the mind

What this possibility raises is the more general question of the role of organizational arrangements in scaffolding the mind. Some of this has been discussed in Chapter 3, and a more general treatment will be given in Chapter 10. For now, we focus on a small set of issues. There are many ways that individual minds can be extended, or scaffolded, by artefacts, technological and cultural. For example, the institutional arrangements posited for the original Caldwell and Spinks model of school-based management required schools to: (1) develop charters that expressed a modest number of priority school goals to be achieved over the three-year life of the charter; (2) to develop implementation strategies that were to be reviewed annually; (3) to use feedback from reviews to modify these implementation strategies where necessary; and (4) to review the accomplishment of charter goals in the light of end result feedback (Caldwell and Spinks 1988). Supported by an extended sense of teacher professionalism, this arrangement could produce a coherent combination of individual and organizational learning.

In a Deweyan democracy, with weak institutional conformity mandating merely liberty, freedom from interference, and some egalitarian distribution of human development infrastructure, a similar coherence between individual and social learning could result, although this would depend on learning arrangements, arguably weakly technical, within socially distributed clusters of people with common interests. To say something more explicit about the institutional environments that would favour learning organizations that in turn may scaffold (or not) individual learning, we need to move to a more fine-grained analysis than that provided by the categories of current social epistemology and the new institutional theory. Some preliminary findings on this issue can be found in the work of Andy Clark in his study of the biotechnology industry (Clark 1999).

According to Clark (1999), relations between the institutional and wider environment on the one hand and the trajectory pursued by the biotechnology organization on the other means that "instead of seeing the environment as simply a source of problems and an arena in which problem-solving processes are played out, it becomes necessary to view aspects of the environment as equal partners in extended, soft-assembled, problem-solving" (Clark 1999, p. 48). Clark then further specifies the nature of the industry as operating in a high-uncertainty market where its processes are research intensive, utilizing high technology.

Given such an institutional and organizational set of constraints, it is possible to argue for certain types of organizational scaffoldings that support both individual and organizational learning. In particular, organizations within this industry typically make use of: (1) 'minimal hierarchical structures' both within organizations and between venturing partners; (2) focus on the development of individuals' specialized skills that lead the organization to articulate in complementary ways with other relevant organizations; and (3) exploit corporate architectures that enable the organization to easily extend itself by permitting high levels of interaction with external resources (Clark 1999, p. 52). Despite the possibility of being able to mount quite detailed arguments for these arrangements that link epistemic considerations with the realities of a particular commercial market, the point that needs emphasizing is the particularity of the example or, indeed, just about any example. There are lessons for schools here, too.

## Conclusion

Theories of educational leadership have tended to be both individualistic and also content centred. We have argued that the explanatory and normative value of leader-centric accounts of leadership needs to be justified and that justification will be context specific. We have also argued that 'content' approaches are seriously compromised by both fallibilism and by context specificity. Individuals, teams, and whole organizations, under these conditions need to build knowledge of leadership through progressive epistemic processes. Hence, our defence of a process approach to leadership as knowledge building. A vital aspect of this approach lies beyond individual psychology and is located on the arena of social epistemology. Such has been the focus of this chapter.

The study of learning in organizational settings is complex. At the most general level is the study of knowledge building in society-wide social formations of the sort that Dewey's social epistemology dealt with. Within particular social formations, institutional constraints are defined for various organizations, and these shape in particular ways the nature of both individual learning and the prospects for learning organizations. Although it was possible, using institutional theory to discern a number of conditions at individual and organizational levels that shaped prospects for learning in each and relations among each in their interaction spaces, a more detailed causal story looked like it would require the resources of both a view of individual learning and cognition as occurring in an extended mind, and an account of how organizational structures and processes operate to scaffold that mind. On this matter, Clark (2001, p. 154) notes:

> The study of these interaction spaces is not easy, and depends both on new multidisciplinary alliances and new forms of modelling analysis. The payoff, however, could be spectacular: nothing less than a new kind of cognitive scientific collaboration involving neuroscience, physiology, and social, cultural, and technological studies in about equal measure.

The study of leadership in context would be well served if placed on this research agenda.

## References

Argyris, C., & Schön, D. (1978). *Organizational learning: A theory of action perspective*. Menlo Park, CA: Addison-Wesley.

Aspin, D.N., & Chapman, J. (2001). Towards a philosophy of lifelong learning. In D.N. Aspin, J. Chapman, M. Hatton, & Y. Sawano (Eds.), *International handbook of lifelong learning. Part one* (pp. 3–33). Dordrecht: Kluwer.

Banks, J., Dragan, V., & Jones, A. (2003). *Chaos: A mathematical introduction*. Cambridge, UK: Cambridge University Press.

Bell, D. (1974). *The coming of post-industrial society: A venture in social forecasting*. London: Heinemann.

Biesta, G.J.J. (2010). *Good education in an age of measurement.* Boulder, CO: Paradigm Publishers.
Boole, G. (1854/1958). *The laws of thought.* New York, NY: Dover Publications.
Burch, P. (2007). Educational policy and practice from the perspective on institutional theory: Crafting a wider lens. *Educational Researcher,* 36(2), 84–95.
Caldwell, B.J., & Spinks, J. (1988). *The self-managing school.* Lewes, East Sussex: Falmer Press.
Chappell, C., Rhodes, C., Solomon, N., Tennant, M., & Yates, L. (2003). *Reconstructing the lifelong learner: Pedagogy and identity in individual, organisational and social change.* London: Routledge/Falmer.
Chitpin, S., & Evers, C.W. (2005). Teacher professional development as knowledge building: A Popperian analysis. *Teachers and Teaching: Theory and Practice,* 11(4), 419–433.
Clark, A. (1999). Leadership and influence: The manager as coach, nanny, and artificial DNA. In J. Clippinger (Ed.), (1999) *The biology of business: De-coding the natural laws of Enterprise* (pp. 47–66). San Francisco, CA: Jossey-Bass.
Clark, A. (2001). *Mindware: An introduction to the philosophy of cognitive science.* Oxford: Oxford University Press.
Dahlgaard, S.M.P. (2004). Perspectives on learning – A literature review. *European Quality,* 11(1), 32–47.
Dewey, J. (1916). *Democracy and education.* New York, NY: Free Press.
Diamond, J. (2011). *Collapse: How societies choose to fail or succeed.* New York: Viking Press.
Dietrich, E., & Fields, C. (1996). The role of the frame problem in Fodor's modularity thesis: A case study of rationalist cognitive science. In K.M. Ford, & Z.W. Pylyshyn (Eds.), *The robot's dilemma revisited: The frame problem in artificial intelligence* (pp. 9–24). Norwood, NJ: Ablex.
Eliasmith, C. (2003). Moving beyond metaphors: Understanding the mind for what it is. *Journal of Philosophy,* 100(10), 493–520.
Engel, C. (2005). *Generating predictability: Institutional analysis and institutional design.* Cambridge, UK: Cambridge University Press.
Evans, N. (2003). *Making sense of lifelong learning: Respecting the needs of all.* London: Routledge/Falmer.
Evers, C.W. (2000a). Connectionist modeling and education. *Australian Journal of Education,* 44(3), 209–225.
Evers, C.W. (2000b). Leading and learning in organizational contexts: A contribution from the new cognitive science. *International Journal of Leadership in Education,* 3(3), 239–254.
Evers, C.W. (2001). Knowing how to lead: Theoretical reflections on inference to the best training. In K.C. Wong, & C.W. Evers (Eds.), *Leadership for quality schooling: International perspectives* (pp. 103–115). London: Falmer Press.
Evers, C.W. (2007). Lifelong learning and knowledge: Towards a general theory of professional inquiry. In D.N. Aspin (Ed.), *Philosophical perspectives on lifelong learning* (pp. 173–188). Dordrecht: Springer.
Evers, C.W. (2012). Organizational contexts for lifelong learning: Individual and collective learning configurations. In D.N. Aspin, J.D. Chapman, K.R. Evans, & R. Bagnall (Eds.), *Second international handbook of lifelong learning* (pp. 61–76). Dordrecht: Springer.
Evers, C.W., & Lakomski, G. (1991). *Knowing educational administration.* Oxford, UK: Pergamon.
Evers, C.W., & Lakomski, G. (2000). *Doing educational administration.* Oxford, UK: Pergamon.
Evers, C.W. & Lakomski, G. (2020). Cognitive science and educational administration. In R. Papa (Ed.), *The Oxford encyclopedia of educational administration.* Oxford, UK: Oxford University Press.
Evers, C.W., & Wu, E.H. (2006). On generalizing from single case studies: Epistemological reflections. *Journal of Philosophy of Education,* 40(4), 511–526.
Fodor, J.A. (1983). *The modularity of mind: An essay on faculty psychology.* Cambridge, MA: MIT Press.

Fodor, J.A. (1990). *A theory of content and other essays*. Cambridge, MA: MIT Press.
Friedman, T. (2010). Going long on liberty in China. *New York Times.* 16 October 2010. http://www.nytimes.com/2010/10/17/opinion/17friedman.html?ref=thomaslfriedman Retrieved 20 October 2010.
Fusarelli, L.D., & Johnson, B. (2004). Educational governance and the new public sector management. *Public Administration and Management: An Interactive Journal*, 9(2), 118–127.
Geeraerts, G. (1998). Non-linear dynamics and the prediction of war. *POLE Paper Series*, 4(1), http://poli.vub.ac.be/pubi/pole-papers/pole0401.htm
Gödel, K. (1931). *On formally undecidable propositions of principia mathematica and related systems.* Translated by B. Meltzer, with Introduction by R.B. Braithwaite (1962). Edinburgh: Oliver & Boyd.
Godfrey-Smith, P. (2009). Dewey and the question of realism, http://www.people.fas.harvard.edu/~pgs/DeweyRealism_S.pdf Retrieved 11 August 2010.
Gutmann, A. (1999). *Democratic education*. Princeton, NJ: Princeton University Press.
Hanson, M. (2001). Institutional theory and educational change. *Educational Administration Quarterly*, 37(5), 637–661.
Hutchins, E. (1995). *Cognition in the wild*. Cambridge, MA: MIT Press.
Jarvis, P. (2004). *Adult education and lifelong learning*. London: Routledge/Falmer.
Kitcher, P. (1990). The division of cognitive labor. *Journal of Philosophy*, 87(1), 5–22.
Kitcher, P. (1993). *The advancement of science*. Oxford: Oxford University Press.
Lagerspetz, E. (2004). Predictability and the growth of knowledge. *Synthese*, 141(3), 445–452.
Millgram, E. (2000). Coherence: The price of the ticket. *Journal of Philosophy*, 97(2), 82–93.
Popper, K.R. (1950). Indeterminism in quantum physics and in classical physics: Part II. *British Journal for the Philosophy of Science*, 1(3), 179–188.
Popper, K.R. (1957). *The poverty of historicism*. London: Routledge & Kegan Paul.
Popper, K.R. (1959). *The logic of scientific discovery*. London: Hutchinson.
Popper, K.R. (1979). *Objective knowledge*. Oxford, UK: Oxford University Press.
Popper, K.R. (1982). *The open universe: An argument for indeterminism*. London: Routledge.
Rowan, B., & Miskel, C.G. (1999). Institutional theory and the study of educational organizations. In J. Murphy, & K. Seashore-Louis (Eds.) (1999). *Handbook of research on educational administration* (pp. 359–383). San Francisco: Jossey-Bass.
Saperstein, A.M. (1999). *Dynamical modeling of the onset of war*. Singapore: World Scientific.
Searle, J. (1995). *The construction of social reality*. New York, NY: The Free Press.
Silins, H., & Mulford, B. (2002). Schools as learning organizations: The case for system, teacher and student learning. *Journal of Educational Administration*, 40(5), 425–446.
Silins, H., & Mulford, B. (2004). Schools as learning organizations: Effects on teacher leadership and student outcomes. *School Effectiveness and School Improvement*, 15(3/4), 443–466.
Simon, H.A. (1976). *Administrative behavior*. 3rd Edition, New York, NY: Free Press.
Splitter, L., & Sharpe, A. (1995). *Teaching for better thinking*. Melbourne: ACER.
Thagard, P. (1992). *Conceptual revolutions*. Princeton, NJ: Princeton University Press.
Watts, D.J. (2004). *Six degrees: The science of a connected age*. London: Vintage.
Watts, D.J., & Strogatz, S.H. (1998). Collective dynamics of 'small world networks'. *Nature*, 393, 440–442.
Weisberg, M., & Muldoon, R. (2009). Epistemic landscapes and the division of cognitive labor. *Philosophy of Science*, 76, 225–252.
Wilkinson, M.H.F. (1999). Non-linear dynamics, chaos-theory, and the "sciences of complexity": Their relevance to the study of the interaction between host and microflora". http://old-herborn-university.de/literature/books/OHUni_book_10_article_11.pdf, pp. 111–130.
Zollman, K.J.S. (2007). The communication structure of epistemic communities. *Philosophy of Science*, 74, 574-587.

# 6
# LEARNING LEADERSHIP THROUGH PROBLEM-SOLVING TRAJECTORIES

## Introduction

Leadership is a form of task engagement in organizational contexts. There are two broad features governing the form it takes. The first is the contingencies of task and organizational context. The second is a normative epistemology for acquiring and applying the necessary knowledge for successful task engagement. In response to the prevailing tendency to see leadership in individualist leader-centric terms, we argue for the modest claim that leader-centric accounts of leadership have an onus-of-proof requirement. There may be other more appropriate units of leadership for successful task accomplishment, and thus leader-centrism is not entitled to be the default position. We also argue the stronger claim that the epistemic constraints for successful task engagement are mostly both distributed and require knowledge building processes. The result is that no one best model of leadership emerges from this analysis. However, we are able to say that some models will be more appropriate than others for certain tasks in specified contexts, and we can even use normative epistemic arguments for organizations to change their own contexts to improve task engagement.

Our claim is that an individual, or team, or organization builds an account of good leadership by responding to the condition of uncertainty in problem-solving tasks through adopting knowledge building processes. These are a matter of intelligent trial and error. They involve choosing a best known starting point for trying something out, and careful attention to the consequences of implementing that choice. There are many examples of this in professional learning. Professional learning by attending to the advice of experts is only one part of the process, but a useful starting point. It needs to be followed by adaption to context, implementation, recognition of where things might have gone wrong, and correcting for these discovered errors, possibly to commence a new round of trial and error. The 'reflective practitioner' model championed by Schön (1983) created a huge industry in understanding and applying this dynamical epistemic framework. Widely accepted and applied versions of action research also fit this broad design (Chitpin and Evers 2005, 2019).

Within this intelligent trial-and-error tradition, we advocate more explicitly for an approach based on the ideas of Karl Popper, with two key modifications. The first of these concerns Popper's anti-psychologism. It had for a long time been customary for philosophers of science to distinguish between contexts of justification and contexts of discovery. Roughly speaking, justification was all about logic, mainly deductive and inductive logic, whereas discovery was often thought to be a psychological process. In his first major work, *The Logic of Scientific Discovery* (1959), Popper argued, as the book's title suggests, that discovery is not a psychological process, but rather a logical process. He later elaborated this position in "Epistemology without a knowing subject" (Popper 1968) and in *Objective Knowledge* (1979). Contrary to this view, we hold that Popper's logic of conjecture and refutation can also function as a psychological process, one that can be consciously adopted by researchers and used to guide their thinking in undertaking scientific and other inquiries (Chitpin and Evers 2005). In training people to use Popper's objective knowledge growth framework, part of the task is showing the advantages of a critical habit of mind, a way to think about growing knowledge to solve problems.

The second key modification we make concerns the process of dealing with feedback from trials or conjectures in the form of errors or refutations. Despite appearances, trials or conjectures are not isolated propositions. They are embedded in a wider context of claims we can usefully call theories, where it is whole theories that face the tribunal of experience, or observation, or empirical evidence. This means that in dealing with feedback that is contrary to theory-driven expectation, we must make a decision over which parts of the theory to hold as background context, and which claim or claims need to be revised. Our coherentism says that there is more to justifying a theory than empirical evidence. There are non-empirical criteria such as consistency, simplicity, comprehensiveness, internal coherence as well as coherence with other well-established theories. Inference from all these sources, empirical and non-empirical, is sometimes called abductive reasoning, or inference to the best explanation. Some of the more technical issues around epistemic holism are canvassed in Chapter 7.

We now turn to a close analysis of a problems-solutions trajectory, why it works, and what lessons can be learned from it in dealing with other problems.

## Example of a problems-solutions trajectory

Consider the case of a Hong Kong high school that is threatened with closure by the government's Education Bureau unless it reaches quota on first year enrolments. (The case is reported in detail in Evers and Katyal 2008, pp. 260–264.) The unit of cognition tasked with solving the problem is the school's leadership team, although this actually understates who is involved once we include all those who participate in actual implementations of solutions. Some of the entities that constitute part of the problem for the school are individuals: there is a lack of potential students, and of parents unwilling to enrol their children. Some are structural, such as the government's Education Bureau and its policies on minimum school sizes. Because social science provides no definitive answer as to how to solve the problem, the first proposed solution is formulated to require minimal resources and effort: they elect to publicize the school in its local district. This plan fails for a mixture of reasons, some clearly to do with individuals (parents are unconvinced) and some structural (the school has a bad reputation). After a further unsuccessful problem-solution iteration with the local community, the school's leadership proposes to recruit students further afield. Structural features, such as subsidized transport and financial support from the school's alumni, now come into play. After more unsuccessful iterations, the enrolment problem is finally solved when the school, with permission from its sponsoring body and the Education Bureau, decides to become co-educational and recruits girls. Any attempt to portray this whole process in narrow leader-centric terms would be misleading because it would seriously understate all of the structural features that constrain what would count as both the process of reaching a solution and the solution itself. The very act of leading in social contexts is constituted by social structures and social facts.

Table 6.1 captures the dynamics of this whole process in terms of a device that makes use of Karl Popper's Objective Knowledge Growth Framework (OKGF).

Each attempt at solving the problem begins with a statement of the problem, P1, followed by a tentative theory, TT1, for dealing with it. The TT1 is then implemented and encounters evidence of its inadequacy. This is known as a process of error elimination, or EE1. The errors highlight a further problem to be solved, P2, a further tentative theory, TT2, and the discovery of further inadequacies now with TT2, recorded as EE2. And so the problem-solving trajectory continues, each step of the process, namely, P1 => TT1 => EE1 => P2, being a Popper Cycle.

The key point to note is that leadership, which is usually construed in terms of agency, is a highly relative notion. The so-called agency/structure issue is better recast in terms of the constraints that define problems, with solutions being framed as a meeting of those constraints or of changing 'soft' constraints so that they can be met. When it comes to explaining and improving organizational functioning, many of these constraints will be relative to the nature and function of the organization and the range of problems which it is tasked to solve. The constraints that define some of the tasks that an army should perform may require quite leader-centric modes of operations, while the tasks that, say, a market solves, namely the selling of products at certain prices, will be mostly leader-less. And within these extremes, we see schools. Some problems will be more or less leader-centric in their mode of solution, but in general we see formal and informal groups as the unit of cognition and epistemic progress, a case we made in Chapter 5. A detailed analysis of this example now follows.

## Learning leadership 95

**TABLE 6.1** An Example of Epistemically Structured Problem-Solving

| Popper Cycle 1 | Popper Cycle 2 | Popper Cycle 3 | Popper Cycle 4 | Popper Cycle 5 | Popper Cycle 6 | Popper Cycle 7 | Popper Cycle 8 |
|---|---|---|---|---|---|---|---|
| **P1:** Recruiting a sufficient number of Form 1 students for the new school year to meet the Education Bureau's requirements. **TT1:** Initiate a pro-active program of publicity and promotion in the immediate neighbourhood. **EE1:** There is little response among prospective parents because of the school's recent poor image on student discipline. | **P2:** How to change parents' perceptions of the school? **TT2:** Approach prospective parents and explain the school's plans to deal with the problem and invite them to visit the school to see what is being done. **EE2:** Some positive responses but there is still evidence of an insufficient intake of new students from the immediate neighbourhood. | **P3:** How to attract students from further afield? **TT3:** Provide convenient transport such as school buses at affordable prices. **EE3:** There is now a need to raise funds to subsidize school transport. | **P4:** How to raise funds to subsidize school transport? **TT4:** Mobilize the school's alumni to raise sufficient funds to cover transport costs for the immediate school year. **EE4:** The extra intake is still insufficient. | **P5:** How to enhance the school's attractiveness? **TT5:** Given the distance of the school from the town centre, this is achieved by providing a free lunch to all students through further financial support from alumni. **EE5:** There is some improvement in enrolments but still not sufficient. | **P6:** How to further expand the size of the Form 1 intake? **TT6:** Change the school from boys only to a co-educational school. **EE6:** This provides a major boost in intake but many school facilities need modification, for example, toilets. | **P7:** How to convert the school to a co-educational mode? **TT7:** Establish a taskforce among the school management to attend to the facilities improvement program with funding from the Education Bureau and the alumni. **EE7:** Immediate targets achieved but the problem now shifts to long-term consolidation. | **P8:** How to strengthen the schools currently fragile position? **TT8:** Mount a sustainable and visible program of quality assurance and improvement on all aspects of the school's performance. **EE8:** New problems are encountered but it is envisaged that a coordinated program of problem-solving in addressing individual problems will be effective in meeting the targets in the future. |

## Defining problems

Leaving aside the question of the nature of the epistemic unit that is tasked with problem-solving, as we have indicated earlier, a problem is defined by a set of constraints plus the demand that something be done. This account is holistic because of the multiple features that go into a problem, thus leaving open a variety of possibilities for resolution. For example, does everyone agree that something must be done? A school that has succeeded in lifting Friday attendance to 92 percent may baulk at the goal of trying further on the grounds that the effort required may be more troublesome than any gains from a higher goal. That is, the goal may be contested. This kind of ground for contestation is common where goal achievement occurs on a sliding scale of costs and pay-offs. Trying to enforce a school dress code beyond a certain level is another example. So, too, are school goals for student learning achievement. At system level, goal setting for student learning through reducing class sizes produces a similar contestation where the trade-off is between financial costs and learning gains. Consensus over the demand that something be done can be difficult to achieve.

In the Table 6.1 case, the consequences for failing to solve the initial problem were more drastic for those in the team with this task. Decision-makers who are directly affected by the consequences of their decisions are said to have skin in the game (Taleb 2018) and this can be a source of goal convergence.

**Problem, P1**: *Recruiting a sufficient number of Form 1 students for the new school year to meet the Education Bureau's requirements.*

Failing to solve the problem would have resulted in the school being closed down within about eighteen months. The problem has another advantage: it is well-structured. For among the constraints is a set of key government regulations that includes a hard constraint on school size. Fortunately, other constraints that shape how the school might respond, such as its budget and staffing resources, or its community and communications options, may be amenable to change. They may be soft constraints.

Well-structured problems possess two principal advantages. They help to delimit the number of tentative theories that can be considered for implementation, and they imply clear criteria for judging progress on solving the problem. A school has many courses of action, but only a limited number will address the declining enrolment problem in a timely manner. And the evidence for success, the kind of feedback that figures in the elimination of errors from tentative theories, is relatively unambiguous in being comprised of actual or promised advanced enrolments. The school had relatively clear data categories for assessing its progress. A problem can also contain useful structure if the data used to show there is evidence of a problem can also function as evidence for later success. Thus, a school may come to know it has a communication problem based on complaints from parents that could be diminished by better communication.

The task of improving communication looks to be relatively open-ended but tracking the number of complaints over a succession of trial solutions will place epistemic pressure on the selection of better methods of communication. Although measuring complaints might seem like a modest proxy function, it can be a good place to start. Our advice is to look for good proxy functions that cohere with important educational values.

A seemingly ill-structured problem can be sharpened up by proxy functions that deliver highly appropriate data that can function to shape tentative theories used to guide implementations of proposed solutions. For example, the perception of low staff morale in a school can be considerably refined by using data from the kind of survey material developed by Wayne Hoy and colleagues (Hoy et al. 1991). One of the simplest measurement proxies for teacher morale is a difference that can be detected by pairing questions with Likert-type answers that explore the difference between what respondents say happens and what they say ought to happen; for example in the pair: the principal supports teachers in disputes with parents, and the principal ought to support teachers in disputes with parents. The validity of this approach depends on the claim that lower morale obtains when the principal is not doing what teachers think the principal ought to be doing. The methodology generalizes to a range of possible sources of morale problems and can be a useful first approximation to where morale problems in a school can lie.

Note that in formulating problems in a way that articulates with the development of theories and evidence of success, or failure, the process is not algorithmic. It calls for professional judgment. In an elementary or primary school the authors were researching, language teachers with a class noticed a discrepancy between students' reading facility, which was quite good, and their comprehension capacity for what they had read, which was low. Despite trying out various ways of improving comprehension, the gap, as measured by a test, remained. And yet, in the judgment of the teachers, students' comprehension had improved. The puzzle was settled when a consultant discovered that the teachers were using an inappropriate comprehension test. Teachers' professional judgment can have wider critical dimensions where, for example, a narrow testing regime goes proxy for educational achievement. But there is a balance here too.

The problem of a school providing a quality education is ill-structured, though it can be made more precise with a specification of what counts as a quality education. It is worth saying more about the kind of balance required to aim for precision. In a tradition that goes back to an articulation in Aristotle's *Ethics*, aspects of what make for a good life are conceived in terms of human flourishing. The virtues that are central to this flourishing are acquired by the process of exercising those virtues. One becomes courageous by doing courageous things. The various social contexts in which these virtues may be acquired as part of the building of wisdom are exceedingly complex and often contested. The sort of cognitive machinery capable of representing such high levels of complexity, we claim, are the representational powers of the brain's neural architecture, its information processing neural networks. In identifying those ways in which education might contribute to human flourishing, the representational powers embodied in the human brain, when functioning as an instrument of measurement and evaluation, are what come into play in assessing the appropriateness of any test for quality education. In formulating problems in what Biesta (2009) calls good education in an age of measurement, the appropriateness of proxy functions needs to be assessed is terms of wider ethical, social, and political values.

## Defining tentative theories

In attempting to solve the problem of falling enrolments, the first tentative theory proposed was:

> **Tentative Theory, TT1**: *Initiate a pro-active program of publicity and promotion in the immediate neighbourhood.*

The heuristic driving this choice of action is ease of implementation. It doesn't require any changes to the school, its practices, its performance, or its teaching. It just needs better promotion in its local community. When outcomes of alternative possibilities are uncertain of success, choose the option that is easiest to implement. After all, it may actually work. This heuristic is a bit stronger since it was the chosen starting point even though the problem-solvers were fairly sure that Tentative Theory 6 would work, which it did. (**TT6:** *change the school from boys only to a co-educational school.*) What they were doing was choosing an uncertain easy option over a relatively certain hard option.

This choice says something important about the link between epistemology and why the resulting trajectory took the form it did. The reason TT1 did not work was because when the publicity program was implemented, the group did not know that the school was held in low esteem by the community. Error elimination occurred. (**EE1**: *there is little response among prospective parents because of the school's recent poor image on student discipline.*) Had this been known beforehand, it would have been included among the constraints that defined the original problem, P1, and would have resulted in the choice of a different TT1. That is, a trajectory arises in part as a result of a growing understanding of the nature of the constraints that existed in defining the original problem. There is a logical feature to problem-solving in a trajectory. In completing a jigsaw puzzle, you don't start by trying to figure out where the centre pieces go. There are not enough constraints, as given by surrounding pieces, to specify what would count as a correct choice of a centre piece. Instead, you start from the corners, then the edges, and then work inward. Similarly, you may not reach a successful tentative theory until through error elimination you reach a sufficient understanding of the constraints that will provide a place in which to fit a workable theory.

Problem-solving in organizational life almost always involves solving multiple problems simultaneously. It is therefore important for different problems-solutions trajectories to cohere in the sense that the implementation of tentative theories for dealing with one problem should not impose additional constraints on the solution of other problems. Sometimes this can be unavoidable, leading to a *de facto* expression of priorities. So, while dealing with the problem of low staff morale might be considered one priority, strategies for improving student learning outcomes might have a higher priority even when those strategies are known to exacerbate the staff morale problem. The public health crisis over Covid-19 contained a dramatic balancing of priorities: a choice of social distancing to halt the spread of the virus versus a severe economic downturn as a consequence of social distancing. Coherent school problem-solving would therefore reflect problems being formulated with awareness of the impact on problem constraint sets by attempts to solve other problems.

One advantage of TT1, in our example, is that it avoids this problem by least disturbing other activities in the school. However, as failures along the trajectory pile up, more engagement with an expanding constraint set is required. Another issue to note, although it is not part of our example, is a way in which resilience can have an effect. It is said that one definition of insanity is doing the same thing again and expecting a different result. Implementing a tentative theory that has failed first time around, or 'doubling-down' can have the effect of changing a problem's constraint set by signaling a determination to solve the problem as an additional constraint. Again, there is no algorithm for this judgment call, just fallible knowledge based on accumulated professional experience, including the experience of when it works and when it doesn't.

Failure to solve the enrolment problem for this school was something that would result in what might be called an extinction level event. When the problem was finally solved by the school going co-educational (TT6), it had reached a point where it had acquired a consensus acknowledgement of a further problem. (***P8:*** *how to strengthen the school's currently fragile position?*) In order to prevent the recurrence of such an event in the future the school developed a tentative theory to deal with that possibility. (***TT8:*** *mount a sustainable and visible program of quality assurance and improvement on all aspects of the school's performance.*) In being more expansive in their self-evaluation, the school was showing awareness that many features of school functioning can lead to it having a poor reputation in the community. Although the original factor was parent perceptions of discipline problems (EE1), other future possibilities could be poor student learning outcomes, poor transitions to further or higher education, unsatisfactory employment outcomes, school-community engagement issues, or adapting to online learning that might be increasingly demanded by parents. Depending on how quickly problems can arise, a good self-evaluation program needs to be more than an effective look in a rear-view mirror. It needs to anticipate and plan for possible problems. Since its brush with extinction, the school has flourished.

## Defining error elimination

Error elimination is the process whereby you find out whether your tentative theory adopted and implemented actually does solve the problem. By engaging in this epistemic process, the distinction between theory and practice is blurred. Theories for solving problems are improved by acting on them and attending to the consequences of their implementation. Because of the nature of theories, the relationship between feedback and holistic evidence, and the dynamics of theory revision, this epistemic process is complex. First, theories are complex wholes. TT1 looks like it contains only one claim, but in fact that claim is only the one chosen to be highlighted from a number of other background claims in which it is nested and with which it shares a range of inferential relations. These background claims will include "the school's achievements are not well-known enough", "the school is generally well regarded in the community", "teaching is adequate", "learning is adequate", "employment prospects for students are adequate", "small changes are relatively easy", "staff and alumni support small changes for improvement". Taken in conjunction, this set of claims comprising the broader theory, meets the heuristic that suggests a promotions and publicity campaign will be effective. The conjunction of hypotheses implies that the enrolment problem could be easily solved. The feedback from implementation is not just a lack of possible enrolments. The feedback includes a further response to the promotions campaign in the form of criticism of the school. Since there is a strong inferential link between criticism of the school and the effectiveness of a publicity campaign, the conclusion that the campaign is doomed unless the criticisms are dealt with is reasonable, and easy to make since feedback did not directly threaten any of the other hypotheses in the network.

The problem of holism becomes more difficult when feedback affects any number of hypotheses in an expanded theory. Although not conspicuous for P1, solving the new problem of improving the standing of the school in its local community (***P2:*** *How to change parents' perceptions of the school?*) even for so-called discipline issues, could involve a wider set of issues responsible for poor discipline. In any case, showcasing the school's plans and improvements to parents (***TT2:*** *Approach prospective parents and explain the school's plans to deal with the problem and invite them to visit the school to see what is being done.*) did not work. (***EE2:*** *Some positive responses but there is still evidence of an insufficient intake of new students from the immediate neighbourhood.*) School discipline is not a narrowly specified target for tentative theories, and their effectiveness, especially where it involves long-term difficulties of teaching and learning school culture, can take considerable time to emerge. Earlier, we remarked that 'doubling down' can soften a constraint that implies resistance to change. The opposite is knowing when to fold. P2 was abandoned, at least within the available timeframe. Acknowledging that theories are complex should function as an invitation to do a critical analysis of the constraints thought to define the problem, since theories chosen for implementation would normally try to change one or more of the constraints. Indeed, that is why the publicity campaign was selected in the example.

In addition to complexity of theories, another area of this epistemic process that requires careful attention is the nature of feedback, or what to count as evidence that a theory is working or not. We saw an example of this in the case of reading comprehension, described earlier. Measuring a student's height is different in important ways from measuring a student's reading comprehension. For a start, a student's height is something you can see. Also, although the act of measurement draws on theoretical notions such as length, there is widespread consensus on the nature of conducting such a measurement. Reading comprehension is less obvious to the senses, needing to be mediated by constructs of a more contested nature. Many observations in education are like this in being theory-laden. What counts as good teaching or good administration is seen through the lens of theories of teaching or administration, including those that are tacit or implicit in the mind of the observer. Sometimes these theories are used to devise instruments, such as tests, that create the very thing that the theory invites us to observe. In assessing feedback from implementing a tentative theory, knowledge of the theory that informs what is being observed is important for assessing error elimination.

In the case of declining student numbers, there was only one type of evidence: promised enrolments. However, even quite straightforward problems can involve multiple types of evidence, leading to the challenge of multi-criteria decision-making. A school has a teaching day of four 80-minute periods. There is a perceived problem of limited student attention over that time, less effective use of the time for student learning, and pressure on staff for meeting the attention span problem. As a result, the school decides to shift to an eight 40-minute period teaching day. In implementing this change, the team monitoring the possibility of errors arising from feedback, will want to attend to a number of indicators. Consider three possible indicators. The school has a crowded campus, and additional noise arising from the change may prove unwelcome. Cutting each lesson time in half may turn out to be less efficient for student learning because of time lost to more beginnings and endings of lessons. Teachers may come to suffer from 'buyer's remorse' and view the change as too disruptive. Each of these indicators – noise (n), efficient learning (e), and teacher's growing unhappiness with the new system (t) – can be regarded as an ordered triplet data set {n, e, t}. Over time, as the implementation is monitored by some agreed set of metrics, the elements in the set will change. For example, {5, 3, 2} might become {5, 4, 7} indicating that the noise has grown, learning efficiency has marginally increased, and teacher dissatisfaction has grown considerably. The difficulty in sorting out gains over time is that the set of ordered triplets is not itself ordered. The only way in which a clear gain emerges between two ordered triplets is if there is a gain for each corresponding indicator: noise becomes less than or of equal concern, learning efficiency rises or remains equal, and teachers' remorse becomes less or equal to previous measures. But this kind of win-win-win is unusual.

Normally, there are trade-offs. We may end up accepting a little more noise in exchange for more efficient learning. The multi-criteria decision problem is difficult because the three indicators are orthogonal; they don't reduce to each other. They are like the three axes in a cube.

One way to deal with this difficulty it to create a measurement that is analogous to the volume of a cube. Define a set of weights to each indicator, n, e, and t, such that we can trade one off against the other. So, this might allow us to specify how much of an increase in noise is acceptable given a corresponding increase in learning or increase in teachers' remorse. An aggregate, A1, for the first set {5, 3, 2} would look like $5*w_1 + 3*w_2 + 2*w_3$ with weights $w_1$ and $w_3$ negative because they reflect unfavourable outcomes and $w_2$ positive because it weights a favourable outcome. Suppose we select as our three weights {-0.2, +0.6, −0.3}. Then the value of A1 would be $5*-0.2 + 3*0.6 + 2*-0.3 = 0.2$. We then compare the result for A2, the second set of indicators: $5*-0.2 + 4*0.6 + 7*-0.3 = -0.7$. Thus, given these indicators and weights, A1 is preferable to A2, and as these are assumed to be shifts over time, the implementation of the eight 40-minute lesson regime is in trouble.

This simple toy model allows us to identify three lessons for multi-criteria problem-solving. The first is that in practice, even where everyone accepts the indicator metrics for n, e, and t, the weights can be unstable, changing over time. People can adapt to increased noise by ignoring it and can similarly adapt to the changed pedagogy. Moreover, there can be a greater appreciation of gains in learning efficiency, even in the context of other perceived disadvantages. The weights that were applied to {5, 3, 2} may have shifted in the context of {5, 4, 7}. And working with these shifts may end up also shifting the teachers' remorse metric. The way the feedback over implementation time is modeled, makes it look like the consequences of a change to the new timetable are getting worse. However, that will be an artifact of the model's assumption that no adaption occurs to the changed context. The second lesson is that the model, in tracking multi-criteria feedback, signals where the next problem, or problems, can occur in making the timetable change work. The emerging P2 from the EE1 is the problem of supporting teachers' adaption to the new teaching arrangements. Solving the problem of promoting greater student learning efficiency relative to available teaching time requires a change in the context of learning giving rise to changes in multiple feedback indicators some of which are problematic. Responding to these consequences of error elimination constitutes the next cycle of the process. The third lesson is that in dealing with orthogonal outcomes, a more global approach to understanding educational leadership is required, namely one that seeks a judgment that aims to maximize the coherence of outcomes with the value of such outcomes and how to trade these off. We discuss some features of maximizing global coherence in Chapter 7.

In responding to feedback from practice, we face the issue of confirmation bias, of interpreting disconfirming evidence as really evidence in support of expected outcomes. While noise might be easily measured (as opposed to perceived noise), along with the breaks to attention by moving from one class to the next, the shift from measured class time to effective class time is exceedingly complex (Darling-Hammond et.al 2020). Many factors are relevant, from the social relations of teaching, to differences among different learning discipline areas, to the school's applied philosophy of teaching, to the availability and use of resources. While one obvious measure to track is student learning, whether either shift actually works to raise student learning will depend on a number of other factors in addition to teaching strategies appropriate for each lesson time. The important point to note is that optimal lesson teaching time is relative to context, as is the notion of what is to be optimized. Once we shift to multiple criteria for optimization – noise, student learning, teaching strategies, staff support – we run into a limit. The analogy of the cube as a weighting of three orthogonal measures fails to scale up in suggesting even an intuitive notion of validity for multiple dimensions with different associated weights. These judgments require leadership to be backed by depth of experience and educational theory. This is what was ultimately required for developing and monitoring TT8. (***TT8:*** *mount a sustainable and visible program of quality assurance and improvement on all aspects of the school's performance.*)

Although the discussion of seeing leadership knowledge building as arising out of context related problem-solving and seeing problem-solving as epistemically progressive trajectories through time, there are a number of advantages in locating even individual leadership in groups. The first, mentioned earlier, is that learning through the consequences of implementing theories not only blurs the theory/practice divide, but that practice invariably involves many hands. Second, the formulation of a problem will be problematic if it is barely recognized as a problem by those who have to participate in solving it. Some group consensus seems desirable for the implementation of proposed solutions. A search for constraints is also assisted by many hands. Third, a search for possible theories can be more comprehensive with the involvement of a number of participants. And finally, there is less scope for confirmation bias in interpreting feedback data during error elimination, subject to the group being able to avoid the 'royal family' effect, namely the effect one dominant individual has on shaping the opinions of all the other participants. This is particularly important to watch where there is tension between the selection of data that can function as proxies in the measurement of educational outcomes, and the more sophisticated role understandings of educational outcomes play in professional knowledge. What we can measure is only part of what we can justifiably understand.

## Conclusion

Acquiring the knowledge for effective educational leadership is a process. Start with what you know best in the context of where you are and engage in problem-solving. Because of the fallibility of our knowledge, this process takes the form of intelligent trial and error that has the epistemic virtue of being self-correcting through the coherent adjustment of our theories in light of feedback from experience. This process bears a close family resemblance to what some would call scientific method. But the constraints that define both educational problems and the limits on proposed solutions that might be enacted, include a powerful array of educational values. In the context of means/ends reasoning, these can appear malleable. Our very Deweyan view is that educational values are quite central to the growth of professional knowledge.

## References

Biesta, G. (2009). Good education in an age of measurement: On the need to reconnect with the question of purpose in education. *Educational Assessment, Evaluation and Accountability*, 21, 33–46.

Chitpin, S. (2003). *The role of portfolios in teachers' professional growth and development: A knowledge building analysis*. Unpublished PhD thesis: University of Toronto.

Chitpin, S., & Evers, C.W. (2005). Teacher professional development as knowledge building: A Popperian analysis. *Teachers and Teaching: Theory and Practice*, 11(4), 419–433.

Chitpin, S., & Evers, C.W. (2012). Using Popper's philosophy of science to build pre-service teachers' knowledge. *International Journal of Education*, 4(4), 144–156.

Chitpin, S., & Evers, C.W. (2019). Decision-making and the school organization. In M. Connolly, D.H. Eddy-Spicer, C. James, & S.D. Kruse (Eds.), *The SAGE handbook of school organization* (pp. 475–488). London: Sage.

Darling-Hammond, L., Flook, L., Cook-Harvey, C., Barron, B., & Osher, D. (2020). Implications for educational practice of the science of learning and development. *Applied Developmental Science*, 24, 97–140.

Evers, C.W. (2012). Organisational contexts for lifelong learning: Individual and collective learning configurations. In D.N. Aspin, J. Chapman, K. Evans, & R. Bagnall (Eds.), *Second international handbook of lifelong learning* (pp. 61–76). Dordrecht: Springer.

Evers, C.W., & Katyal, K. (2008). Educational leadership in Hong Kong schools: Critical reflections on changing themes. *Journal of Educational Administration and History*, 40(3), 251–264.

Evers, C.W., & Lakomski, G. (2000). *Doing educational administration*. Oxford: Elsevier.

Heap, S.H., Hollis, M., Lyons, B., Sudgen, R., & Weale, A. (1992). *The theory of choice: A critical guide*. Oxford: Blackwell.

Hoy, W.K., Tarter, C.J., & Kottkamp, R.B. (1991). *Open schools/healthy schools: Measuring organizational climate*. Newbury Park, CA: Sage.

Hoy, W.K., & Tarter, J. (1995). *Administrators solving the problems of practice*. Needham Heights: Allyn and Bacon.

Kahneman, D. (2011). *Thinking fast and slow*. New York: Penguin Books.

Klein, G.A. (1997). Applying hybrid models of cognition. In C.E. Zsambok, & G.A. Klein (Eds.), *Naturalistic decision making* (pp. 331–370). Mahwah: Lawrence Erlbaum.

Lakomski, G., & Evers, C.W. (2010). Passionate rationalism: The role of emotion in decision-making. *Journal of Educational Administration*, 48(4), 438–450.

Popper, K.R. (1950). Indeterminism in quantum physics and classical physics: Part II. *British Journal for the Philosophy of Science*, 1(3), 179–188.

Popper, K.R. (1957). *The poverty of historicism*. London: Routledge and Kegan Paul.

Popper, K.R. (1959). *The logic of scientific discovery*. London: Hutchinson.

Popper, K.R. (1968). Epistemology without a knowing subject. *Studies in Logic and the Foundations of Mathematics*, 52, 333–373.
Popper, K.R. (1979). *Objective knowledge*. Oxford: Oxford University Press.
Schön, D. (1983). *The reflective practitioner: How professionals think in action*. New York: Basic Books.
Silver, N. (2011). *The signal and the noise*. New York: Penguin Press.
Simon, H.A. (1947/1976). *Administrative behavior* (3rd edition). New York: The Free Press.
Simon, H.A. (1991). Bounded rationality and organizational learning. *Organization Science*, 2(1), 125–134.
Simon, H.A. (1993). Altruism and economics. *The American Economic Review*, 83(2), 156–161.
Taleb, N.N. (2018). *Skin in the game: Hidden asymmetries in daily life*. Toronto: Allen Lane.

# 7
# CONSTRAINTS, STRUCTURE, AND REASONING

## Introduction

The argument presented here takes the following form. We first explore claims that human reasoning exhibits systematic irrationality when it comes to some tasks. These claims are based on a number of well-known empirical studies that describe reasoning tasks where what people do diverges from accepted normative accounts of what they should do. We also consider some evidence from social psychology showing divergences due to culture in reasoning performance. This raises the question of cognitive pluralism, which we also explore.

In meeting these claims, we argue for the value of well-structured problems in generating a commonality of approach for leadership problem-solving tasks. We give examples that cover mathematics, physics, and social science, while also noting limits that cognitive holism places on too close a specification of the nature of common reasoning strategies. But where leadership can employ common reasoning approaches to task achievement, this will be mostly due to the common structure of the tasks to be achieved. These reasoning approaches are central to a process view of leadership, namely one where solutions to educational and other problems emerge from progressive epistemic practices.

## Evidence for human irrationality

There is a substantial body of literature in empirical psychology that reports analyses and findings about how people reason. Typically, such studies employ well-defined cognitive tasks about which good and bad reasoning can easily be adjudicated. Perhaps the most frequently discussed is what is known as the selection task, first devised by Peter Wason (1966) and designed to test an understanding of logical relations. The task consists of four cards with a letter on one side and a number on the other. Two are shown with the letter face up, two with the number face up, thus:

| A | B | 7 | 6 |
|---|---|---|---|

Experiment participants are then invited to say which cards have to be turned over in order to determine the truth of the claim: "If a card has a vowel on one side, then it has an odd number on the other side" (Samuels and Stich 2004, p. 280). Participants – usually university undergraduates – have no trouble choosing the 'A' card. But then many fail to choose the '6' card since they do not realize that its failure to have a consonant on the other side would falsify the truth of the conditional. That is, people fail to see that "if x then y" is equivalent, by modus tollens, to "if ~y then ~x".

One explanation for this failure that has been explored by a number of writers – e.g. D'Andrade (1989) and Hutchins (2005) – is that people can make correct logical inferences if the problems they are dealing with are embedded in culturally coherent mental schemas. Thus, if participants are shown the premise "if x is true then y is true", and they are told "y is not true" and invited to choose, among alternatives, what follows logically from that, only 15 percent of respondents in the study chose correctly "x is not true" as their answer. On the other hand, if participants are given the premise "if this is a garnet, then it is a semi-precious stone", and told 'this is not a semi-precious stone', they have no trouble choosing, from among alternatives, the correct answer "this is not a garnet" (Hutchins 2005, p. 1558).

The suggested difference between cognitively processing the abstract premise, with its x's and y's, and the premise about the semi-precious stone is that "unless x and y are associated with particular known concepts, our culture has nothing in particular to say about the relationship between x and y" (Hutchins 2005, p. 1558). A coherent linking of concepts for x and y, however, allows the transformations involving x into y, y into ~y and ~y into ~x to be held stably in memory while the inferences are performed.

Another well-studied cognitive illusion concerns how people reason about probability. Tversky and Kahneman (1982, p. 92) presented participants in an experiment with the following description of Linda:

> Linda is 31 years old, single, outspoken, and very bright. She majored in philosophy. As a student, she was deeply concerned with issues of discrimination and social justice, and also participated in anti-nuclear demonstrations.

Participants were then asked to rank from most probable to least probable a set of eight statements about Linda. The key result was that most people thought that 'Linda is a bank teller and is active in the feminist movement' to be more probably true than the statement 'Linda is a bank teller', even though a conjunction of two features is never more probable than either of the features.

Here, the explanation for this result, which was robust, holding up over many trials, was that people thought of Linda in terms of prototypes, where a prototype is a cluster of features that coheres in a characteristic way. It is the plausibility of the prototype that misleads over the probability of the conjunction of features.

Notice that just as the absence of culturally coherent mental models functioned as an explanation for poor cognitive performance on abstract logical reasoning tasks, so the presence of culturally coherent mental models, in the form of prototypes, is claimed to be responsible for errors over probability judgments. Evidently, to improve human reasoning on these and many other tasks, it is vital to possess normatively appropriate representations, or mental models, something that the empirical literature implies many of us do not possess.

## Some philosophical responses

In response to this pessimistic prognosis, there are several important philosophical arguments that attempt to show that the very concept of systematic human irrationality is incoherent. These arguments do not deny that some errors of reasoning occur. Rather they deny the possibility of error being endemic in human thought.

The first group of arguments focusses around the methodology of attributing conceptual schemes to people. Much discussed in the 1960s, Quine (1960, pp. 26–79) explores the conditions that determine how to do radical language translation, in particular, how to translate an unknown language into English with no more resources except observational evidence about the conditions under which utterances are made and responded to. One of the maxims he emphasizes for translating logical connectives is that any translation that posits the speaker to hold wildly implausible views is more likely to be a mistranslation than a confusion in the mind of the speaker: "The common sense behind the maxim is that one's interlocutor's silliness, beyond a certain point, is less likely than bad translation..." (Quine 1960, p. 59). Without the assumption of some minimal rationality, there are insufficient constraints on translation to make the job meaningful. Almost anything will count as an adequate translation if we cannot impose the condition that a translation preserves for the speaker a coherent scheme of thought.

Davidson (1984) offers similar considerations in understanding what others are saying. Suppose you use the word 'proton' everywhere that we would use the word 'electron'. For you, protons are negatively charged particles that occupy places in a configuration around an atom's nuclear material. For us it is electrons that do that. The same for atomic weights, quantum spin number, and so on. At some point, it is more reasonable to assume that you have a coherent world view, similar to ours, and that the difference between us is purely linguistic: you are ascribing truth to the same claims that we do and are merely using the word 'proton' where we would use the word 'electron'. Indeed, Davidson goes further. In order to interpret the utterances of another about, say, atomic theory, we are obliged to assume some broad agreement of truths between us. He thinks that charity in interpreting others "is forced on us; whether we like it or not, if we want to understand others, we must count them right in most matters" (Davidson 1984, p. 197). This implies that conceptual relativism is false; we cannot make sense of the idea that different cultures have radically different conceptual schemes. Instead, the business of interpretation proceeds by reading our requirements for the truth of their claims into the process of translation. Thus, their beliefs are as coherent as ours if we interpret their 'proton' as our 'electron'.

Dennett (1978) imposes sterner requirements on the link between interpretation of a person's beliefs and desires, of their intentionality, and rationality. In order to make sense of the behaviour of people, he supposes we posit them as possessing a coordinated framework of beliefs and desires. So, when you go to the fridge to retrieve a beer, one understands that behaviour in terms of positing your desire for a beer and your belief that the beer is in the fridge. That is, the fridge-going behaviour, construed as intentional behaviour, is a rational consequence of the link between the belief and the desire. But according to Dennett (1978, p. 20), "when a person falls short of perfect rationality ... there is no coherent intentional description" of a person's mental states.

The core claims being made by these arguments are that we cannot do radical translation, or we cannot impute conceptual schemes, or we cannot impute intentional behaviour without also imputing a large amount of rationality to people's words, thoughts, and behaviour.

There are several points that we would like to make in response. First, with the possible exception of Dennett's requirements, the amount of imputed rationality seems to be fairly fault tolerant. Problems with modus tollens or probability assignments seem to be easily detectable in the process of interpretation, perhaps owing to the fact that under the given experimental conditions, normative standards of rationality are not in question. Participants' judgments are clearly errors. Of course, once cognitive tasks move beyond examples from toy universes into those that offer more complex challenges, such as multi-criterial decision-making, then the adjudication of rationality becomes more controversial.

Second, despite their talk of rationality and coherence, these arguments fail to achieve a defence of a unitary conception of rationality. Rather, they merely imply that the interpreter must project his or her concept of rationality into the task of making sense of others. But as Stich (1990) often asks: whose concept of rationality is being used? For there are very many possible concepts of rationality that can be invoked, from individuals with their idiosyncratic differences to whole societies with broad cultural differences. The shift to a more ubiquitous concept may again be due to background agreement about the data exhibiting evidence of reasoning errors.

An influential argument that purports to settle this matter and establish a unitary view of human reason has been offered by Cohen (1981). To deal with the objection that lapses in human reasoning compromise the claim that humans are fundamentally rational, Cohen distinguishes between competence and performance in much the same way that linguists draw the distinction. Mistakes in reasoning are like uttering the occasional ungrammatical sentence – they are performance errors made under particular circumstances that occur against a broader context of underlying, or tacit, reasoning competence. That is, people possess the capacity to reason well but circumstances such as distractions or forgetting prevent that capacity from being manifested. Rules of inference are part of our reasoning capacity as rules of grammar are part of our linguistic capacity.

But why should this tacit knowledge of rules of inference be normatively appropriate, given the evidence for human irrationality? Cohen's answer is that these tacit rules arise out of a process of reflective equilibrium. We revise our intuitions about rules if they lead to inferential consequences we cannot accept, and we revise our views about the unacceptability of consequences if they are entailed by rules that we cannot revise (see also Stich 1990, pp. 79–86). Now if reflective equilibrium yields all of the justification there is to be had, if there is no justification procedure for reasoning beyond that emerging from the processes of reflective equilibrium, then the empirical evidence for posits of rational competence is the same as that given in descriptions of human reasoning performance in all their variegated detail.

Needless to say, this argument has been extensively discussed and debated (see, for example, Open Peer Commentary 1981, pp. 331–359). For our purposes, we can again ask the question: whose rationality is in reflective equilibrium? Because the acquisition of rationality, in common with most learning, is mediated by wider social processes beyond the level of the individual, where a person reaches what appears to be an idiosyncratic equilibrium, it may be easier to argue the case that this is a matter of performance errors than a lack of competence. However, where entire cultural traditions settle into equilibria that manifest as judgments contrary to the sorts of simple normative reasoning rules captured by modus tollens or elementary probability theory, the distinction between performance errors and reasoning competence becomes more problematic.

## Cultural differences in reasoning

There is an extensive body of empirical research on cultural differences in reasoning that has been gathered and analysed by Nisbett and his co-authors. In a major review of findings on patterns of reasoning among East Asians and Westerners (mainly North Americans), they offer the following summary:

> The authors find East Asians to be holistic, attending to the entire field and assigning causality to it, making relatively little use of categories and formal logic, and relying on "dialectical" reasoning, whereas Westerners are more analytic, paying attention primarily to the object and the categories to which it belongs and using rules, including formal logic, to understand behaviour.
>
> *(Nisbett et al. 2001, p. 291)*

Although their review contains many kinds of examples to illustrate their thesis, two in particular can be singled out for discussion. The first, what they regard as "one of the best established findings in cognitive social psychology" is the "fundamental attribution error, ... the tendency to see behaviour as a product of the actor's dispositions and to ignore important situational determinants of the behaviour" (Nisbett et al. 2001, p. 298).

Here is an example of an experiment that purports to show evidence of cultural differences in causal attribution. The first part of the experiment sets the scene. Consider a situation in which participants, both Americans and Koreans, are invited to read an essay that either supports or opposes some important social issue. Participants are told that the author of the essay had no choice in determining what view to take. They then had to say what the author really believed about the issue. Those reading the affirmative essay were much more inclined to say that the author believed the affirmative position than those who had read the opposing essay. In the second stage of the experiment, participants themselves were asked to write such an essay and given no choice as to which side of the issue they took. They were then told that the author of the essay they were to read had been through a similar 'no choice' situation. Once again, participants were asked to indicate what view the author held. For the American participants, the experience of having to write such an essay themselves made no difference in their willingness to attribute affirmative views to the author. But for the Korean participants, their identical experience made a substantial difference. The Americans appeared to be assuming a narrower, more individualistic, causal field for their attribution judgements, while the Koreans took a more holistic perspective in which factors outside the individual were relevant (Choi and Nisbett 1998; Nisbett et al. 2001, pp. 298–299).

Although the evidence for a performance error of causal attribution may be utterly ambiguous in a scaled up complex world, in the restricted universe of this experimental set-up, it is normatively clear.

A different set of examples, one removed from attributions, concerns the assessment of arguments and argument strategies. Here is one study that again uses Korean and American participants, this time university students. Two sorts of logic exercises were constructed for the groups. The first consisted of a set of abstract syllogisms with no content. The second consisted of a set of meaningful syllogisms with both plausible and implausible conclusions. The task was to classify the syllogisms as either valid or invalid. Both groups performed equally well on the abstract syllogisms, but on the second task, Korean students showed a stronger belief bias than American students. That is, they were more willing to classify valid arguments as invalid if the arguments had an implausible conclusion. "[T]he results indicate that when logical structure conflicts with everyday belief, American students are more willing to set aside empirical belief in favour of logic than are Korean students" (Nisbett et al. 2001, p. 301.)

If these sorts of studies provide any indication of culture-wide reasoning processes, then it is plausible to suppose that what can arise out of reflective equilibrium can be at odds with normative rationality.

## Normative cognitive pluralism

In a wide-ranging discussion of all these issues, Stich (1990) draws a more radical conclusion. He thinks that empirical evidence for cultural diversity in cognitive practices undermines claims to there being just one normative standard of rationality. His argument is complex since he considers a variety of philosophical positions, but the core idea is this. Consider how one would ever defend a candidate set of norms of rationality. Presumably, some justificatory arguments would need to be made that involved appeal to reasons. Let's call these reasons 'second order reasons'. But now a regress threatens, because second order reasons have to come from somewhere. And unless they can be quarantined, or shown to enjoy some special privileged cognitive status, they will be affected by the same processes of reflective equilibrium that apply to the first order culture-laden reasons. But the empirical data on human reasoning shows that reflective equilibrium does not logically guarantee normative appropriateness. Hence, the second order principles of rationality required to justify first order principles of rationality are not known to be normatively appropriate (Stich 1990, pp. 89–100).

Stich explores various strategies for dealing with the problem. For example, he considers the idea that there may be some conceptual link between the nature of rationality, which would have normative force, and some proposed collection of second order reasoning principles. Unfortunately, concepts have to come from somewhere too, and are subject just as much to culture-ladenness as are reasons. Views of rationality, defended in this way, are in the same boat as principles used to justify principles.

Another possible defence of second order principles of reasoning is a consequentialist approach: for example, choose those principles that lead to the most satisfactory outcomes. It seems unlikely, however, that the specification of satisfactory outcomes can proceed in a cultural vacuum. And yet, the principles of elementary logic and probability theory that provided such a useful normative corrective to commonly made inferences about Linda the bank teller or the selection task are unlikely to lose their utility where people want to navigate their way through life-making decisions whose outcomes are more reliably known than those based on the toss of a coin.

Building on the apparent capacity of these modest tools for being pressed into wider service of utility, the strategy that we wish to pursue here develops the thought that there may be enough structure in some of the problems that different groups face to defend a view of reason that can have normative force across these groups.

## Problems, solutions, and objectivity

In his dialogue, the Meno, Plato asks the question "How is inquiry possible?" and poses a paradox in response. If we know what it is we seek, then we have no need for inquiry. But if we don't know what it is we seek, then we would never know

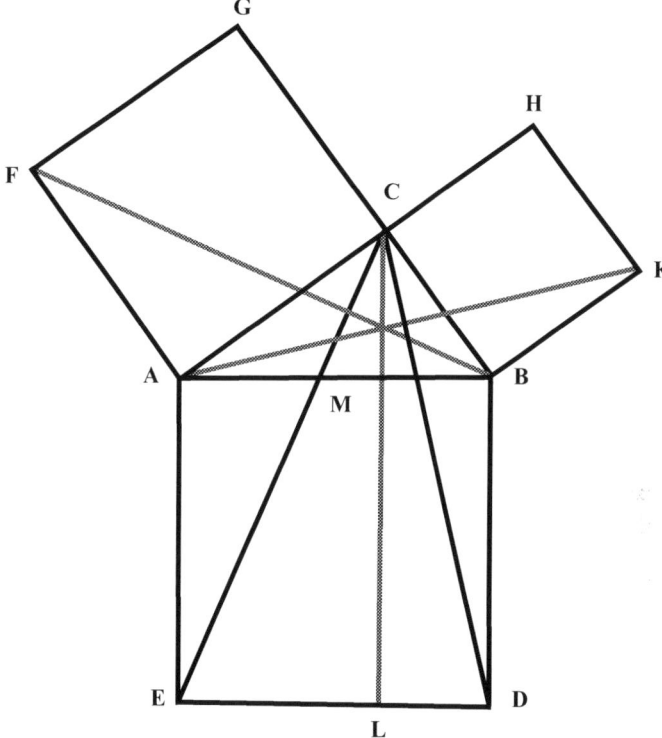

**FIGURE 7.1** Euclid's first proof that $AB^2 = AC^2 + BC^2$

if we found it. Therefore, inquiry is either unnecessary or pointless. For Plato, the way out of the dilemma was to say that inquiry was really just recollection of what we already knew. And to prove his point, the dialogue shows how a slave boy, under close questioning, knows the proof of Pythagoras' theorem. Simon (1977), in the company of many others, has proposed another resolution, one that involves arguing that we know we have found what we seek when it solves the problem we are inquiring to solve. (See also Haig 1987, for a discussion of this matter.) The more well structured the problem, the easier it is to know that we have a solution. Euclid's first proof is probably the most famous (Figure 7.1).

The reasoning is as follows. The area of triangle ABK is half the square BCHK and also equals the area of triangle CBD which equals half LDxDB. Similarly, the area of triangle AFB is half the square AFGC and also equals the area of triangle AEC which equals half AExEL. But EL+LD equals AE, the side of the largest square. So BCHK plus AFGC equals AEDB.

Perhaps the earliest proof on record is that given by ancient Chinese mathematicians, by some estimates as early as 1100BC, although a more generally accepted date is the sixth century BC. Known as the 'Gougu Theorem' in traditional Chinese geometry, and appearing in both the Zhou Bi and Jui Zhang

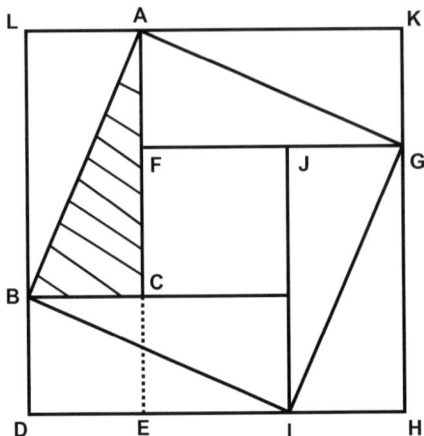

**FIGURE 7.2** The Gougu theorem

texts, the strategy (illustrated in Figure 7.2) is slightly different, although again it involves showing that the areas of squares drawn on the sides of the triangle add in the required way (Wu 1983, pp. 70–72).

Here is the reasoning. BDEC is the square on the 'gou', or shorter, arm, while EFGH is equal to the square on the 'gu' or longer arm. Now from the figure BDHGFC, which is the sum of the squares of these two arms, cut the triangle BDI and place it at AFG, to make the new square ABIG, which is the square of the hypotenuse.

The problem of finding the length of the hypotenuse of a right angle triangle given the lengths of the other two sides is sufficiently well-structured to admit of the same answer, although often via different proofs, regardless of culture or history.

There is also a surprising amount of structure in physics problems, as can be seen even when two fundamentally different worldviews are in dispute. For example, against an Aristotelian view of motion, which was the dominant position in his cultural landscape, Galileo employed a very minimalist argument that made use of premises embedded in the structure of both that view and his opposing perspective. A consequence of Aristotelian dynamics was a theory of inertia that implied that heavy objects fall faster than light ones. Against this, Galileo devised the following thought experiment (See Popper 1957, pp. 442–443).

Begin by hypothesizing that heavier objects fall faster than light objects. Imagine two masses, M and m, connected by a light inelastic string (Figure 7.3).

Let us suppose that the heavy object, M, begins to fall rapidly, with velocity VM, on being released, but its downward motion is then impeded by the slower motion, Vm, of the lesser mass, m, to which it is tethered. The two masses connected by the string thus move more slowly than the heavier mass alone and faster than the lesser mass. Let us wind in the string. When separated by an infinitely

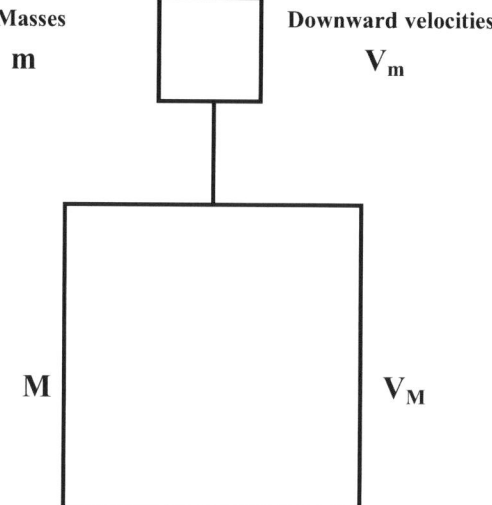

**FIGURE 7.3** Galileo's thought experiment

small distance, the total moves more slowly than the larger mass, but when the two objects meet, by hypothesis, their velocity, $V_{M+m}$, should exceed that of the larger mass. Since the string can be made vanishingly small, this implies that, in the limit, the combined mass is moving both faster and more slowly, which is a contradiction. Therefore, the Aristotelian hypothesis is false.

That such a powerful empirical conclusion can emerge from such modest premises, including principles of reasoning that were common to both worldviews, is a lesson in how important structure can be. Popper (1957, p. 443), in his commentary on this reasoning, says: 'I see in Galileo's imaginary experiment a perfect model for the best use of imaginary experiments'.

In addition to mathematics and physics, a vast amount of technology is heavily constrained by the way the world is, rather than simply by culture or individual mindset. (For an impressive inventory of ancient Chinese inventions, Needham's multivolume work, Science and Civilization in China, should be consulted.) The technology for providing a water supply for ancient cities needed to come to terms with water's key properties, including its propensity to flow downhill. This constrained the design of aqueducts in the Roman world and prompted the invention of water-locks for canals in China. Developments in transportation, agriculture, metallurgy, currency, bridge and building construction, shipbuilding, navigation, moveable print presses, the spinning wheel and the loom are all similarly constrained by the properties of the materials that figure in their construction and composition. The fact that many of these ideas and inventions arose independently in different times, places and cultures, again points to the existence of common constraints that define problems and similarities among ways of reaching solutions, including cognitive ways and means. Whatever the theoretical limits of cognitive pluralism, its practical limits are clearly evident, unless there are grounds for thinking the similarities are entirely accidental.

To explore this matter a little further, we need to take a closer look at how problems and solutions might be characterized. We begin with Nickles (1981, p. 109), who asks the question "What, then, are problems" and responds:

> My short answer is that a problem consists of all the conditions or constraints on the solution plus the demand that the solution (an object satisfying the constraints) be found. For this reason ..., I call it the constraint-inclusion model of problems. The constraints characterize – in a sense 'describe' – the sought-for solution.

The first point to note about this answer is that it does not rule out different ways of solving a problem within a given constraint set. Thus, there are currently some 40 different ways of proving Pythagoras' Theorem. They all yield the same result, but some manage to be strikingly different while still falling within touchstone, or common, or agreed requirements for mathematical proof.

However, there is another source of difference that is more substantial. It concerns the prioritizing, or ranking, of constraints. Take a simple decision problem: whether to make a big move of household in order to take a better job. There are various constraints: the attraction of more money, more prestige, and more interesting challenges. Then, there are the difficulties of making the move, disrupting one's family, giving up valuable friendships, and so on (Thagard and Millgram 1995, p. 446). The solution that different people come to – whether to take the job or not – will depend on the different priorities or levels of importance they attach to the various considerations. That is, this conception of ranking determines, to some extent, the structure of a web of belief, with least revisable or most heavily prioritized claims towards the centre of the web and more revisable ones at the periphery. Cultural differences can present in the form of systematic differences in priorities to the point where solutions can be characteristically different. Research on Chinese and American approaches to management problems, for example, implies that maintaining harmony in the workplace acts as a more powerful priority, and hence constraint, on the decisions that Chinese managers make than it does on their American counterparts (Wong 2001).

The way to deal with this issue would be to see the rationality of solving problems by satisfying constraints as a process that operates in much the same way regardless of the priorities people assign to claims or the different weights they give to the constraints. Then the cognitive task boils down to trying to secure a kind of best fit, or most coherent course of action. Of course, not everyone would actually behave in this way. But not everyone assigns the normatively appropriate probabilities to the descriptions of Linda the bank teller either. So the normative requirement here is to solve problems that an epistemic unit's own system of priorities says are worth solving, in a way that respects the priorities that define the problem.

## Problems of scale

Whether this can be done with large-scale problems is a difficult issue. As a refinement of Nickles's analysis that involves some further reconceptualization of key terms, consider a proposal by Thagard and Verbeurgt (1998) for computing best fit in a constraint satisfaction theory choice model. Imagine that we have a set of claims, E, that contains the following elements: $e_1, e_2, e_3, \ldots e_n$. Suppose that some of these claims, say ei and ej, are positively constrained in the sense that we can accept both or reject both, or negatively constrained, in the sense that if we accept one we would want to reject the other. So, if ei explains ej then we would want to accept (or reject) both, whereas if ei is contradicted by ej, we would want to accept one and reject the other. Let the strength of the link between two positively or negatively constrained elements, ei and ej, be called the weight, wij, of the pair. Now a best fit on the set of claims E, is a partition of its elements that maximizes some way of summing of all the weights.

One way in which Thagard (1992) implements this abstract model in computer simulations of real theory choice problems in the history of science is by treating it as a harmony artificial neural network, as follows. Each proposition of a theory, or its main rival, ei, corresponds to a node in the network. The initial priority, or importance, of the proposition would be given by its level of activation, ai, at that node. The weights, wij, between nodes correspond to the influence one node has on the activation of another node. A best-fit choice of theory would be those nodes with higher activation values that emerged subject to the requirement to maximize the sum of all the weighted products of pairs of activation values:

Best Fit = Maximizing $\Sigma i \Sigma j w_{ij} a_i a_j$.

The idea is that over the duration of learning a best-fit solution, some nodes will be turned off and some will be increased, leaving the active nodes representing a maximally coherent set of true propositions.

From a computational perspective, the main problem is the sheer number of calculations that have to be performed. For n propositions, the computer would have to calculate 2n possible solutions (Thagard and Verbeurgt 1998, pp. 7–8). In general, mathematical modelling of constraint satisfaction problems for even a relatively modest set of considerations appears to be formally intractable. The computations cannot be done in polynomial time, or as Millgram (2000, p. 87) colourfully puts it, "there are reasonably sized inputs for which you will not be able to solve the problem – at any rate, not before the universe freezes over". This means that under these conditions the rationality of a course of action, construed as the best fit of a number of constraints, can never in principle be known if that number is sufficiently large. Given the enormous amount of background knowledge that we bring to any problem, that number of constraints will indeed be large. Clearly, we must find some way of framing problems-solutions so that much of this background does not figure, or better, does not need to figure, in cognitive processing.

From having earlier faintly disparaged toy universes and hinted at the virtues of wielding large coherent conceptual schemes to deal with life's complexities, it is time to champion the virtues of smaller cognitive worlds.

That we can often solve problems, or at least make epistemic progress, by effectively bracketing much background and focusing on just one or two aspects of a situation, is a commonplace. In asking whether this kind of approach will support claims for the trans-cultural objectivity of small cognitive world problems, it is worth distinguishing two issues. If it makes sense, in this context, to abstract altogether from the question of agreement over background knowledge, so that both problems and solutions can differ for different cultures, then what remains of a common approach to rationality is just the procedural apparatus of securing a best fit of whatever subset of claims is in play. This would be analogous to proposing the trans-cultural validity of a logical argument while waiving consideration of its soundness, or the truth of its premises.

However, if we wish to construe rationality in a broader epistemic sense, such as the sense in which best-fit models are used to sustain inferences to the best explanation, or to justify clusters of claims, then we need to pursue the possibility of touchstone, or agreed bodies of background knowledge. The central difficulty turns on the fact that, as Fodor (1983, pp. 104–119) puts it, the total body of knowledge that is involved in setting our beliefs is isotropic and Quinean. It is isotropic because evidence or theory that is relevant to the justification of our beliefs can come from anywhere in our system of thought. And it is Quinean because the global properties of the whole system are relevant to the determination of the epistemic value of a piece of evidence. Selecting what knowledge to avoid revising in light of additional evidence is an instance of what is known as the 'frame problem' (See Dietrich and Fields 1996). As the literature on this is both voluminous and mostly unhelpful (but see Shanahan 1997), we shall focus on just one line of inquiry that seems promising.

In his book, *The View from Nowhere*, Nagel (1986, p. 5) posits a continuum between subjectivity and objectivity in the following way:

> A view or form of thought is more objective than another if it relies less on the specifics of the individual's makeup and position in the world, or on the character of the particular type of creature he is. The wider the range of subjective types to which a form of understanding is accessible – the less it depends on specific subjective capacities – the more objective it is.

Since there is no such thing as a view from nowhere, an alternative task for anyone attempting to defend some account of objectivity is to specify circumstances under which specific subjective capacities and circumstances do not result in a relativity of epistemic judgments. One such attempt at specification is that proposed by Sen (1993, pp. 466–467), where he introduces a further distinction between objectivity that is position-dependent ("positional objectivity") and that which is trans-positional, involving "synthesizing different views from distinct positions". Sen explains positional objectivity with the aid of an example: "The sun and the moon look similar in size". This claim is position-dependent because to someone on the moon, Neil Armstrong perhaps, the claim would not be true. It would depend on the position of the observer. But if the observer were in a similar position, they would agree with the claim. Hence, a claim can be person-invariant and position-dependent, and can enjoy a certain amount of objectivity in that it is relatively independent of the individual, idiosyncratic features of observers.

Unfortunately, this account becomes problematic when, as Sen wishes, we expand the notion of positionality to include additional, non-spatial parameters that may affect perceptions: living in a particular society, bearing a particular culture, experiencing a particular kind of education. Then it looks like, for example, "belief in women's inferiority in particular skills" (Sen 1990, p. 10) enjoys positional objectivity for people in a society where the prevalence of these ideas is an outcome of such positional parameters. Sen (1990, p. 10) attempts to block this conclusion by arguing that there is always the possibility of internal critique, even in that society, and hence the view is non-necessary, and so is not positionally objective. Our worry, however, is that if we came into the debate with concerns about culture affecting the objectivity of reason, we'll have much the same concerns over the objectivity of internal critique. Under these circumstances, the view from nowhere is best countered by defending the possibility of a view from everywhere.

Defending the possibility of a view from everywhere amounts to arguing that there is enough common human experience to render plausible the notion of a common, or touchstone, view of reasoning about similar things across cultures. Take, for example, a small cognitive world embedded in the operation of a set of variably linked binary switches. Because this world is so constrained, anyone contemplating and interacting with the setup in its limited pattern of operation should reach the same conclusion about how it might work as a set of logic gates for truth tables, or for adding or multiplying binary numbers. It would be like a jigsaw puzzle, or a set of Sudoku numbers that fit together in a unique way. And its algebraic properties could be extracted and described at the appropriate level of abstraction.

Now consider the case of an initial learner who is interacting with middle-sized dry physical objects. Following Grandy (2006, p. 2), let's propose that these objects satisfy the criterion of "maximal dynamic cohesiveness – meaning roughly that moving one part of the object tends to move it all". More precisely, 'maximal' means that the object is not part of another object, and 'dynamic cohesiveness' means that if a force acts on one part of the object it can be regarded as acting on all of the object. Although examples of these objects will vary from culture to culture, a vast portion of an infant's time will be spent in interaction with elements of this kind. In common with the binary switches, these elements exhibit a characteristic pattern of behaviour in interactions. Take the behaviour of a collection of variously shaped blocks of different sizes and place them into groups A, B, C, and so on. Gathering together groups A and B first and then group C has the same effect on the total number of blocks as gathering together B and C first and then A. This is the associative law of addition. Switching two piles around and adding them has no effect on the total number of blocks either. Hence, addition is commutative. Placing blocks in columns and rows, and interchanging these (simply by rotation or change of viewing perspective) shows that multiplication is commutative. More impressive manipulations will give the associative law of multiplication, and less impressive ones will yield up additive identity, additive inverses, and the distributive law.

These characteristic patterns, and others to do with causation and the physics of objects, arguably underwrite patterns in elementary forms of reasoning and logic (See Halmos 1962; Halmos and Givant 1998). That the infant's arms and hands may also be included among the objects appropriate for such a developing abstract model of the world adds a useful reflexiveness to these thoughts. Just as the cross-cultural studies, considered earlier, pointed to cultural diversity in some cognitive matters, so there is much research in developmental psychology that tends to support the cross-cultural ubiquity of other features of cognition. (For a survey of much of the literature, see Karmiloff-Smith 1992). Recent work on the role of cognitive artifacts in sustaining thought processes in social practices further develops this last point (see Fauconnier and Turner 2002, pp. 201–203 on the invention of money; Chapter. 3, this volume). This blend of artifact and cognition for the solution of small-scale practical problems can further be seen in cross-cultural inventions such as sundials, gauges, and compasses. The suggestion is that the trans-culturally common patterns inherent in the manipulation of material objects can scaffold upwards into more elaborate artifactually supported shared cognitive processes; measurement apparatus and procedures for determining property boundaries can even develop a conceptual life of their own as geometry.

If this kind of story is approximately true, then not only does it provide the cognitive conditions for a view from everywhere, but it also provides a way of dealing with the frame problem. Experience should be seen as relevant both to the setting of priorities among claims, and the way claims cluster – that is, the weights among them. The fact that our rationality is bounded in the sense of our having limited computational, memory and informational resources means that although in principle our web of belief may be isotropic and Quinean, in practice the cognitive task would begin with the highest priority claims and pursue relevant reasoning along axes determined by the greatest weights. Shanahan (2004, p. 4) avails himself of this sort of solution when he argues that "the computational theory of mind can be relieved of the frame problem" if the account of rationality on which it depends is "suitably modified to allow resource-boundedness".

Problems are thus scaled down and made more tractable by a process of selective attention to a limited number of features perceived to be most relevant.

That from culture to culture, it is roughly the same background knowledge that is bracketed-off as not central with regard to certain particular, small, well-structured problems, is due in part to the common causal genesis of priorities among these claims and the weights that bind the claims together into a structure. Thus, the mathematicians that proved the Gougu Theorem would understand Euclid's proof of Pythagoras' Theorem, we may safely assume. And the Korean inventors of the moveable type printing press, whose invention preceded Gutenberg's by 200 years, would have appreciated the nature of the European's problem and his solution. That these and other common patterns of reasoning might be said to have normative value could be argued from the fact that a solution is found, or that all the constraints, in Nickles's sense, are satisfied.

## Conclusion

There is much evidence that human reasoning is not normatively appropriate. Many experiments are able to show significant differences between how people actually reason and the correct way of reasoning in those experimental set-ups. However, once we move beyond small-scale reasoning experiments, it becomes harder to specify with the same precision what counts as normatively appropriate cognition. In response, some philosophers have argued that when it comes to larger scale reasoning tasks, the concept of reason itself is tied in with the conceptual schemes invoked for these tasks, and that it is a confusion to question the rationality of human cognition under these broader conditions. Against this conclusion, it has been argued that the notion of reason, in both its descriptive and normative dimensions, fragments precisely where larger conceptual schemes reflect significant cultural differences. The objectivity of reason seems therefore to be compromised by there appearing to be culturally relative standards.

Against this line of argument, we have urged that we look for cross-cultural objectivity in reasoning about well-structured, small-scale issues and problems, where the normative once again becomes clearer and the computational intractability of the large is not a significant factor. Unfortunately, scaling real problems back down from the richer cognitive contexts in which they are almost always embedded requires dealing with the frame problem; that is, knowing the appropriate body of beliefs to hold constant, or as background. Our suggestion is that this knowledge occurs naturally, by dint of the cognitive development of creatures with limited reasoning resources. Furthermore, for some small cognitive tasks, there is cross-cultural evidence that these are seen in much the same way, this time by virtue of the common run of experiences with the world of material objects in early childhood by creatures with similar cognitive endowments. These tasks thus present as similarly structured sets of claims that have similar priority. This is indeed a modest sense of objectivity, but the high level of intercultural articulation that is able to occur among people of different backgrounds suggests that it provides cognitive scaffolding for a lot of other reasoning tasks as well.

Leadership in problem-solving by cognitive agents comprised of individuals, teams or whole organizations are advised to develop their problem-solving trajectories from a close examination of the constraints that define the problem and give it its causal features.

## References

D'Andrade, R. (1989). Culturally based reasoning. In A. Gellatly, D. Rodgers, & J. Sloboda (Eds.), *Cognition and social worlds*, Oxford: Oxford University Press.

Chitpin, S., & Evers, C.W. (2005). Teacher professional development as knowledge building: A Popperian analysis. *Teachers and Teaching: Theory and Practice*, 11(4), 419–433.

Choi, I., & Nisbett, R.E. (1998). Situational salience and cultural differences in the correspondence bias and in the actor-observer bias. *Personality and Social Psychology Bulletin*, 24, 949-960.

Cohen, J. (1981). Can human irrationality be experimentally demonstrated? *Behavioral and Brain Sciences*, 4(3), 317–329, 359–367.

Davidson, D. (1984). *Inquiries into truth and interpretation*. Oxford: Clarendon Press.

Dennett, D. (1978). *Brainstorms*. Cambridge, MA: MIT Press.

Dietrich, E., & Fields, C. (1996). The role of the frame problem in Fodor's modularity thesis: A case study of rationalist cognitive science. In K.M. Ford, & Z.W. Pylyshyn (Eds.), *The robot's dilemma revisited: The frame problem in artificial intelligence* (pp. 9–24). Norwood, NJ: Ablex.

Fauconnier, G., & Turner, M. (2002). *The way we think: Conceptual blending and the mind's hidden complexities*. New York, NY: Basic Books.

Fodor, J.A. (1983). *The modularity of mind: An essay on faculty psychology*. Cambridge, MA: MIT Press.

Grandy, R.E. (2006). Soft borders, bright colors: The cognition and metaphysics of everyday objects http://www.ruf.rice.edu/~rgrandy/Project.pdf.

Haig, B.D. (1987). Scientific problems and the conduct of research. *Educational Philosophy and Theory*, 19(2), 22–32.

Halmos, P. (1962). *Algebraic logic*. New York, NY: Chelsea Publishing.

Halmos, P., & Givant, S. (1998). *Logic as algebra*. New York, NY: The Mathematical Association of America.

Hutchins, E. (2005). Material anchors for conceptual blends. *Journal of Pragmatics*, 37, 1555–1577.

Karmiloff-Smith, A. (1992). *Beyond modularity: A developmental perspective on cognitive science*. Cambridge, MA: MIT Press.

Millgram, E. (2000). Coherence: The price of the ticket. *Journal of Philosophy*, 97(2), 82–93.

Nagel, T. (1986). *The view from nowhere*. Oxford: Oxford University Press.

Needham, J. (1954). *Science and civilization in China, Volumes 1–5*. Cambridge, UK: Cambridge University Press.

Nickles, T. (1981). What is a problem that we may solve it? *Synthese*, 47, 45–118.

Nisbett, R.E., Peng, K., Choi, I., & Norenzayan, A. (2001). Culture and systems of thought: Holistic versus analytic cognition. *Psychological Review*, 108(2), 291–310.

Open Peer Commentary (1981). *Behavioral and Brain Sciences*, 4(3), 331–359.

Popper, K.R. (1957). *The poverty of historicism*. London: Routledge & Kegan Paul.

Quine, V.W.O. (1960). *Word and object*. Cambridge, MA: MIT Press.

Samuels, R., & Stich, S. (2004). Rationality and psychology. In A.R. Mele, & P. Rawling (Eds.), *The Oxford handbook of rationality* (pp. 279–300). Oxford: Oxford University Press.

Sen, A. (1990). Objectivity and position: Assessment of health and well-being, http://www.grhf.harvard.edu/HUpapers/90_01.pdf.

Sen, A. (1993). Positional objectivity. *Philosophy and public affairs*, 22, 126–145. (Cited as reprinted in Sen, A. (2003). *Rationality and freedom* (pp. 463–483). Cambridge, MA: Harvard University Press.

Shanahan, M. (1997). *Solving the frame problem: A mathematical investigation of the common sense law of inertia.* Cambridge, MA: MIT Press.

Shanahan, M. (2004). The frame problem. *Stanford Encyclopedia of Philosophy.* http://plato.stanford.edu/entries/frame-problem/

Simon, H.A. (1977). *Models of discovery.* Dordrecht: Reidel.

Stich, S. (1990). *The fragmentation of reason.* Cambridge, MA: MIT Press.

Thagard, P. (1992). *Conceptual revolutions.* Princeton: Princeton University Press.

Thagard, P., & Millgram, E. (1995). Inference to the best plan: A coherence theory of decision. In A. Ram, & D.B. Leake (Eds.), *Goal-driven learning* (pp. 439–454). Cambridge, MA: MIT Press.

Thagard, P., & Verbeurgt, K. (1998). Coherence as constraint satisfaction. *Cognitive Science*, 22(1), 1–24.

Tversky, A., & Kahneman, D. (1982). Judgments of and by representativeness. In D. Kahneman, P. Slovic, & A. Tversky (Eds.), *Judgment under uncertainty: Heuristics and biases*, Cambridge: Cambridge University Press.

Wason, P.C. (1966). Reasoning. In B. Foss (Ed.), *New horizons in psychology*, London: Penguin Books.

Wong, K.C. (2001). Culture and educational leadership. In K.C. Wong, & C.W. Evers (Eds.), *Leadership for quality schooling: International perspectives* (pp. 36–53). London: Routledge/Falmer.

Wu, W. (1983). Out-in complementary principle. In Y. Mao (Ed.), *Ancient China's technology and science*, Beijing: Foreign Language Press.

# PART III
# Individuals in context – reason, emotion, organization

# 8
# NATURALIZING EMOTION

## Introduction

The idea of reason and emotion as separate and opposing faculties is a myth about human nature that has a very long history (Damasio 1994; Dixon 2003; Solomon 2008; Scarantino 2016) and continues to be a fundamental assumption in mainstream educational leadership theory and practice where reason traditionally has won out over emotion, especially in administrative decision-making. However, the rationalist emphasis has recently been challenged resulting in a sharper focus on the importance of the emotions in education and leadership (see Berkovich and Eyal 2014 for an extensive overview). In the eyes of Yamamoto et al. (2014, p. 167), this emphasis is overdue, and the reasons they offer are instructive: "How can theory in educational administration be worthy of its scientific stature if it neglects the human dimension of emotion in leadership?", adding, "A theory that neglects the role of emotion in leadership is under-theorized and not informed by practice".

In this chapter we address this justified concern and propose a naturalistic account of emotion as an important component of leadership theory in education and elsewhere.

As brains reside in skulls, and skulls are attached to bodies, and bodies inhabit sociocultural environments, understanding emotions requires explanations at multiple levels that are interconnected: the psychological, sociocultural, and neural (Thagard 2010; Rogers et al. 2014; Thagard and Schröder 2015). The psychological is important because it provides the categories and concepts of folk psychology that give meaning to emotional experience in everyday life; the sociocultural matters in that emotions are shaped by social relations in specific sociocultural contexts, and the neural level is of fundamental importance because neural processes provide the causal account of how emotions are constructed by the human brain. (Neural processes are also importantly shaped at the molecular level, but this cannot be addressed here.) The upshot of such a multilevel view of emotions, we argue, is that emotions are best understood as *constructions*; that is, they are neither hard-wired and invariant, nor completely socially constructed.

The discussion of what emotion is, whether there are 'basic' emotions, where 'they' are located or generated, and what 'they' are 'for' is the core business of emotion science, aptly described by de Gelder (2017, p. 4) "as a loosely organized collection of research endeavors each working with its own notion of emotion". Given such fragmentation, the account we present is an attempt at unifying the various strands in emotion science. At the same time, in some fundamental sense, emotions seem quite straightforward and unproblematic as we all *feel* emotion/s rather than just have them, and deal with them in our personal and work lives in the pursuit of our goals. Emotions matter because they make us move and act in the world. In addition, the discussion is also made difficult because the only language we have are the folk psychological terms and concepts that while thoroughly familiar, have little in common with the scientific explanations now available. Familiar words, for example, fear, love, disgust, happiness are (English language) tokens for neurobiological events and processes we do not yet fully understand. We therefore think it important to discuss what scientific evidence there is about emotion at the three different but interconnected levels, and thus to provide a more comprehensive account rather than considering emotions from one perspective alone.

The chapter is divided into six sections. In the first section we examine a new theory for an affective paradigm for educational leadership theory and practice by James et al. (2018). Drawing attention to the need to connect affect, actions, power, and influence, this theory is an important development in that it presents a theoretical, rather than merely descriptive, account of emotion in educational leadership.

In Sections two and three we discuss a prominent, contemporary, perspective in emotion (or affective) science that argues for the *psychological* (e.g. Barrett 2006; Barrett et al. 2010; Gross and Barrett 2011, 2014, 2017) and *sociocultural construction* of emotions respectively (e.g. Markus and Kitayama 1991; Mesquita and Boiger 2014; Mesquita et al. 2015; 2016) in opposition to the traditional view of emotions as 'essences' or 'natural kinds'. (e.g. Izard 1992; Ekman 1999). A further extension of sociocultural constructionism is an emphasis on *social institutions* in the construction of emotion through *social interaction*, a perspective developed in Affect Control Theory (ACT) (e.g., Heise 2007; Rogers et al. 2014) which we discuss in Section four. ACT proposes a formal model for measuring cultural meanings and suggests a methodology that offers an important steppingstone for the development of a neurocomputational theory of emotion, the *Semantic Pointer Theory of Emotion* (Thagard and Schröder 2015; Kajić et al. 2019), outlined in Section five.

Given that psychological constructionism links the construction of emotions to brain mechanisms, we take a closer look at a recent neuroscientific model of brain structure and function in section six: the network model of the emotional brain to see how compatible the former is with the network model characterized as a dynamical system (Pessoa 2017, 2018; also Anderson 2014). We conclude that as the brain basis of emotion is but part of general cognitive processes, emotions are 'cognitive', just as cognition is 'emotional'.

## Emotion in education and educational leadership

Emotion research in education has generally been empirical, qualitative, and descriptive and has focussed on the emotional experiences of teachers and principals, educational outcomes, and teacher education programs. (See Schutz and Zembylas 2009; Crawford 2009; Samier and Schmidt 2009; Special Issue of the *Journal of Educational Administration*, 48(5) 2010; Berkovich and Eyal 2014).

The rise of emotion studies in leadership has been described as a counter movement to the dominant scientific-empiricist and bureaucratic approach in educational administration and leadership (e.g. Bush 2014). As Bush (2014, p. 163) sees it, like distributed and instructional leadership, emotional leadership is another *alternative model* to the scientific-bureaucratic approach. It is exemplified in Crawford's (2009) landmark book *Getting to the Heart of Leadership* in which she describes how school leaders experience emotion in their daily lives by way of narratives and case studies. The suggestion that emotional leadership can be considered as an *alternative* model clearly assumes that emotion exists separately from reason and can be discussed as an independent entity. Yamamoto et al.'s (2014, p. 168) view regarding decision-making in educational leadership echoes this perspective and is representative of the field: "Emotion has a role to play in decision-making. Acknowledging emotion, we can look at it critically and ascertain whether logic or emotion should help with the decision-making. Every decision should not be based on logic. Emotion can be a powerful tool, just as logic and rationality can be". In the most recent proposal for a new affective paradigm for educational leadership theory and practice by James et al. (2018), this general dualist view continues to characterize the discussion.

Understanding leadership in the traditional sense of "influencing others", James et al. (2018) emphasize that "the various forms of affect – feelings, moods, and emotions – have yet to be accorded the significance they warrant in understandings of educational leadership ... Without that recognition, the understandings of leadership theory and practice will only ever be partial and will be limited in nature and scope" (James et al. 2018, p. 1). The core of their theory is that:

> feelings and moods are central in initiating and motivating social actions, which take place during the emotion process. In those actions, power is experienced, which influences others. As the practice of educational leadership is an influencing act, affect, actions, power and influence are connected and the central role of feelings in motivating educational leadership practices is established.
>
> *(James et al. 2018, p. 1)*

The definition of emotions they accept is that of Matsumoto and Ekman (2009, p. 69), advocates of the discrete or basic theory of emotions that considers emotions as species-universal and hardwired. Emotional reactions, or the emotion process, as James et al. (2018) call it, is a highly complex interplay between an individual's affective current state and how the individual appraises the context, that is, the 'emotional zones' with their respective rules, norms, and expectations that determine the type of emotional reaction that is appropriate. In the school context, it is readily apparent that there are many such zones – for example, expressing certain feelings or emotions in the classroom may be inappropriate to expressing the same emotions in the staffroom.

A critical aspect of their paradigm is the assertion that "feelings cannot be ascertained and communicated about easily for ontological, epistemological and methodological reasons …[but] feelings nonetheless influence actions in the emotion process". (James et al., p. 6). The solution is to *interpret* those actions on the assumption of the "underpinning affective emotional processes and on the assumption that actions have affective rationales. Interpretations within such a paradigm gives a deeper understanding of the rationales for leadership action". (p. 6). Only interpretation will be able to explain the meaning of social phenomena in question, in this context educational leadership practices. By the same token, what cannot yet be explained is "a way of knowing, explaining and theorizing the role they [affects] play in specific and observed educational leadership practices". (p. 6). To anchor those hidden meanings, affective aspects of organizing can be determined by means of four interpretive frameworks: organizational psychodynamics, social constructionism, Marxist and feminist frameworks. The authors claim that the nature of leadership actions, when interpreted from an "affective standpoint" "can give insights into the individual's feelings and moods". (James et al., p. 8).

Ambitious in scope, the affective paradigm raises important considerations for emotions in leadership theory and practice, but it also raises significant problems. The latter are due to: (1) its tacit assumption of commonsense emotion; and (2) its theoretical-epistemological framework of empiricist science with its associated methodology that shows in the acceptance of the observational/non observational divide which ramifies all the way back to emotions that, as non-observables, escape the grasp of (empiricist) science. While social actions or organizational processes are said to be observable, their meaning – 'explanation' in the authors' view – has to be established by interpretation. But it is by now well established that the observation/non-observation distinction does not hold in virtue of the theory-ladenness of all observation; no observation is ever free of interpretation. On this account, establishing the 'meaning' of a social action, or organizational process, is a matter for the interpretive frame adopted, and as each frame has its own rules for what counts as evidence, there is no disciplined way to choose among interpretations. School leaders may give different accounts of what they felt, or what motivated them to act, and no account is any 'truer' or more 'authentic' than another. Subjective accounts may have personal therapeutic value, but as they are non-cognitive, they provide no reasons for actions taken, nor do they lead to proposals for organizational change.

Although the affective paradigm draws on relevant psychological science and emotion science, its epistemological framework does not have the theoretical resources that allow it to consider affect and emotions as natural mental phenomena amenable to scientific investigation. For example, there is substantive neuroscientific research on how emotions are believed to travel between people, that is, how 'influence' works, investigated via the concept of 'empathy' for one (e.g., Hatfield et al. 1994; Hatfield et al. 2009). That is to say, there is no need for different interpretive perspectives – just for a better account of science (e.g., Evers and Lakomski 1991, 1996, 2000).

In the next sections we turn to the discussion of the construction of emotions at the psychological and sociocultural levels.

## From emotions as essences to emotions as constructions

Definitional difficulties and the inability to define emotions as an analytical construct, as mentioned in the proposal for affective leadership, reflect the dilemma of contemporary emotion research that continues to trade in traditional dichotomies such as "emotional vs rational or cognitive processes, … emotions related or not to appraisal and cognition; personal vs. sub-personal processes; body vs. brain vs. mental processes", to name just a few of the many identified by de Gelder (2017, p. 1).

The very quest for essences, or natural kinds, characteristic of the classical approach to emotion (e.g. Izard 1992; Ekman 1999), supported by faculty psychology with its assumption of modular brain architecture, continues in affective neuroscience (for discussion, see Lindquist and Barrett 2012). With regard to emotion concepts such as fear, anger, sadness and disgust, affective neuroscience attempts to find the "elusive biological essences (that is, their neural signatures or fingerprints), usually in subcortical regions. This inductive approach assumes that the emotion categories we experience and perceive as distinct must also be distinct in nature". (Barrett 2017, p. 1; for discussion see Thagard and Schröder 2015). But just because we have invented a word for a mental phenomenon, it does not follow that that word is an "essence holder" (Barrett et al. 2010, p. 1) for some material entity instantiated in a particular brain profile (Kagan 2018, p. 79). The simple assumption of one-to-one mapping – emotion concept/behavior to brain area – is theoretically and empirically unsupported. It is not surprising that experimental research within the natural kinds paradigm has failed to surface evidence of emotion types as "brain regions are involved in many functions, and … functions are carried out by many regions … the mapping between structure and function is both *pluripotent* (one-to-many) and *degenerate* (many-to-one)" (Pessoa 2012, p. 158; for a comprehensive discussion of the brain basis of emotion see Lindquist et al. 2012). As we will see later, it is not the brain region that should be the focus of analysis, but the whole brain network itself.

Departing from the assumptions of faculty psychology, Barrett's *constructionist theory of emotion* (formerly also known as the conceptual act theory; e.g., Barrett 2014) draws on an understanding of the brain as consisting of large-scale neural networks 'intrinsic' (or domain general) to the brain's architecture (Barrett and Satpute 2013, p. 363, 365). According to Lindquist and Barrett (2012 p. 1), "common sense mental states such as … emotions [e.g. anger, disgust, etc.] are created (or 'constructed') out of the combination of more basic psychological operations or 'ingredients.'" Earlier these were described as "psychological primitives", psychological categories that "are psychologically irreducible and cannot be redescribed as anything else psychological". (Barrett 2009, p. 331). Three phenomena are identified (amongst others) as important, such as affect, categorization, and a "matrix consisting of different sources of attention", that is, "as anything that can change the rate of neuronal firing". It is a fundamental claim that a "constructionist approach assumes that these operations can be mapped to intrinsic networks in the brain". (Lindquist and Barrett 2012, p. 533).

Physical changes in our bodies and sensory changes in the external environment including such things as other people's facial muscle movements, their actions, as well as the physical surroundings, etc. "become *real as emotion* (as fear, anger, etc.) when they are categorized as such using emotion concept knowledge… learned from language, socialization and other cultural artifacts within the person's day-to-day experience". (Barrett 2014, p. 293). Categorization is a central component of the constructionist account, and is represented in the concept of *situated conceptualization,* adapted from Searle's (1995, 2010) framework of social ontology, where conceptualizations are 'situated' in that they use "highly context-dependent representations that are tailored to the immediate situation". (Barrett 2014, p. 293); the importance of context is described thus:

> Mental events and human behaviors can be thought of as states that emerge from moment-by-moment interaction with the environment rather than proceeding in autonomous, invariant, context-free fashion from preformed dispositions or causes. *Inherently, a mind exists in context.* … the observables of psychology – thoughts, feelings, actions – are not driven by single causes but are the emergent results of multiple transactive processes". (emphases added).
>
> *(Barrett et al. 2010, p. 5; also pp. 5–8 for a brief account of the history of the context principle in psychology)*

Importantly, for emotions to count as emotions and be recognized by others as part of social reality assumes *collective intentionality,* a second concept Barrett derives from Searle (Barrett 2014; for discussion see Schweikard and Schmid 2013). Any emotion that is acknowledged as an emotion of a particular type derives its meaning from the specific situation or cultural context in which it occurs, most often without conscious awareness. It is a feature of Barrett's account that "the act of seeing, feeling or thinking is at once a perception, an emotion, and a cognition".

(see Lewis 2005, pp. 175–176 for a brilliant description of how the emotion of road rage emerges).

Even on such a brief characterization, it is clear that psychological constructionism's account of mental states such as emotions, situated conceptualizations, anchored in a conception of functional distributed brain networks, is a far cry from faculty psychology's assumption of the modular brain and one-to-one mapping between behaviour and emotion category. Instead, emotions are said to emerge, are thoroughly context-dependent, and are, in this specific sense, socially constructed.

## The sociocultural construction of emotions

Although the psychological constructionist theory of emotion explicitly acknowledges the importance of the *sociocultural* context, it does not discuss it explicitly. The sociality of emotion, however, constitutes a different level of analysis as it includes specifically social and cultural elements. The interest in and concern over emotion in education and leadership becomes most salient at the sociocultural level.

Building on the claim that there are no universal, essentialist emotions or natural kinds, *social* constructionists postulate a universal "emotion potential" (e.g. Boiger and Mesquita 2012; Mesquita and Boiger 2014; Mesquita et al. 2015; Mesquita et al. 2016). In particular, Mesquita et al. (2015, p. 542) suggest that the constituents of emotion are shaped "in culture-specific ways that are meaningful and predictable, resulting in systematic cultural differences in 'emotional practices' (i.e. people's actual emotional lives). Whereas emotions are not universal, the underlying rule of emotional life is: Culturally adaptive emotions are more prevalent and intense". Furthermore, such 'emotional fit' contributes to general wellbeing as it supports cultural identity and belonging (e.g. De Leersnyder et al. 2014; Mesquita et al. 2016, p. 31). For example, in Western cultures where individual achievement is highly prized, including school achievements, anger helps individuals to achieve their goals, if frustrated or thwarted, and is more frequent in contrast to other cultures that value interpersonal harmony. Similarly, the experience of happiness in Western cultures tends to be just an individual's personal experience which in turn is congruent with overall cultural meanings that emphasize individual autonomy. In Japanese society, in contrast, happiness has broader and more social elements in keeping with the prevailing cultural model of harmony in relationships (Mesquita et al. 2016, p. 31). "In addition, the *patterns* of emotional experience appear to be culturally normative ... meaning that there are cultural differences in the typical profiles of emotional responses in particular types of situations". (p. 31).

Within the sociocultural perspective of emotion construction, Boiger and Mesquita (2012) suggest, emotions are constructed within three embedded contexts of which the cultural is the widest and represents the macro level. At the micro level, emotions are constructed in moment-to-moment interactions, in that the emergence of emotions is contingent on what happens in a situation. In a conflict situation between two people, whether or not anger develops depends on the reaction of the other who may show mere indifference, or anger, or something else. The construction of emotion always happens during social interaction. Take the relationship between Principal Y and Teacher X which is an established one; it has a certain pattern, e.g. 'X believes that Y is never happy with her work'. This pattern will emotionally shape any new encounter on both sides of the relationship. It will also be shaped by implicit projections of the future of the relationship; that is, for X, "Is it worth repressing my anger to maintain a relationship or not?" The quality of the relationship itself is shaped by emotions. As emotions are mutually constructed 'in the moment' within a social relationship, they are also always constructed within sociocultural frameworks and cultural models that differ in terms of what is or is not congruent with the prevailing cultural model, resulting in different emotions being constructed in the same interactions, and also defining what are appropriate emotion expressions.

The sociocultural constructionist perspective thus adds another layer to the psychological by explaining further how and why emotions are not simply "in the head", innate, hard-wired, or invariant, as presupposed in the essentialist tradition. Emotions, in Boiger and Mesquita's (2012, p. 224) perspective, emerge as "self-organizing social processes" over time, and variability within an emotion category, and in cross cultural categories is the key to their model.

What becomes evident is that such complexity is difficult to research empirically if we want to find out exactly how emotion constitution happens in specific instances in everyday life as opposed to what happens in the laboratory. Boiger and Mesquita (2014) and Mesquita et al. (2017) acknowledge this problem and note that the best evidence they have gathered is by way of qualitative cross-cultural interviews, despite the inherent dangers of self-reports and retrospective bias.

## The sociological construction of emotion

There is a further aspect to specifying the interconnections between the three embedded layers emphasized by the sociocultural perspective – moment-to-moment interactions, relationships, and sociocultural contexts – that is, explaining the mechanisms that account for their interrelationship. Our previous example of the Principal-Teacher relationship indicates that social interaction always takes place in the context of some social institution. What is missing in the sociocultural perspective is an account of sociality in terms of agents' embeddedness in a multitude of diverse social institutions that shape their identities through various roles that are tied to them. Teachers, principals, and students, for example, are labels/names for individuals who are members of a social institution, the education system, which comes with its own roles and identities and the shared affective meanings of the concepts of teacher, student, and principal. The construction of emotions through the layer of social institutions with their associated roles and identities that come with more or less typical affective meanings, is the focus of Affect Control Theory (ACT) (e.g. Heise 2007; Robinson et al. 2007, 2010; Rogers et al. 2014).

While largely complementary to the sociocultural perspective and derived from symbolic interactionism (e.g. Mead 1934), ACT is a mathematically formalized theory in the sociology of emotion, originally proposed by Heise (2007). ACT wants both to explain the *social construction* of emotion as well as the *individual-level mechanisms* of such constitution. (See Robinson et al. 2007; Part I of Heise 2007, sets out the theory in non-technical terms.)

ACT is based on three assumptions: (1) actors use cognitive labels ('culturally shared linguistic categories') to interpret the meaning of social situations; (2) every cognitive label comes with an affective meaning; we cannot separate our cognitive understandings of the situation from how we feel about it; and (3) people act to maintain the affective meanings that are evoked by the definition of the situation (Rogers et al. 2014, p. 125). Taken together, this means that "affect control theory makes the control of *affect* the key feature underlying social life" (Robinson et al. 2007, p. 179). Affect here is understood broadly as (core) affect is in the constructionist perspective whereas emotions "are culturally given labels that we assign to experiences in the context of social interaction that is self-referential. They are signals about how we feel within a situation and how that feeling compares to the stable affective meanings that are usually associated with our self-identity" (Robinson et al. 2007, p. 183; Heise 2007, Ch. 8).

A person's identity is the main source of emotion, say that of 'professor' that has affective meanings attached to it, such as respected and important member of the university, which when confirmed, makes us feel valued, positive, and good about ourselves. But these meanings are not static and they can fluctuate given the situation and relationships, and we may make adjustments, or change, or abandon the relationship (Rogers and Smith-Lovin 2012, p. 233). Affective processing is at the very core of ACT.

An important part of managing affect which is central to maintaining the social and cultural order is the fact that actors often manage affect to comply with expected emotion norms although they do not themselves feel the expected emotion (e.g. Hochschild 1983). For example, teachers might enthusiastically respond to the principal's proposal for restructuring the senior leadership team although this initiative is widely believed to be a mistake. Such a display of inauthentic emotion is, as Heise (2007, pp. 57–58) points out, "… work – masking the emotion you really feel, and then shaping your face and body and voice to simulate a different emotion" (Also Turner and Stets 2006). This is difficult to maintain over time, and has psychological costs. Hochschild (1983) coined the term 'emotional labor' to describe this aspect of the management of emotion.

In addition to asserting the primacy of the dynamics of affective processing, ACT differs from constructionism in the claim that meaning can be quantified and measured (Osgood 1962; also Heise 2007, Part II, for details of the formal, mathematical theory). The basic building blocks for measurement are grounded in the three aspects that shape the feelings we have about certain concepts:

Evaluation, Potency, and Activity. As Heise (2007, p. 7) explains: "Evaluation concerns goodness versus badness, Potency concerns powerfulness versus powerlessness, and Activity concerns liveliness versus quietness. …". These dimensions have provided the framework for empirical studies, using the semantic differential methodology (Osgood et al. 1957; Osgood et al. 1975) that made possible the compilation of cross-cultural 'affective dictionaries' that represent socially shared affective meaning that are cross-cultural universals (Heise 2007, p. 10). These are treated as vectors in a three-dimensional EPA space.

In summary, the main contention of Affect Control Theory is that "emotions in social situations result from the transient fluctuations of identity meanings in affective space that accompany interpretations of social events. As the affective meanings of the concepts that people use to make sense of events follow cultural patterns, the individual experience of emotion is inherently social" (Rogers et al. 2014, p. 126; Heise 1997).

## The semantic pointer theory of emotion

The updated version of Affect Control Theory presented by Rogers et al. (2014) and psychological constructionism both link their accounts to the neural level of analysis, a link not made explicit by social constructionism. Psychological constructionism (as in Barrett's theory) proceeds on the assumption of biological features of brain networks while ACT adopts the hypothesis of emotions as semantic pointers. In contrast, the Semantic Pointer Theory of Emotion (SPTE) developed by Thagard and Schröder (2015) and its recent application in the computational model POEM (POinters–EMotions) outlined by Kajić et al. (2019), is a neurocomputational theory that aims to integrate physiology, appraisal, and construction. It offers a solution to the relationship of language and emotions and to the embodiment of emotions (central to psychological constructionism) and specifies the computational mechanisms that underlie the generation of emotions in the brain, thus going further than the other theories discussed. The ambitious aim of SPTE is to attempt to "unify the mind", to explain emotion and cognition within the one theory. (Duncan and Barrett 2007). To that end, the semantic pointer architecture (SPA) was not primarily developed to explain emotion but to present a biologically realistic model of cognitive processes in general. SPA is an example of a cognitive architecture, a "general theory of the mechanisms of thought, proposing parts (representations) and interactions (computations) that aim to explain the full range of mental phenomena" (Eliasmith et al. 2012; Eliasmith 2013; Kajić 2019 et al. p. 3). It proceeds on the assumption that the neural processes underlying the psychological construction of emotion cannot be separated out from those constructing cognition, an assumption supported by very recent accounts of (biological) brain function and architecture, discussed later.

Central to SPA is the idea of semantic pointers, a concept adopted from computer science. Semantic pointers simulate the neural mechanisms that are involved in the processing of emotions and "consists of spiking patterns in a large population of neurons that provide a kind of compressed representation analogous to JPEG picture files ... [it] is a neural process that compresses information in other neural processes to which it points and into which it can be expanded when needed" (Eliasmith 2013, p. 19; Thagard and Schröder 2015, p. 148). Explained slightly differently, they are "patterns of neural firing that bind neural representations of physical inputs, evaluations of situations, and cultural/linguistic context" (Kajić et al. 2019, p. 36). Semantic pointers are able to explain, through *binding*, accomplished by the mathematical operation of *circular convolution*, how neural processes can solve the symbol/subsymbol problem, that is, it can explain the relations between (high-level) symbols such as words and concepts ('propositional knowledge') and (low-level) distributed representations in neural networks ('tacit knowledge'). This means that semantic pointers that take two patterns of firing produce a new pattern, and the new pattern in turn can continue the process by binding with other patterns, creating more and more complex representations through repeated bindings (Thagard and Schröder 2015, provide an example, pp. 154–155). An important feature of binding by convolution is that it can be undone, making possible an approximation of the original neural patterns (perceptual inputs) that were bound; e.g. 'white leg' becomes again 'white' and 'leg' as separate neural patterns (Kajić et al. 2019, p. 37).

Semantic pointers provide both shallow and deeper meanings. The former are provided "through symbol-like relations to the world and other representations" (Thagard and Schröder 2015, p. 148), e.g. 'cat', while the latter is not just a physical representation but is also related to other representations and beliefs such as 'cats eat mice', 'some cats are pets', etc. Such higher representations are also produced by convolution in binding 'cat', 'eat', 'mice', etc. In this way, Kajić et al. (2019, p. 37) argue, "semantic pointers bridge the gap between neural network cognitive architectures and ones based on rules using symbols".

Employing the same process of binding by convolution, *emotions are semantic pointers* that bind embodied experience (external stimuli), physiological changes (e.g. increased heart rate), stored concepts ('love'), and linguistic knowledge. (For detail see Kajić et al.'s example of "falling in love ...", 2019, p. 39). But there is one further consideration here that needs to be mentioned. There are cases where self-reference is important, that is, where the 'I' needs to be represented.

The example Thagard and Schröder (2015, p. 157) provide is the emotion of happiness when a paper has been accepted for publication, as in: "I am happy that my paper is accepted". Bypassing the enormous social psychological literature on the self (e.g., James 1890; Baumeister 1987; Schlenker 2003, 2011; see Thagard 2014, and Thagard and Wood 2015 for discussion of self as a multilevel system), self-representation, too, can be understood as a semantic pointer. Binding by convolution is again the central mechanism: "Self-representation = BIND(self-concepts, experiences, memories)" (Thagard and Schröder 2015, p. 157). "I am happy" in this specific context is explicable in the context of sociocultural norms and constructed meanings, as we saw both in social constructionism and

Affect Control Theory. The application of semantic pointers here makes clear how the neural construction of emotions is simultaneously culturally constrained.

While we have highlighted only some central features of the semantic pointer theory and POEM, the important general point to make is that POEM has been successful in simulating six important aspects of emotions (for detail see Kajić et al. 2019, p. 36). It has thus demonstrated its explanatory power and biological plausibility and represents the most realistic model of how the brain generates emotion.

In summary, the semantic pointer theory of emotion roughly complements and significantly expands psychological constructionism by providing "a computational specification of mechanisms used by the brain for the generation of emotion" (Kajić et al. 2019, p. 48). Insofar as SPTE and POEM integrate the techniques of Affect Control Theory that treats emotions as mathematical transformations in a vector space of EPA, it is able to demonstrate how "representations and transformations can be achieved in biologically plausible neural networks". (Kajić et al. 2019, p. 48). In doing so, POEM also accounts for cultural variation in emotional experience since it uses as input the empirically-based sentiment/affective dictionaries referred to earlier. As Kajić et al. (2019, p. 48) note, "Emotion generating brains are sensitive to culture through the learned semantic relationships between specific patterns of neural activity". Finally, although we did not expressly discuss appraisal perspectives, the notion of appraisal, integral to Barrett's psychological constructionism, could be modeled as "a parallel process of identification of emotions based on parallel satisfaction of many goal-related constraints" (Thagard and Aubie 2008; Kajić et al. 2019, p. 49).

Given that psychological constructionism, the updated Affect Control Theory, and especially the semantic pointer theory of emotion argue for biological plausibility, we consider next how they dovetail with the proposal of the network brain before we conclude this chapter.

## The neural construction of emotion

The traditional assumption that the brain is a hierarchical model that consists of the phylogenetically newer "higher primate" brain responsible for cognitive processes, and the lower, older, and more primitive "reptilian brain" where the basic emotions are located, with information flowing from lower to higher systems, is no longer supported (Kiverstein and Miller 2015, p. 3).

Following Pessoa's recent model, brain organization is better characterized as consisting of large-scale neural network interactions that span the whole neuroaxis (Pessoa 2014; Pessoa 2017, p. 357; also Churchland and Sejnowski 1994). The network brain is characterized by "multiple anatomical and functional principles … that lead to the concept of 'functionally integrated systems', cortical–subcortical systems that anchor the organization of emotion in the brain". It is on the basis of this organization that the brain is 'emotional'.

Pessoa (2017, pp. 358–362) identifies five principles that characterize brain organization: (1) massive combinatorial anatomical connectivity between cortical and subcortical regions; (2) cortical-subcortical anatomical connectional systems (how brain regions are connected); (3) high distributed functional connectivity, in addition to anatomical (structural) connectivity regions are functionally connected in that "a region affiliates (or clusters) with a set of other regions, thereby defining a momentary circuit" (Pessoa 2017, p. 359); (4) networks "are made of interwoven sets of overlapping communities" (p. 361); and (5) dynamic brain networks, that is, "functional connections vary as a function of context, and are altered by cognitive, emotional, and motivational variables" (p. 361). This means that networks are dynamic and that functional connectivity operates moment-by-moment (Churchland 1986; Churchland and Sejnowski 1994; Anderson 2014). As brain organization is not hierarchical but heterarchical, the central challenge becomes one "of understanding how inter-region coordination dynamics" come into being, that is, "how signals from multiple regions collectively evolve". (Pessoa 2017, p. 365). As these are suggested to be the general principles of brain organization, it follows that the "mechanisms of emotion" should be consistent with them, including anatomical connectivity to and from the body.

Here, we might mention in passing that the brain basis of emotion in emotion research has generally been studied by focusing on a small number of brain structures. *Subcortically*, the focus was on amygdala, hypothalamus, periaqueductal grey, and ventral striatum while *cortically,* the insula, orbitofrontal cortex, and medial PFC were the focus of investigation. This recent research is able to explain that these are indeed important regions for the emotional brain, but they do not represent the brain basis of emotion. They are *hub* regions, meaning they are particularly well connected (Pessoa's Principle 4), and are subject to all the other principles of connectivity and overlap previously mentioned.

Considering the account of brain function and architecture outlined by Barrett's constructionism earlier, the significant point of difference with the dynamic systems perspective is that the latter disavows any 'intrinsic' networks. The brain is built from *dynamic emerging processes*, and not from "finite primitives" (Pessoa 2017, p. 366). On the network model with its functionally integrated, flexible, and dynamic systems that are highly context-dependent, the mapping proposed by Lindquist and Barrett (2012) is thus neurally implausible. (For further discussion see Kiverstein and Miller 2015). As an example of high context-dependence, Pessoa (2017, p. 366) cites the cortex-amygdala system that does not have a core function of "affect generation", although it is traditionally presumed that 'fear', for example, is generated there (see Poldrack 2010; especially LeDoux 1996). Rather, it is its particular functional state at a moment in time that will determine "how it will contribute to multiple mental operations, and these involve not only arousal, vigilance, and novelty but also attention, value determination, and decision–making more broadly". The role of the amygdala on this account is thus much broader than traditionally assumed and turns out to be a multiple-purpose and multiple-function system that *inter alia* includes emotion generation.

Despite the differences we have mapped above between a psychological constructionist account of emotion and the model of the network brain, a view arises that converges on an understanding of emotion as emerging moment by moment, as thoroughly distributed, and as instigating action. This has been demonstrated by the simulations made possible by POEM which in turn means that the computational specification of neural mechanisms successfully approximate how the biological brain generates emotion.

## Conclusion

Given a dynamic systems view of the brain, and the acknowledgment of the sociocultural context of emotion construction, it is now easier to understand why the impact of emotion is so wide-ranging and can be so varied in scope and intensity. The question of whether there are specialized emotion circuits, a question of central concern for classical emotion theories, can, with a high degree of confidence, be answered in the negative. It follows that labels such as emotion and cognition are not helpful in the context of a dynamic view of brain function. "What matters", Pessoa and McMenamin (2017p. 395) argue, is "the coordinated neural action that supports behaviors".

To emphasize this important point, although the neurobiological (and biochemical) machinery of emotion is in the head and body, what makes an emotion experience what it is (for us) depends on the kind of social interactions in which it is created, given that the (fluctuating) affordances of the situation are always shaped by the broader sociocultural contexts that sanction some cultural models over others.

Given the intricacies and complexity of emotion generation, it follows that we cannot simply decide to turn the emotional mechanism off. As Thagard (2010, p. 114) notes, "You can no more decide to operate in a fully nonemotional mode than you can decide to cut your left hemisphere off from your right hemisphere without highly destructive neurosurgery". Without emotional processes in the brain, we would not be able to assess what is, or is not, of value to us from situation to situation in our ongoing encounters with one another, and the world in general. While we cannot turn the emotional mechanism off, we are not entirely at the mercy of our emotions either. We do manage to self-regulate emotional responses, both consciously and subconsciously, and we can do this well or poorly. (On the complexities of emotion regulation, for example, see Gross and Barrett 2011.) In Chapter 9 we will discuss how and why emotions are relevant and indeed necessary for *rational* decision-making to occur.

## References

Anderson, M.L. (2014). Complex function in the dynamic brain. Comment on understanding brain networks and brain organization by Luiz Pessoa. *Physics of Life Reviews*, 11, 436–437.
Barrett, L.F. (2006). Solving the emotion paradox: Categorization and the experience of emotion. *Personality and Social Psychology Review*, 10(1), 20–46.

Barrett, L.F. (2009). The future of psychology: Connecting mind to brain. *Perspectives on Psychological Science*, 4(4), 326–39.

Barrett, L.F. (2014). The conceptual act theory: A précis. *Emotion Review*, 6(4), 292–297.

Barrett, L.F. (2017). The theory of constructed emotion: An active inference account of interoception and categorization. *Social Cognitive and Affective Neuroscience*, 12(1), 1–23.

Barrett, L.F., & Satpute, A.B. (2013). Large-scale brain networks in affective and social neuroscience: Towards an integrative functional architecture of the brain. *Current Opinion in Neurobiology*, 23(3), 361–72.

Barrett, L.F., Mesquita, B., & Smith, E.R. (2010). The context principle. In B. Mesquita, L.F. Barrett, & E.R. Smith (Eds.), *The mind in context* (pp. 1–23). New York and London: The Guilford Press.

Baumeister, R.F. (1987). How the self became a problem: A psychological review of historical research. *Journal of Personality and Social Psychology*, 52(1), 163–176.

Baumeister, R.F. (2011). Self and identity: A brief overview of what they are, what they do, and how they work. *Annals of the New York Academy of Sciences*, 1234, 48–55.

Berkovich, I., & Eyal, O. (2014). Educational leaders and emotions: An international review of empirical evidence 1992–2012. *Review of Educational Research*, 20(10), 1–39. doi: 10.3102/0034654314550046.

Boiger, M., & Mesquita, B. (2014). A socio-dynamic perspective on the construction of emotion. In L.F. Barrett, & J.A. Russell (Eds.), *The psychological construction of emotion* (pp. 377–398). New York, NY: Guilford Press.

Boiger, M., & Mesquita, B. (2012). The construction of emotion in interactions, relationships, and cultures. *Emotion Review*, 4, 221–229. doi:10.1177/1754073912439765.

Bush, T. (2014). Emotional leadership: A viable alternative to the bureaucratic model? *Educational Management Administration & Leadership*, 42(2), 163–164.

Churchland, P.S. (1986). *Neurophilosophy*. Cambridge, MA: MIT Press.

Churchland, P.S., & Sejnowski, T.J. (1994). *The computational brain*. Cambridge, MA: The MIT Press.

Crawford, M. (2009). *Getting to the heart of educational leadership*. London: Sage.

Damasio, A.R. (1994). *Descartes' error*. New York: Putnam.

De Gelder, B. (2017). Going native. Emotion science in the twenty-first century. *Frontiers in Psychology*, 8,1212. doi: https://doi.org/10.3389/fpsyg.2017.01212.

De Leersnyder, J., Mesquita, B., Kim, H., Eom, K., & Choi, H. (2014). Emotional fit with culture: A predictor of individual differences in relational well-being. *Emotion*, 14(2), 241–245.

Dixon, T. (2003). *From passions to emotions: The creation of a secular psychological category*. Cambridge: Cambridge University Press.

Duncan, S., & Barrett, L.F. (2007). Affect is a form of cognition: A neurobiological analysis. *Cognition & Emotion*, 21, 1184–1211.

Ekman, P. (1999). Basic emotions. In T. Dalgleish, & M. Power (Eds.), *Handbook of cognition and emotion* (pp. 45–60). Chichester, UK: Wiley.

Eliasmith, C. (2013). *How to build a brain*. Oxford: Oxford University Press.

Eliasmith, C., Stewart, T.C., Choo, X., Bekolay, T., DeWolf, T., Tang, Y., & Rasmussen, D. (2012). A large-scale model of the functioning brain. *Science*, 338, 1202-1205.

Evers, C.W., & Lakomski, G. (1991). *Knowing educational administration*. Oxford: Elsevier.

Evers, C.W., & Lakomski, G. (1996). *Exploring educational administration*. Oxford: Elsevier.

Evers, C.W., & Lakomski, G. (2000). *Doing educational administration*. Oxford: Elsevier.

Gross, J.J., & Barrett, L.F. (2011). Emotion generation and emotion regulation: One or two depends on your point of view. *Emotion Review*, 3, 8–16.

Hatfield, E., Cacioppo, J., & Rapson, R. (1994). *Emotional contagion*. Cambridge: Cambridge University Press.

Hatfield, E., Rapson, R.L., & Le, Y.C. (2009). Emotional contagion and empathy. In J. Decety, & W. Ickes (Eds.), *The social neuroscience of empathy* (pp. 19–31)). Cambridge, MA: MIT Press.

Heise, D.R. (1997). INTERACT: Introduction and software. Affect Control Theory website, University of Indiana. Retrieved from http://www.indiana.edu/~socpsy/ACT/interact.htm

Heise, D.R. (2007). *Expressive order: Confirming sentiments in social action.* New York: Springer.

Heise, D.R. (2010). *Surveying cultures. Discovering shared conceptions and sentiments.* New York: Wiley.

Hochschild, A. (1983). *The managed heart: The commercialization of human feeling.* Berkeley, CA: University of California Press.

Izard, C.E. (1992). Basic emotions, relations among emotions, and emotion-cognition relations. *Psychological Review*, 99(3), 561–565. https://doi.org/10.1037/0033-295X.99.3.561

James, C., Crawford, M., & Oplatka, I. (2018). An affective paradigm for educational leadership theory and practice: Connecting affect, actions, power and influence. *International Journal of Leadership in Education Theory and Practice*, ISSN: 1360-3124 (Print) 1464-5092 (Online) Journal homepage: http://www.tandfonline.com/loi/tedl20 pp. 1–12.

James, W. (1890). *The principles of psychology.* New York, NY: Holt

Kagan, J. (2018). Brain and emotion. *Emotion Review*, 10(1) 79–86.

Kiverstein, J., & Miller, M. (2015). The embodied brain: Towards a radical embodied cognitive neuroscience. *Frontiers in Human Neuroscience*, 9(237), 1–11. doi: 10.3389/fnhum.2015.00237

Kajić, I., Schröder, T., Stewart, T.C., & Thagard, P. (2019). The semantic pointer theory of emotion: Integrating physiology, appraisal, and construction. *Cognitive Systems Research*, 58, 35–53.

LeDoux, J. (1996). *The emotional brain.* New York, NY: Simon & Schuster.

Lewis, M.D. (2005). Bridging emotion theory and neurobiology through dynamic systems modeling. *Behavioral and Brain Sciences*, 28, 169–245

Lindquist, K.A., & Barrett, L.F. (2012). A functional architecture of the human brain: Emerging insights from the science of emotion. *Trends in Cognitive Sciences*, 16, 533–540.

Lindquist, K.A., Wager, T.D., Kober, H., Bliss-Moreau, E., & Barrett, L.F. (2012). The brain basis of emotion: A meta-analytic review. *Behavioral and Brain Sciences*, 35, 121–143.

Markus, H.R., & Kitayama, S. (1991). Culture and the self: Implications for cognition, emotion, and motivation. *Psychological Review*, 98, 224–253.

Matsumoto, D., & Ekman, P. (2009). Basic emotions. In D. Sander, & K.R. Scherer (Eds.), *Oxford Companion to emotion and the affective sciences* (pp. 45–49). Oxford: Oxford University Press.

Mead, G.H. (1934). *Mind, self, & society.* Chicago: University of Chicago Press.

Mesquita, B., & Boiger, M. (2014). Emotions in context: A sociodynamic model of emotions. *Emotion Review*, 6(4), 298–302.

Mesquita, B., Vissers, N., & De Leersnyder, J. (2015). Culture and emotion. In J. D. Wright (Editor-in-chief), *International encyclopedia of the social & behavioral sciences.* 2nd edition, (pp. 542–549). Vol. 5. Oxford: Elsevier.

Mesquita, B., Boiger, M., & De Leersnyder, J. (2017). Doing emotions: The role of culture in everyday emotions. *European Review of Social Psychology*, 28(1), 95–133, DOI: 10.1080/10463283.2017.1329107.

Mesquita, B., Boiger, M., & De Leersnyder, J. (2016). The cultural construction of emotions. *Current Opinion in Psychology*, 8, 31–36. doi:10.1016/j.copsyc.2015.09.015

Osgood, C.E. (1962). Studies of the generality of affective meaning systems. *American Psychologist*. 17, 10-28.

Osgood, C.E., May, W.H., & Miron, M.S. (1975). *Cross-cultural universals of affective meaning.* Urbana, IL: University of Illinois Press.

Osgood, C.E., Suci, G.C., & Tannenbaum, P.H. (1957). *The measurement of meaning.* Urbana, IL: University of Illinois Press.

Pessoa, L. (2012). Beyond brain regions: Network perspective of cognition–emotion interactions. *Behavioral and Brain Sciences,* 35, 158–159.

Pessoa, L. (2014). Understanding brain networks and brain organization. *Physical Life Review,* 11, 400–435.

Pessoa, L. (2017). A network model of the emotional brain. *Trends in Cognitive Sciences,* 21(5), 357–371.

Pessoa, L. (2018). Emotion and the interactive brain: Insights from comparative neuroanatomy and complex systems, special section: Brain and emotion. *Emotion Review,* 10(3), 204–216.

Pessoa, L., & McMenamin, B.W. (2017). Dynamic networks in the emotional brain. *Neuroscientist,* 23(4), 383–396.

Poldrack, R.A. (2010). Mapping mental function to brain structure: How can cognitive neuroimaging succeed? *Perspectives on Psychological Science,* 5(6), 753–761.

Robinson, D.T., Smith-Lovin, L., & Wisecup, A.K. (2007). Affect control theory. In J.E. Stets, & J.H. Turner (Eds.), *Handbook of the sociology of emotions* (pp. 179–202). New York, NY: Springer Science.

Rogers, K.B., & Smith-Lovin, L. (2012). Answering the call for a sociological perspective on the multilevel social construction of emotion: A comment on Boiger and Mesquita. *Emotion Review,* 4(3), 232–233.

Rogers, K.B., Schröder, T., & von Scheve, C. (2014). Dissecting the sociality of emotion: A multi-level approach. *Emotion Review,* 6(2), 124–133.

Samier, E., & Schmidt, M.(Eds.) (2009). *Emotional dimensions of educational administration and leadership.* New York: Routledge.

Scarantino, A. (2016). The philosophy of emotions and its impact on affective science. In M. Lewis, J. Haviland–Jones, & L.F. Barrett (Eds.) *The handbook of emotions* (pp. 3-47). 4th edition. New York: The Guilford Press.

Schlenker, B.R. (2003). Self-presentation. In M.R. Leary, & J.P. Tangney (Eds.), *Handbook of self and identity* (pp. 492–518). New York, NY: Guilford Press.

Searle, J.R. (1995). *The construction of social reality.* New York, NY: The Free Press.

Searle, J.R. (2010). *Making the social world: The structure of human civilization.* Oxford: Oxford University Press.

Schutz, P.A., & Zembylas, M.(Eds.) (2009). *Advances in teacher emotion research.* London: Springer.

Schweikard, D.P., & Schmid, H.B. (2013). Collective intentionality. In E.N. Zalta (Ed.), *Stanford encyclopedia of philosophy.* (Summer 2013 edition), URL = <https://plato.stanford.edu/archives/sum2013/entries/collective-intentionality/>.

Solomon, R.C. (2008). The philosophy of emotions. In M. Lewis, & J. M. Haviland (Eds.), *Handbook of emotions.* 3rd edition (pp. 3–16). New York: Guilford Press.

Turner, J.H., & Stets, J.E. (2006). Sociological theories of human emotions. *Annual Review of Sociology.* 32, 25–52.

Thagard, P. (2010). *The brain and the meaning of life.* Princeton, NJ: Princeton University Press.

Thagard, P. (2014). The self as a system of multilevel interacting mechanisms. *Philosophical Psychology,* 27(2), 145–163.

Thagard, P., & Aubie, B. (2008). Emotional consciousness: A neural model of how cognitive appraisal and somatic perception interact to produce qualitative experience. *Consciousness and Cognition,* 17, 811–834.

Thagard, P., & Schröder, T. (2015). Emotions as semantic pointers: Constructive neural mechanisms. In L.F. Barrett, & J.A. Russell (Eds.), *The psychological construction of emotions*, New York: Guilford.

Thagard, P., & Wood, J. (2015). Eighty phenomena about the self: Representation, evaluation, regulation, and change. *Frontiers in Psychology*, 6(334), 1–15.

Yamamoto, J.K., Gardiner, M.E., & Tenuto, P.L. (2014). Emotion in leadership: Secondary school administrators' perceptions of critical incidents. *Educational Management Administration & Leadership*, 42(2), 165–183.

# 9
# THE ROLE OF EMOTION IN EDUCATIONAL DECISION-MAKING

## Introduction

How do we make good decisions? That "Deciding is a sine qua non of educational administration", as Hoy and Miskel (2008, p. 325) note, is an observation that is hardly contentious. But when it comes to identifying by which means, procedures or strategies we get to make good decisions – in schools as indeed in all formal organizations – consensus soon vanishes, as is evident in the history of decision-making that has produced a multitude of models. Although these vary in their specific features, they nevertheless share considerable common ground (Buchanan and O'Connell 2006, provide an excellent, brief overview; Shapiro and Stefkovich 2005, offer case studies of ethical decision-making; also Hoy and Tarter 1995, who discuss eight prominent models applied in educational decision-making).

Decision-making has long been identified with the rational coordination of beliefs and desires, both in its non-technical, folk psychological expression, and in the more arcane models of maximizing expected utility, or multi-criterial modelling under various epistemic conditions. (Hoy and Miskel 2013, provide a good description of various models in the opening pages of Chapter 9.) Because the medium of analysis of what goes on inside the heads of decision-makers is linguistic/symbolic, these processes are usually treated in a way that abstracts from the causal machinery of cognition, what cognitive (neuro)scientists fondly refer to as our 'wetware', and instead focusses on certain normative canons of reasoning defined over symbolic representations.

The modern legacy of the assumption that rationality is defined by the human ability to use language and other symbolic representations such as, for example, mathematical or logical notations, is played out in many domains of the social sciences, and especially in economic theory and theories of social

DOI: 10.4324/9781003241577-12

choice. In the domain of administrative-organizational theory and educational administration, Herbert Simon's (1976) view of decision-making is one prominent example that continues to be influential. However, we have good reasons for re-examining such approaches in light of our greater understanding of the causal processes of thought. We now know a lot more of what actually goes on between our ears to challenge the very conception of rational thought and reasoning that has dominated our understanding of these matters for a long time. (See Chapter 8 for detail.) Subsequently, we also have occasion to doubt that the models of decision-making currently on offer cohere with what we now know.

The aim of this chapter is to demonstrate that knowledge of the causal mechanisms of decision-making is relevant for the development of any satisfactory normative model of human decision-making. We argue for this in five sections, beginning with a discussion of normative versus descriptive accounts of decision-making, followed by considering classic accounts of decision-making in section two. We show how emotion appears even in classical accounts in section three. In Section four, we introduce the Somatic Marker Hypothesis (SMH) that offers an important explanation of the critical role emotion has in attempts to understand rational decision-making. Section five presents a brief outline of what a theory of emotional decision-making might look like, and why such a theory is indeed rational.

## Normative versus descriptive accounts of decision-making

There is a useful distinction to be drawn in the study of all forms of reasoning where we wish to consider prescriptions or canons of good reasoning. In the study of formal logic, for example, it has long been recognized, certainly from the time of Frege, and arguably in the logical writings of Aristotle, that the case for identifying forms of argument as valid or invalid, can be made independently of considerations of human psychology. Roughly speaking, valid forms of argument allow true conclusions to be deduced from true premises. That is, valid forms of argument are truth preserving. Admittedly, the reasoning that goes into producing valid arguments must occur in some physical medium, such as a human brain, but the nature of the medium – whether it be ensembles of neurons, arrays of vacuum tubes, or silicon chips – is irrelevant to the issue of validity. The so-called laws of thought in this sense are not about the details of the causal operation of thinking machines. Rather, they concern the classification of abstract rules for determining deductive validity, or more generally, with how logical reasoning ought to proceed.

In the history of logic, this anti-psychologism has enjoyed a fairly comprehensive victory. When it comes to the question of how logical proofs are discovered, there is some scope for appeal to psychology. But when it comes to the matter of justification, the prevailing view is that psychology has no role to play (Cohen 1981). As we noted in Chapter 5, Karl Popper even extended the anti-psychologism thesis to the matter of scientific discovery in his most influential book *The Logic of Scientific Discovery* (1959).

This normative/descriptive distinction also goes over smoothly into the study of decision-making. Accounts of how people actually think and reason have therefore tended to have a descriptive, not normative, focus with particular attention being given to human lapses in normative rationality and decision-making, while much effort has gone into developing various mathematical models of normative decision-making. (See Heap et al. 1992, for examples from game theory, utility maximization models, consumer choice theory, and collective choice.) Where the relevance of these descriptive accounts is invoked normatively, it has been mainly in the context of how to proceed as best we can in decision-making given all of the revealed cognitive limitations. (But see also Oaksford and Chater 2007.) The central argument in this chapter is that the descriptive/normative distinction has been overplayed and that some appeal to the causal mechanisms of human decision-making must be made in order to be able to construct any plausible normative theory of decision-making. The causal story we describe here pushes explanation not only beyond psychology and into computational neuroscience, but in the direction of showing the significance of emotion for reasoning about choices.

## High reason, classical decision-making, and bounded rationality

Let us begin with a well-known normative view that is also informed by important details about the psychology of decision-making, namely Herbert Simon's theory of decision-making under bounded rationality. Unlike classical optimization theories, it accepts some limitations in the way humans come to their decisions and also accepts that perfect rational choice is not possible.

An anecdote told by Thagard and Millgram (1997) serves nicely to illustrate the dilemma of classical decision theories:

> … an eminent philosopher of science once encountered a noted decision theorist in a hallway at their university. The decision theorist was pacing up and down, muttering, "What shall I do? What shall I do?"
> "What's the matter, Howard??" asked the philosopher.
> Replied the decision theorist: "It's horrible, Ernest – I've got an offer from Harvard and I don't know whether to accept it".
> "Why Howard," reacted the philosopher, "you're one of the world's great experts on decision–making. Why don't you just work out the decision tree, calculate the probabilities and expected outcomes, and determine which choice maximizes your expected utility?"
> With annoyance, the other replied: "Come on, Ernest. This is serious."

As advocated by classical decision theories, maximization of a person's utility is governed by three broad conditions under which the rationality of individual preferences can be expressed:

i. Under conditions of uncertainty, where some or all probabilities are unknown, and
ii. Under conditions of risk, where all probabilities of outcomes are known, an individual's preferences are assumed to maximize expected utility.
iii. Under conditions of certainty, where all outcomes are known, an individual's preferences are assumed to maximize utility.

*(Harsanyi, as cited in Evers and Lakomski 1991, p. 177)*

The above definition covers classical decision theory in general terms and despite the fact that it has been subjected to substantial critique (e.g. Goldstein and Hogarth 1997; Tversky and Kahneman 1999; Kahneman et al. 1999; Bechara and Damasio 2005), it continues to be influential, especially in modern economic theory. Simon's account of decision-making under conditions of bounded rationality (Newell and Simon 1972) provides a somewhat less austere theory in that he acknowledges the limitations of human rationality and human information processing without, however, sacrificing the possibility of making a correct decision. Compared with the requirements of classical choice theory to make *optimal* choices (that come with high costs), he advocates that we *satisfice* rather than *optimize*. Human behaviour falls short of rationality in the following ways:

1. Rationality requires a complete knowledge and anticipation of the consequences that will follow on each choice. In fact, knowledge of the consequences is always fragmentary.
2. Since these consequences lie in the future, imagination must supply the lack of experienced feeling in attaching value to them. But values can be only imperfectly anticipated.
3. Rationality requires a choice among all possible alternative behaviours. In actual behavior, only a very few of all these possible alternatives ever come to mind.

*(Simon 1976, p. 81)*

However, despite bounded rationality, correct administrative decisions are possible insofar as the domain where values and preferences are arbitrated is avoided. This domain deals exclusively with policy decisions.

In general, a correct administrative decision for Simon is one that makes for the realization of certain 'given' values in a given situation. Accomplishing these given values itself is a factual matter of assessing whether the resources applied have been employed effectively or efficiently. Values and human preferences, since they are non-observable, are externalized in this instrumental way and their origins or status is of no concern in scientific administrative decisions but are to be adjudicated in the area of policy. (For extensive discussion on Simon's empiricist philosophical framework, see Evers and Lakomski 1991, Chapter 1; also Lakomski 2005, Chapter 7). Questions of policy are questions of arbitrating between different values, and value judgments are a matter of 'human fiat' (Simon 1976, p. 56). Validating a factual proposition, on the other hand, is a matter of 'its agreement with the facts'. The affective side of human behaviour, i.e. subjective feelings, preferences, values are excluded from rational decision-making which, true to empiricist doctrine, has no purchase on rational decision-making.

This is not to deny that Simon acknowledges human values and preferences as important. He comments explicitly on the limitations of human choice imposed by their psychological environment. To overcome these limitations, he notes, human beings have developed some working procedures that "…consist in assuming that he [human being] can isolate from the rest of the world a closed system containing only a limited number of variables and a limited range of consequences" (Simon 1976, p. 82). Successfully manipulating these variables, that is, our factual knowledge is what defines human rationality and intelligence.

In a nutshell, while symbol systems manage to be successful in executing a range of (narrowly defined) thinking tasks, they are subject to computational limits in information processing such as speed and organization of a system's computations and size of its memories. Even such a well-specified game as chess cannot be played perfectly by a symbol system because this would require analysis of more chess moves than there are molecules in the universe, a feat that is computationally impossible. Simon acknowledges that if exact computation in chess is impossible, then so are the problems of everyday life. Therefore, he concludes, "… *intelligent systems must use approximate methods to handle most tasks. Their rationality is bounded*". (Simon 1990, p. 6; emphases in original). Bounded rationality remains a key to his theory of rationality. Most tellingly, amongst the issues that still need to be resolved, Simon and colleagues acknowledge as a problem "how to integrate emotion, feeling and affect into cognitive architecture". (Newell et al. 1996, p. 127). In other words, what is at issue are precisely those features that we ordinarily consider as truly human.

The problems with this influential perspective are many but are not the subject of this discussion (see Evers and Lakomski 1996, 2000, Ch. 3; Clark 1997, 2001). We might just note in passing that among philosophically inclined writers within educational administration, Donald Willower had dedicated much of his career to argue against Simon's version of rationalist decision-making and advocated a Deweyan process – and values-oriented approach. Christopher Hodgkinson has defended values 'über Alles' in the administration enterprise, and Thomas Greenfield had fought passionately for the importance of human subjectivity as the basis for social choice (see Evers and Lakomski 1991). All three have in their ways attempted to redress the emotion/values imbalance in educational administration theories, with Willower coming closest to a naturalistic solution in the wake of Dewey's pragmatism. But there is now a lot more to be said about emotion.

## Emotion enters the equation

Even on classical accounts of decision-making, the relevance of emotion is undisputed, although it is always portrayed as compromising rationality. To see the arguments for this portrayal, consider again the basic machinery of much decision-making (see Hoy and Tarter 1995; Hoy and Miskel 2013). This consists of choosing that course of action that is most likely to realize what we value most whether described in familiar folk-psychological terms or in the more arcane terminology of mathematics.

One of the constraints that is in operation here is the requirement that we are able to value alternatives in a relatively clear way. That is, it assumes a stable value, or preference, structure over the alternatives being adjudicated. But if values are construed broadly as conceptions of "the desirable with motivating force", as Hodgkinson (1978, p. 105), was fond of putting it, then it will be difficult, conceptually, to find a clear demarcation between values and emotion. For if it is about anything at all, emotion is a source of motivation and affects what we regard as desirable. The problem is that emotions fluctuate and can change with the passing show of experience, and with a range of bodily influences. (Some of the causal mechanisms that account for such fluctuations are explained in Chapter 8). Since decision-making regularly assumes deferred alternatives, an unstable value structure compromises the theoretical basis on which alternatives are being ranked. One's preferences may change well before any outcomes come into play as alternatives.

Worse still, emotion can render values inconsistent. For example, people can value procedural impartiality in evaluating alternatives but want to give short shrift to the consideration of some alternatives to which they have very strong feelings of opposition. This problem spills over into the very nature of specifying decision alternatives, since we are prone to evaluate differently equal situations that are described differently. Thus, people tend to say they would prefer a surgical procedure with an 80 percent survival rate rather than one with a 20 percent mortality rate, even though the two are actuarially equivalent.

Emotion also figures in such fundamental epistemic processes as learning from experience, a requirement for fixing on reasonable estimates concerning the likelihood of alternative outcomes of possible actions, or decisions. Consider how we might adjust our theories of the world in the light of evidence. The key issue is resolving what is known as the "stability/plasticity dilemma" (Carpenter 1989, pp. 25–26; Carpenter and Grossberg 1991). We have views on many issues, and we change our minds from time to time as a result of discovering new information. But what is the correct balance here? How, for example, do we assess the teaching-by-lecture mode when compared with teaching-by-discovery learning mode? Do we throw out all lecturing on the basis of new evidence? If we err on the side of plasticity, our minds will be like a beach with every new wave of experience washing over and obliterating all that was previously written in the sand, and we accept any new education fad that comes along.

On the other hand, if we err on the side of stability, our minds are more like concrete with engravings almost entirely unsusceptible to successive waves of experience. We continue with the lecture method, regardless of new evidence that might require that we modify our approach in some way. In epistemology, and methodology, this latter condition is known as confirmation bias, with even evidence contrary to expectation being interpreted as supporting one's viewpoint. Holding one's views with a passion inclines us to confirmation bias with its corresponding limitations on learning. But being disinterested in one's views can result in a failure to accumulate knowledge, a necessary condition for developing intellectual structures that can match the complexity of the world in which we live. In the absence of an agreed methodological solution to these problems, it is important that we at least try to develop an understanding of the role of emotion in decision-making in general, and subsequently for educational decision-making in particular.

The neglect of emotion in serious scientific study until recently can largely be accounted for by the general trend to study the mind/brain as if it had nothing to do with evolution. Simon's theory is only one well-known example amongst many that reflect this view. The last three decades of research in cognitive and affective neuroscience, however, have seen a remarkable change (see LeDoux 1996, 1999; Damasio 2000; Lane and Nadel 2000; Minsky 2006). The idea that emotion and cognition are two separate systems that interact only occasionally, and usually to the detriment of rationality, is no longer accepted in light of behavioural and neuroscience data that demonstrate not just their interaction but, more strongly, the view that their integrative operation is necessary for adaptive human functioning (e.g. Thagard 2006; Churchland 2002, 2007; Churchland and Churchland 1998; Ochsner and Phelps 2007; Pessoa 2012).

In Damasio's (2000, p. 14) words, "Well-tuned and deployed emotion … is necessary for the edifice of reason to operate properly". From an evolutionary perspective, of course, this is hardly surprising. Emotions, in fact, have quite unique qualities. They are embodied, and as Dolan (2002, p. 1191) notes, they "manifest in uniquely recognizable, and stereotyped, behavioural patterns of facial expression, comportment, and autonomic arousal. Second, they are less susceptible to our intentions than other psychological states insofar as they are often triggered unawares; and thirdly, and most importantly, they are less encapsulated than other psychological states as evident in their global effects on virtually all aspects of cognition".

The renewed emphasis on the scientific study of emotion has already led to significant developments evidenced by the emergence of neuroethics (e.g. Illes and Raffin 2002; Gazzaniga 2005; Glannon 2007) and affective neuroscience (Dolan 2002; Davidson 2003), to mention just two prominent fields of research. In the sections to follow, we consider the connection between cognition and emotion as presented in the so-called Somatic Marker Hypothesis (SMH). Although this is one approach among several (see, for example, Montague 2006), it serves to illustrate new thinking about the important explanatory role emotion has in attempts to understand rational decision-making. The Somatic Marker Hypothesis to date remains a highly influential, albeit controversial, hypothesis. (For discussions see Linquist and Bartol 2013; Bartol and Linquist 2015; TenHouten 2016).

## The somatic marker hypothesis

To begin with, in everyday life we commonly conflate emotions and feelings. Such conflation has caused difficulties with the research on emotions. It appears that what we call *emotions* is a bundle consisting of *background emotions*, *primary or basic emotions* (fear, anger, disgust, surprise, sadness, and happiness) and *social emotions* (sympathy, embarrassment, shame, guilt, pride, jealousy, envy, gratitude, admiration, indignation, and contempt). The latter Damasio (2003, p. 43 onwards) calls the *emotions-proper*. Background emotions in contrast are not prominent in behaviour but are in evidence when we, for example, detect whether someone is enthusiastic about or bored by a task we asked them to perform; or, they are present in the experienced diagnostician who by merely observing a patient is able to make an assessment of the illness. Although it is still early days in our understanding of how the brain triggers *social emotions*, given the evidence we discussed in Chapter 8, we now have more plausible and comprehensive accounts of how this happens. These are based largely on more advanced knowledge of the brain's interconnectivity and ways of processing, combined with a better understanding of the social and cultural contexts in which we live. Nevertheless, Damasio (2003, p. 46) is right to note that deeply engrained in the organism's brain, social emotions are "a gift of the genome of certain species".

Given their evolutionary history, is seems that the brain machinery for emotion and for feelings was assembled in instalments (Damasio 2003, p. 80; for a stimulating albeit controversial discussion of the origins of the modern mind, see Donald 1993). The machinery of emotion came first which facilitated reactions to an object or event, and then the machinery for feelings came after. Feelings seem to emerge when something like a critical 'body' mass of mapped detail gets to a critical point. Their substrate is thus the set of neural patterns that map the body state, and which give rise to a mental image of the body state. A simple way to differentiate between emotions and feelings is that the term 'feeling' refers to the private, mental experience of an emotion; the term 'emotion' refers to the responses whose perception we call feeling (Damasio 2000, p. 15). Practically speaking, "you cannot observe a feeling in someone else. Likewise, no one can observe your own feelings, but some aspects of the emotions that gave rise to your feelings will be patently observable to others". (Damasio 2000, p. 15). Here, it is also important to note that there is a difference between feeling and knowing that we feel; these are separable processes. What happens when the brain machinery relevant to the production of emotions has been injured is a matter of enormous interest. The most famous, classical case study is that of Phineas Gage whose sad fate presents one of the earliest examples of the impact of brain injury on everyday decision-making and personality (Restak 1984, Ch. 4; Damasio 1996, Ch. 1).

When Gage was working as a construction foreman for a railroad company in Vermont in 1848, an iron bar he used to tamp down explosives shot out of the hole. The charge blew up in his face, and the iron bar entered Gage's left cheek, shot through his skull diagonally, and exited through the top of the head. Amazingly, he was not killed. Gage recovered after a few months, but it was observed that his personality had changed significantly. After the accident he no longer seemed to care for either work or friends, had become prone to fly off the handle, and no longer showed respect for social conventions. Also, his decision-making ability regarding what was or was not in his best interests, and planning for the future, had disappeared so that he made poor choices that turned out badly for him. A second important aspect in Gage's story is the discrepancy (dissociation) between his negative character changes and the seemingly normal state of his cognitive capacities and behaviours that showed no impairment. In other words, his value or ethical system that shaped his (former) character had become split from his cognitive faculties and behaviour. The Somatic Marker Hypothesis (SMH) offers a possible explanation for such dissociation.

What knowledge we now have of how the (healthy) brain makes decisions (e.g. Sanfey and Cohen 2004; Coltheart 2004; Thagard 2006) is in large part due to the modern neuroscientific research methods of functional magnetic resonance imaging (fMRI), positron emission tomography (PET), electroencephalography (EEG), direct neuronal recordings, and clinical work with brain damaged patients. In particular, the work of Damasio and his colleagues with patients who suffered lesions in the ventromedial prefrontal cortex (VMPFC; the 'underbelly' of the frontal lobe right behind our eyebrows, Damasio 1996, p. 32) showed what was presumed to have happened in Gage's case. These patients, including the modern Phineas Gage, Damasio's patient 'Elliot', demonstrated normal cognitive abilities as per standard tests, but also showed poor decision-making behaviour. Personality changes were described by their families as 'emotionally flat', 'decides against his best interest', 'doesn't learn from his mistakes', 'is impulsive', etc. (Sanfey and Cohen 2004, p. 16709).

The SMH maintains that emotions have a significant influence on decision-making, that is, people make decisions, sometimes primarily at gut or emotional levels rather than engaging in what is portrayed as a rational assessment of the future outcomes of weighing options and alternatives in some kind of cost-benefit analysis, as standardly assumed in theories of choice (see Clore and Huntsinger 2007). SMH "provides a system–level neuroanatomical and cognitive framework for decision–making and suggests that the process of decision–making depends in many important ways on neural substrates that regulate homeostasis, emotion, and feeling." (Bechara et al. 2000; Bechara 2004, p. 30; a good non-technical overview is given by Morse 2006).

What happens in ordinary life goes something like this. You contemplate a bad outcome in connection with a particular response option, let's say you, the school principal, picture informing your Deputy that she is not getting the financial support she was expecting to attend an international education conference, and you experience a negative, unpleasant gut feeling. A somatic marker 'marks' a body image. In doing so, it makes you attend to the negative consequences of the action you contemplated – anger and/or disappointment on the part of your deputy; a threat to leave the school; accusations of unfairness, etc. The somatic marker, your negative gut feel, serves as a kind of alarm signal. Having experienced such examples of markers before, you might immediately reject your planned decision without giving it any further thought. The considerable benefit of such an early warning system, according to Damasio and colleagues is that it stops you in your tracks, so to speak, and thus immediately eliminates a negative option thus reducing the pool of available options for selection.

This does not mean, however, that you may not also carry out a kind of rational cost-benefit analysis – e.g. financial costs that will be incurred by your Deputy's trip and absence, tasks that need to be reallocated, but also the gains in education knowledge and expertise she will bring back to the school, continued good will towards you, and the school, and so on – but if and when you do, you have fewer alternatives to crunch through. In this manner, Damasio and colleagues believe that somatic markers make decision-making more accurate and efficient. Specifically, *"somatic markers are a special instance of feelings generated from secondary emotions*. Those emotions and feelings *have been connected, by learning, to predicted future outcomes of certain scenarios"* (Damasio 1996, p. 174; emphases in original). A negative somatic marker functions like an alarm bell while a positive somatic experience serves as an incentive. Both kinds can be said to pre-sort efficiently and quickly what options are available in a potentially unlimited option space.

These advantages need to be emphasized as advantages of rationality. The point is that, from a purely logical point of view, there is an arbitrarily large number of options that need to be included in any decision-making calculus. But this results in combinatorial explosion, the sort of thing that happens in evaluating chess moves by looking ahead more than just a few moves at a time. The number of possible moves to be evaluated very quickly outruns any real-time computational process. Much of the resulting indecision observed in patients with Gage-like affective disorders is the result of combinatorial overload, there being no basis for sifting all the possible options.

A second advantage for rationality is that the acquisition of somatic markers is linked to experience, thus facilitating reinforcement learning. One mechanism for avoiding emotion-driven confirmation bias, that is, where one particular experience leads to a permanent filtering of a class of experiences, is having emotions that are relatively labile, or subject to change. Rather than compromising rationality, it improves plasticity in the stability/plasticity trade-off, which is an epistemic virtue in a dynamic and changing environment of the sort we inhabit, though perhaps not one in a static environment. (Some gradient-descent neural network models of learning implement plasticity by introducing a percentage of randomness into the network's learning algorithms, thus preventing the network from getting stuck in a local minimum on its way to a better solution. See Evers 2000, p. 215.) Nevertheless, a systematic bias against bad experiences has its evolutionary advantages for cognizing agents. Being risk averse is epistemically useful as a generic strategy in that it means we live to learn another day. It is therefore rational in this broader sense even if the result is that we favour a surgical procedure that is 80 percent successful over one that is 20 percent unsuccessful.

When somatic markers do not become conscious, this does not mean that no evaluation of a contemplated choice has been undertaken. It is just that the evaluation did not rise to consciousness, and hence did not become a feeling. While the explicit imagery related to, say, a negative outcome is generated it would not produce a perceptible body state but instead inhibit those neural circuits in the brain which mediate approach behaviours. This mechanism might well be the source for what we call intuition. As a result of inhibition of the tendency to act, chances of making a bad decision may be reduced, as we noted above in our example. Such inhibition might well buy time for conscious deliberation and possibly making a more appropriate decision or avoiding a negative one altogether. It is in this sense that somatic markers are said to bias cognitive processes of decision-making. Indeed, it is this very biasing function of somatic markers, it is claimed, that makes decision-making possible at all.

The most telling experimental support for the SMH, and the most often cited study, is the *Iowa Gambling Task* (IGT) (Damasio et al. 1991; Bechara et al. 2000; Bechara 2004; Bechara and Damasio 2005). Administered to a group of *normals* and a group of brain-impaired subjects, this task required subjects to choose between four decks of cards that either yield high immediate gains but result in future loss, or that yield modest immediate gains and result in lower long-term loss. The details of the task need not concern us here (for a fuller description see Bechara 2004, p. 31), but the point of this exercise was to test the decision-making abilities of both groups. When compared with *normals* subjects with lesions in the VMPFC did not avoid choosing the bad deck, indeed they preferred it, even after they had figured out what the bad deck was. In other words, they continued to make decisions that were not to their long-term advantage. This behaviour pattern was also characteristic in their ordinary lives in relation to personal and social matters where it is normally not possible to calculate exact future outcomes, and where we have to make decisions based on hunches and guesses. Further support for this result was gained by administering a psychophysiological measure while patients made decisions during the task in order to ascertain their skin conductance response (SCR); for example, did they get sweaty palms, or not? Interestingly, after learning how the task works, *normals* began to generate SCRs *before* they were contemplating from which deck to choose, with more pronounced SCRs evident when selecting risky cards. In stark contrast, no SCRs were generated by the VMPFC group before picking up any card. These outcomes were seen to provide strong support for the claim the somatic marker hypothesis postulates, i.e., that decision-making is guided by emotional signals, generated in the anticipation of future events. (For a contemporary application of the SMH to investment choices see Cantarella et al. 2018.)

As we noted earlier, the SMH is controversial and has given rise to considerable debate (e.g. Maia and McClelland 2004; Dunn et al. 2005; Quartz 2009; Quartz and Sejnowski 2002). There is no scope in this chapter to engage in any of the complex discussions, but there seems little disagreement regarding the general claim that not only do emotions influence decision-making, but that this influence is essential for the rationality of decision-making. What is contested particularly though is the further claim that *normals* choose advantageously before being consciously aware of the advantage of one pair of decks over the other (e.g. Maia and McClelland 2004). Of what consequence these criticisms are remains to be seen. It is, however, noteworthy that Thagard (2006, Ch. 6) has not only provided support for the SMH but has also developed a neuro–computational model of SMH that extends Damasio's earlier findings by adding two new dimensions missing from Damasio's earlier work, that of time and context. This is a remarkable development that we can only note in the present context.

## Emotional decision-making

In the previous sections we have endeavoured to show that the knowledge we gain from (affective) neuroscience helps us understand what enables the human organism to select from an infinite array of goals and options that which seems most advantageous. We learn that when faced with a range of often conflicting and ill-defined choices our hunches or gut feels, our sweaty palms or increased heart rates, are indications of covert decision processes our brains and bodies generate from past experience. Tempting though it is, we must not conclude from this that we should simply 'trust our gut', but rather that we should treat our hunches or other bodily manifestations as instances of an early warning system to reconsider planned action (e.g. Bonabeau 2003). If the SMH is generally correct, then emotion in our decision-making is part and parcel of our biological make-up, whether we become conscious of this or not. If so, the task of figuring out how to make good decisions shifts to developing models of thought that are holistic and include values and emotion in both our substantive theories of the world and shape our epistemic processes for improving those theories. (The semantic pointer architecture discussed in Chapter 8 is an example of an integrative, computational, model of the mechanisms of thought.)

Part of theorizing about the consequences of incorporating emotion into our understanding of rational decision-making is seeing how the distinction between descriptive accounts of rationality and normative accounts can be made mutually supporting. The strategy is to focus not so much on cognitive illusions and other less systematic manifestations of human irrationality for which it is easy to pit emotion against reason, but to combine the most powerful descriptive accounts of human cognition, which now include emotion, with the fact that this cognition also very often yields normatively very good decisions.

So, given what we have learnt about the fundamentally emotional nature of deciding anything, the task now becomes one of determining how adequately to theorize of how we go about making good decisions that properly incorporate our emotions or intuition and are rational at the same time. In other words, it is not sufficient just to decide on the basis of a hunch or an intuition, especially when serious matters like educational options are at stake (rather than choosing between brands of chocolates, for example); hunches can lead you astray badly. On the other hand, decision-making by calculation does not attend to the things that really matter to us. Therefore, it is important to find a way that accommodates both our emotions and design overtly rational procedures that allow us consciously to rank order options.

A useful way of approaching this is to return to the idea that decision-making can best be considered as a task that has to satisfy different multiple constraints. This idea, (e.g. Thagard and Millgram 1997; Thagard and Verbeurgt 1998, 2000; Thagard 2001) assumes that people come to their decisions by considering various often competing goals and actions, and rank order them in light of some accepted goals. Rational decision-making consists in making decisions that cohere best with our current objectives and goals; that is, they satisfy the most constraints we are aware of. For example, you really want to watch a favourite TV show, but you also have to finish marking a number of student papers that are due tomorrow. You cannot easily accomplish both goals since enjoyment of the program and the accomplishment of your professional responsibilities, plus satisfying your professional ethos of marking papers on time, are not consistent with one another. In this instance you may apply a 'decision rule' that means you make an 'inference to the best plan', as Thagard and Millgram put it (1997). In other words, you engage in a holistic assessment of what is important to you.

In real life, unlike the classical decision theoretic approaches that presume a fixed ultimate goal, and also unlike Simon's more moderate approach, we always have many conflicting goals simultaneously, and deciding between them is not a straightforward linear calculation, as nicely illustrated in the anecdote about the philosopher and his decision theory friend. But by what procedure is it possible to make an inference to the best plan, and what is an inference here? Simply put, you opt for that interpretation or action that coheres best with all your other beliefs. (See Thagard 2006, Ch. 2 for a fuller account.) That is, you make a judgment of what fits together best regarding your goals and possible actions. The important difference between this model and the rationalist decision theories noted is that goals can and do change, they are not fixed. What is being described is a decision trajectory, a dynamical ongoing process. This feature is not unlike Dewey's conception of the means-ends relationship that remains open-ended in the light of changing circumstances, or the 'flux of experience'. Importantly, this process is not accessible to your consciousness. What is conscious is the result: the realization of which action you want to take. But there is more to coherence decision-making than accepting or rejecting certain elements. There is also what Thagard (2006) calls an *emotional valence* attached to the elements in decision-making, picking up Damasio's concept of somatic markers. In addition to accepting or rejecting certain elements, or their degree of acceptability, they are also related to one another by positive or negative valences, or 'emotional tags'. The more important our values or goals, the stronger the markers or emotional tags (Barnes and Thagard 1996). Thagard tested out these elements in a computational model based on the performance of neural nets, 'HOTCO' (Hot Coherence), and while it is not a general model of emotional cognition, it did capture the production of emotional decisions, similar to how the human brain would do this.

Although this model of emotional coherence is psychologically more realistic, it also harbors a danger, in fact the same danger that attaches to making decisions simply on the basis of a hunch. Given that our emotional choices are hidden from consciousness, our intuitions may be stuck on what we like best or crave most, and what we like best might prevent us (that is, the circuitry of our neural nets and body loops) from considering a range of other goals and actions. So how can we counterbalance what we earlier called confirmation bias? Putting the question positively: how can we tutor our intuitions? There is no foolproof way, but we might follow the procedure Thagard (2006, p. 22) proposes:

## Informed intuition

1. Set up the decision problem carefully. This requires identifying the goals to be accomplished by your decision and specifying the broad range of possible actions that might accomplish those goals.
2. Reflect on the importance of the different goals. Such a reflection will be more emotional and intuitive than just putting a numerical weight on them but should help you to be more aware of what you care about in the current decision situation. Identify goals whose importance may be exaggerated because of jonesing [strong craving] or other emotional distortions.
3. Examine beliefs about the extent to which various actions would facilitate the different goals. Are these beliefs based on good evidence? If not, revise them.
4. Make your intuitive judgment about the best action to perform, monitoring your emotional reaction to different options. Run your decision past other people to see if it seems reasonable to them.

These are, of course, modest heuristics. But they do incorporate the decision-maker's emotional reactions into the decision process in a way that is iterative, epistemically progressive, and realistic. Your intuition might become a lot more informed as a result.

## Conclusion

What we have sketched here is far from a comprehensive theory of emotional decision-making. But what is possible on the present account is that it allows us to assess the results of unconscious evaluations, that is, beliefs about what we should do, but also a positive emotional attitude toward the action to be undertaken. What needs to be worked out in future, amongst other issues, is how this personal procedure might be applied to the kind of decision-making groups of people engage in. In the meantime, tutoring our own intuitions so that they are better informed is a considerable advance in the business of making rational choices whether applied in informal or formal contexts such as schools.

## References

Barnes, A., & Thagard, P. (1996). Emotional decisions. In G.W. Cottrell (Ed.), *Proceedings of the eighteenth annual conference of the cognitive science society* (pp. 426–429). Mahwah, NJ: Lawrence Erlbaum.

Bartol, J., & Linquist, S. (2015). How do somatic markers feature in decision making? *Emotion Review*, 7(1), 81–89 DOI: 10.1177/1754073914553000.

Bechara, A. (2004). The role of emotion in decision–making: Evidence from neurological patients with orbitofrontal damage. *Brain and Cognition*, 55, 30–40.

Bechara, A., & Damasio, A.R. (2005). The somatic marker hypothesis: A neural theory of economic decision. *Games and Economic Behavior*, 52, 336–372.

Bechara, A., Damasio, H., & Damasio, A.R. (2000). Emotion, decision–making and the orbitofrontal cortex. *Cerebral Cortex*, 10, 295–307.

Bonabeau, E. (2003). Don't trust your gut. *Harvard Business Review*, 81(5), 116–123.

Buchanan, L., & O'Connell, A. (2006). A brief history of decision making. *Harvard Business Review*, 84(1), 32–41.

Cantarella, S., Hillenbrand, C., Aldridge–Waddon, L., & Puzzo, I. (2018). Preliminary evidence on the somatic marker hypothesis applied to investment choices. *Journal of Neuroscience, Psychology, and Economics*, 11(4), 228–238. http://dx.doi.org/10.1037/npe0000097.

Carpenter, G.A. (1989). Neural network models for pattern recognition and associative memory. *Neural Networks*, 2, 243–257. *Cited as reprinted in Carpenter and Grossberg (1991).*

Carpenter, G.A., & Grossberg, S.(Eds.) (1991). *Pattern recognition by self-organizing neural networks.* Cambridge, MA: MIT Press.

Churchland, P.M. (2007). *Neurophilosophy at work.* Cambridge, MA: Cambridge University Press.

Churchland, P.S. (2002). *Brain-wise.* Cambridge, MA: MIT Press.

Churchland, P.M., & Churchland, P.S. (1998). *On the contrary.* Cambridge, MA: MIT Press.

Clark, A. (1997). *Being there: Putting brain, body, and world together again.* Cambridge, MA: MIT Press.

Clark, A. (2001). *Mindware.* New York: Oxford University Press.

Clore, G.L., & Huntsinger, J.R. (2007). How emotions inform judgment and regulate thought. *Trends in Cognitive Sciences*, 11(9), 393–399.

Cohen, J. (1981). Can human irrationality be experimentally demonstrated? *Behavioral and Brain Sciences*, 4(3), 317–329, 359–367.

Coltheart, M. (2004). Brain imaging, connectionism, and cognitive neuropsychology. *Cognitive Neuropsychology*, 21(1), 21–25.

Damasio, A.R. (1996). *Descartes' error*. London: Macmillan.
Damasio, A.R. (1999). *The feeling of what happens*. New York: Harcourt Inc.
Damasio, A.R. (2000). A second chance for emotion. In R.D. Lane, & L. Nadel (Eds.), *Cognitive neuroscience of emotion*, New York: Oxford University Press.
Damasio, A.R. (2003). *Looking for spinoza*. New York: Harcourt Inc.
Damasio, A.R., Tranel, D., & Damasio, H. (1991). Somatic markers and the guidance of behaviour: Theory and preliminary testing. In H.S. Levin, H.M. Eisenberg, & A.L. Benton (Eds.), *Frontal lobe function and dysfunction*, New York, NY: Oxford University Press
Davidson, R.J. (2003). Seven sins in the study of emotion: Correctives from affective neuroscience. *Brain and Cognition*, 52, 129–132.
Dolan, R.J. (2002). Emotion, cognition, and behaviour. *Science*, 298(5596), 1191.
Donald, M. (1993). Précis of origins of the modern mind: Three stages in the evolution of culture and cognition. *Behavioral and Brain Sciences*, 16, 737–791.
Dunn, B.D., Dalgliesh, T., & Lawrence, A.D. (2005). The somatic marker hypothesis: A critical evaluation. *Neuroscience and Biobehavioural Reviews, xx*, 1–33.
Evers, C.W. (2000). Connectionist modelling and education. *Australian Journal of Education*, 44(3), 209–225.
Evers, C.W., & Lakomski, G. (1991). *Knowing educational administration*. Oxford: Elsevier.
Evers, C.W., & Lakomski, G. (1996). *Exploring educational administration*. Oxford: Elsevier.
Evers, C.W., & Lakomski, G. (2000). *Doing educational administration*. Oxford: Elsevier.
Gazzaniga, M.S. (2005). *The ethical brain*. New York/Washington, DC: Dana Press.
Glannon, W. (2007). *Bioethics and the brain*. Oxford: Oxford University Press.
Goldstein, W.M., & Hogarth, R.M. (Eds.) (1997). *Research on judgment and decision–making*. Cambridge: Cambridge University Press.
Heap, S.H., Hollis, M., Lyons, B., Sugden, R., & Weale, A. (1992). *The theory of social choice: A critical guide*. Oxford: Blackwell.
Hodgkinson, C. (1978). *Towards a philosophy of administration*. Oxford: Blackwell.
Hoy, W.K., & Miskel, C.G. (2008). *Educational administration: Theory, research, and practice*. 8th edition. New York: McGraw-Hill.
Hoy, W.K., & Miskel, C.G. (2013). *Educational administration: Theory, research, and practice*. 9th edition. New York: McGraw-Hill.
Hoy, W.K., & Tarter, C.J. (1995). *Administrators solving the problems of practice: Decision-making concepts, cases, and consequences*. Boston: Allyn and Bacon.
Illes, J., & Raffin, T.A. (2002). Neuroethics: An emerging new discipline in the study of brain and cognition. *Brain and Cognition*, 50, 341–344.
Kahneman, D., Slovic, P., & Tversky, A. (Eds.) (1999). *Judgment under uncertainty: Heuristics and biases*. Cambridge: Cambridge University Press.
Lakomski, G. (2005). *Managing without leadership*. Oxford: Elsevier.
Lane, R.D., & Nadel, L. (Eds.) (2000). *Cognitive neuroscience of emotion*. New York: Oxford University Press.
LeDoux, J. (1996). *The emotional brain*. New York: Simon & Schuster Paperbacks.
Linquist, S., & Bartol, J. (2013). Two myths about somatic markers. *The British Journal for the Philosophy of Science*, 64(3), 455–484.
Maia, T.V., & McClelland, J.L. (2004). A reexamination of the evidence for the somatic marker hypothesis: What participants really know in the Iowa gambling task. *Proceedings of the National Association of Sciences of the USA (PNAS)*, 101(45), 16075–16080.
Minsky, M. (2006). *The emotion machine*. New York: Simon & Schuster Paperbacks.
Montague, R. (2006). *Your brain is (almost) perfect: How we make decisions*. New York: Penguin.
Morse, G. (2006). Decisions and desire. *Harvard Business Review*, 84(1), 42–51.

Newell, A., & Simon, H.A. (1972). *Human problem solving*. New York: Prentice Hall.
Newell, A., Rosenbloom, P.S., & Laird, J.E. (1996). Symbolic architectures for cognition. In M.I. Posner (Ed.), *Foundations of cognitive science*, Cambridge, MA: MIT Press
Oaksford, M., & Chater, N. (2007). *Bayesian rationality*. Oxford: Oxford University Press.
Ochsner, K.N., & Phelps, E. (2007). Emerging perspectives on emotion–cognition interactions. *Trends in Cognitive Sciences*, 11(8), 317–318.
Pessoa, L. (2012). Beyond brain regions: Network perspective of cognition–emotion interactions. *Behavioral and Brain Sciences*, 35, 158–159.
Popper, K.R. (1959). *The logic of scientific discovery*. London: Hutchison.
Quartz, S.R. (2009). Reason, emotion and decision–making: Risk and reward computation with feeling. *Trends in Cognitive Sciences*, 13(5), 209–215.
Quartz, S.R., & Sejnowski, T.J. (2002). *Liars, lovers, and heroes*. New York, NY: HarperCollins.
Restak, R. (1984). *The brain*. Toronto, New York: Bantam Books.
Sanfey, A.G., & Cohen, J.D. (2004). Is knowing always feeling? *Proceedings of the National Association of Sciences of the USA (PNAS)*, 101(48), 16709–16710.
Shapiro, J.P., & Stefkovich, J.A. (2005). *Ethical leadership and decision making in education: Applying theoretical perspectives to complex dilemmas*. 2nd edition. Mahwah, NJ: Lawrence Erlbaum.
Simon, A. (1990). Invariants of human behaviour. *Annual Review of Psychology*, 41, 1–19.
Simon, A. (1976). *Administrative behavior*. Third edition. New York, NY: The Free Press,
Thagard, P. (2000). *Coherence in thought and action*. Cambridge, MA: MIT Press.
Thagard, P. (2001). How to make decisions: Coherence, emotion, and practical inference. In E. Millgram (Ed.), *Varieties of practical inference*, Cambridge, MA: MIT Press.
Thagard, P. (2006). *Hot thought*. Cambridge, MA: MIT Press.
Thagard, P., & Verbeurgt, K. (1998). Coherence as constraint satisfaction. *Cognitive Science*, 22, 1–24.
Thagard, P., & Millgram, E. (1997). Inference to the best plan: A coherence theory of decision. http://cogsci.uwaterloo.ca/Articles/Pages?Inference.Plan.html
TenHouten, W.D. (2016). Embodied feeling and reason in decision-making: Assessing the somatic-marker hypothesis. *Revista Latinoamericana de Estudios sobre Cuerpos, Emociones y Sociedad*, 20(8), 87–97.
Tversky, A., & Kahneman, D. (1999). Judgment under uncertainty: Heuristics and biases. In D. Kahneman, P. Slovic, & A. Tversky (Eds.), *Judgment under uncertainty: Heuristics and biases*, Cambridge: Cambridge University Press.

# 10
# A NATURALISTIC VIEW OF ORGANIZATIONS

## Introduction

The study of organizations as a discipline, as opposed to the study of an individual organization such as a hospital or school is a relatively recent phenomenon that emerged within the discipline of sociology in the late 1940s (e.g., Perrow 1973; Scott 1998). Its significance was signalled by the founding of a new journal, the *Administrative Science Quarterly*, in 1956, which has remained a flagship of organization and administrative studies ever since. Its first edition contained what might be called the sociological manifesto of organization studies in a two-part series by Talcott Parsons (1956a, 1956b). At the same time the study of organizations also developed as a multi/interdisciplinary inquiry, through the (then) Carnegie Institute of Technology associated with the work of Simon (1947), March and Simon (1958), and Cyert and March (1963). The importance of this development was that organizations were to be studied "at the level of *theoretical abstraction* sufficiently general to call attention to similarities in form and function across different areas of activity … [and] encourage[d] *empirical investigation*". (Scott 1998, p. 9). In a society characterized by increasing specialization, so Parsons (1956b, p. 225) argued, "… the development of organizations is the principal mechanism by which, in a highly differentiated society, it is possible to 'get things done' …" A less sociologically tinted definition that is generally accepted by contemporary organization theorists is of organizations "as *social structures created by individuals to support the collaborative pursuit of specific goals*" (Scott 1998, p. 10. Emphases in text).

There are many differences between organizations as well as common characteristics. In this chapter we concentrate on one central issue in organization theory: the conceptualization of the relationship between environment and organization, which ranges from considering the environment as external and insignificant, to the view that organizations have permeable boundaries, and thus make the environment a significant concern not only for organizational functioning but for the very definition of organization itself. How to conceive of the environment, and thus of organization, is a debate in organization theory that continues and is unresolved (e.g., Meyer and Scott 1992.)

In this chapter we offer a solution that presents a unified account in which both 'organization' and 'environment' are conceived of as interconnected parts of a broader, culture-based cognitive system. The argument we pursue here is a continuation and extension of the theory of distributed cognition as presented in Chapter 3. As a consequence of the broadening of cognition from skull- and skin-bound to distributed, we argued that the tension between leader cognition and context dissolves. Similarly, just as leader cognition is part of a wider cognitive system, so are organizations as social-cultural collectivities that are not only characterized by the standard division of labour but, fundamentally, by the distribution of cognitive labour. While in Chapter 3 the emphasis is on the individual extended mind, in this chapter we consider what is, so to speak, on the other side of the skull/skin divide, that is, the role of external representations – symbolic, non-symbolic, artifactual and natural – in relation to onboard cognition. Specifically, the argument is that external representations are not only helpful but necessary scaffolds that not only support limited memory and computation but facilitate vastly extended cognition, of which 'organization' and 'organizations' are the external and durable manifestations.

The development of this argument requires a number of steps. In the first section, we explain how organization theory conceived of organizations and their environment, including social organizations such as schools. Given that the theoretical framework for organization studies is that of General Systems Theory including both closed and open perspectives, we raise some epistemological problems in section two for why a systems perspective has no explanatory value to determine where 'organization' ends and 'environment' begins, leaving that determination to subjective assessment. In section three we outline how the environment/organization nexus was substantially refashioned by the original and brilliant work of Simon (1947, 1955, 1956) and Newell and Simon (1972), based on the conception of *bounded rationality* that provided a specific answer as to how organization and environment were integrally linked through the cognitive abilities of the decision-maker. In Section four we expand Newell and Simon's conceptualization of task environment that while analytically brilliant is too narrow and introduce the wider notion of *environment as activity space* supported by the theory of distributed cognition (Kirsh 1999). We explain what role external representations and memory play for everyday problem-solving in terms of scaffolding and anchoring conceptual structure. Finally, in Section five, we make some comment regarding the challenges organizations such as schools face regarding their very nature and design, as well as that of leaders, when considered as thoroughly distributed cognitive systems.

## Organizations and environment

The nexus between organizations and environment was initially framed by the functionalist (orthodox) perspective of organization theory that saw organizations either as machines or as organisms, or a combination (e.g., Selznick 1948; March and Simon 1958; Katz and Kahn 1966; Lawrence and Lorsch 1967; Perrow 1973; Egri and Pinfield 1997, p. 471; Scott 1998; Morgan 2006). Organizations (without environment) were seen as ubiquitous (Simon 1991) and as the most important focal point for analysis, a perspective described as 'orgocentric' (Egri and Pinfield 1997, p. 471). 'Environment' was generally and generically understood as everything that happens 'outside' of an organization, as 'all phenomena that are external to and potentially or actually affect the form or size of a community's [organization's] populations' (Bidwell and Kasarda 1985, p. 224.)

In the case of the organization-as-machine metaphor, the environment had no role to play as the organization was seen as a rational entity able to accomplish its internal objectives, including managing change or adjustment limited to internal routines or processes much like the way the internal workings of a machine could be fixed. Where organizations were seen as an organism (in the functionalist approach), attention was paid to the organization's environment by acknowledging an interdependent relationship insofar as the organization's survival was threatened.

The lack of attention to, or concern for, the role of environment in orthodox organization theory was based on the assumption of a closed boundary between organization and environment, so that the environment was seen as immutable having no effect on the organization's goals and objectives. The formal organization in this perspective is in Selznick's (1948, p. 25) admirably parsimonious phrase, "the structural expression of rational action" whose main features are rational planning and design".

The view of organizations as closed, rational systems was for a while also prominent in educational administration theory, where the idea of the school as a closed system was initially presented by Bidwell (1965) but later revised (Bidwell 1979). More recently still, Bidwell (2001, pp. 103–104) remarks that by the time his (1965) article had appeared, the theoretical climate had begun to change markedly, largely attributable no doubt to the influence of Simon's notion of bounded rationality that led to "envisioning a permeable organizational boundary and discovering that limitations of the human mind set limits to rational planning and decision making".

Reflected in Bidwell's views is the organization theory perspective that conceptualized organizations as grounded in General Systems Theory (von Bertalanffy 1950; Scott 1961, 1972; Kast and Rosenzweig 1972) that defines both closed and open systems. According to von Bertalanffy (1950, p. 155), "... a system [is] closed if no materials enter or leave it. It is open if there is inflow and outflow, and therefore change of the component materials". The main characteristic of a general system is that it consists of interrelated objects, events, and attributes – as the phrase goes, everything is related to everything else – and this is true of mechanical, biological, and social systems. It follows that all living systems are (by definition) open and schools as social organizations fit the bill. (Kast and Rosenzweig 1972, p. 450, provide a helpful summary of key system concepts.) The best-known, prominent, advocates in educational administration are Hoy and Miskel whose landmark text *Educational Administration: Theory, Research, and Practice* has appeared in its ninth edition (2013). Hoy recently (2019, p. 1) reiterated his commitment to the open systems view in all relevant characteristic features.

For present purposes, the most important result of the shift from a closed to an open system perspective is the fact that 'environment' had become an important explanatory variable in accounting for organizational functioning and survival. Organizations could no longer be studied in isolation from their environments. This point was made especially by Emery and Trist (1965) whose work is credited with having set the agenda for subsequent conceptualizations of organizational environments (Egri and Pinfield 1997, p. 471). Not only are organizations closely interrelated with their environments, but also they argued, organizational environments have a 'causal texture', a concept borrowed from Tolman and Brunswick (1935).

Although they accept von Bertalanffy's general systems perspective, Emery and Trist (1965, p. 22) point out that the stipulated exchange processes characteristic of open systems between organism/organization and environment have been left unspecified. Specifically, "it does not deal at all with those processes in the environment itself which are among the determining conditions of the exchanges. To analyse these an additional concept is needed – *the causal texture of the environment'*–." (p. 22). By this they mean that organizational environments are changing towards greater complexity, driven by technological advances, and it is therefore important to consider the former's characteristics *in their own right*. In brief, the 'causal texture' of organizational environments consists of transactional dependencies among organizations, primarily from the perspective of a focal organization, the 'first-order' environment, and the 'second-order' environment which comprises relationships between all other organizations and with the focal organization.

While Emery and Trist have drawn attention to the importance of researching organizational environments as fundamental aspects of organizational functioning and survival, the "conceptual map of the causal linkages" is, however, no more than a map *between organizations* where environment has no independent role to play and is in fact identical with organizations. The nature of linkages – *de facto* between organizations – and what causality might consist in is not further defined or explained.

Conceptualizing environments independent of organizations has not been a significant development in organization theory, but Scott (1998, Ch. 6) proposed to analyse levels of environments such as, for example, organization sets and organizational populations, and characteristics of environments such as institutional and technical environments (for discussion see Freeman 1978; Meyer and Scott 1992; Scott 1998, Ch. 8 provides a good overview of main perspectives). However, despite these attempts at further specifications, underlying conceptualizations of organizational environments is the key notion of permeable boundaries between organizations and environments, and therefore the theoretical and empirical problem of determining where to do draw the line between them.

## Epistemological problems

The roots of these difficulties are enshrined in von Bertalanffy's (1950) original conception of General Systems Theory which he developed as a practicing biologist and conceived of as "a logico-mathematical field whose task is the formulation and derivation of those general principles that are applicable to 'systems' in general." (Bertalanffy 1972, p. 411). A system is defined as "a set of elements standing in interrelation among themselves and with the environment". (p. 417.) Bertalanffy (1972, p. 421) acknowledges that it is far from easy to define and describe what counts as a system, and the way he states the issue makes clear what the fundamental epistemological problem is in attempting to define 'system': "It will be readily agreed that a galaxy, a dog, a cell, and an atom are 'systems'. But in what sense and what respects can we speak of an animal or human society, personality, language, mathematics, and so forth as 'systems'"?

The answer he does provide is insufficient to settle the matter of what a 'system' is, how to demarcate one from another, and subsequently, how to determine an 'environment': "Ultimately, all boundaries are dynamic rather than spatial … [and] the distinction between 'real' objects and systems as given in observation and 'conceptual' constructs and systems cannot be drawn in any common-sense way." (Bertalanffy 1972, p. 422). Eschewing the epistemology of logical positivism and empiricism, Bertalanffy argues for "the investigation of organized wholes of many variables [which] requires new categories of interaction, transaction, organization, teleology, and so forth, with many problems arising for epistemology, mathematical models and techniques". (p. 423). Truth or reality in his view is established in the interaction between knower and known and depends "on a multiplicity of factors of a biological, psychological, cultural, and linguistic nature". All of this leads him to affirm a scientific attitude, but to consider science as only one 'perspective' amongst others.

The elaborate and ambitious theoretical framework of General Systems Theory in its open system expression fails for a number of reasons. Most importantly, it fails to provide a specification of what a system is. Having stated that we commonsensically 'know' a system when we see one, anything and everything can count as a system if we name it as such. Given the vagueness of the system definition that does not specify the nature of the relations in question, the notion of system is trivial as any collection of objects can in principle be related. We can always specify similarities based on our point of view, and system determination is therefore a subjective matter. (For critical discussion see Phillips 1969; Evers and Lakomski 1991, pp. 60–73, 1996, pp. 43–55, 2012).

The fundamental epistemological problem is that in order to identify a galaxy or a dog as a 'system' we must already know what either is in order to identify it and to see it as a 'whole'. How do we know this? The specifications of the relations in question pertaining to 'galaxy' and 'dog' have already been established by the concepts and theories of the relevant sciences of physics and evolutionary and biological theory, reflecting our claim in Chapter 4 that theory precedes classification. Whatever plausibility systems theory has in fact depends on the background theories that provide the classification schemas for either entity. The problem with general and open systems theory is thus not that it is too abstract, but that it is vacuous. The explanatory heavy lifting is done by the relevant sciences that provide the substance of whatever 'system' is being discussed. When it comes to illuminating the 'organized complexity' of real organizations in the open systems perspective, the theoretical burden is carried by the social and behavioural sciences. For example, early adopters such as Katz and Kahn (1966, p. 31) counselled paying attention to "the essential social–psychological facts of the highly variable, loosely articulated character of social systems". The 'cement' which holds these contrived systems together, they observe, "is essentially psychological rather than biological. Social systems are anchored in the attitudes, perceptions, beliefs, motivations, habits, and expectations of human beings". (Katz and Kahn 1966, p. 33). Their work, as one of the most prominent examples of the open systems view of organizations and environments, shows clearly that the language and concepts of social psychology have replaced those of physics and mathematics, characteristic of the closed view (also Katz and Kahn 1983).

Our particular concern here is not a general examination of the success or otherwise of the open systems perspective in organization theory, but to draw attention to the difficulties in accounting for the nature of environment/s, largely driven by the basic theoretical assumptions of open systems theory that stipulates the permeability of boundaries. Organization theorists have addressed the issue of what is an organizational environment in different ways, variously drawing on social, economic, institutional, ecological, and political concepts and theories to deal with the boundary issue. But in the absence of clear specification of what a system is and the nature of its internal relations, the distinction between different systems as well as environments, and what 'environment' is independent of organization, is analytically impossible to draw, empirically indeterminate and epistemologically subjective. The general point to make is that General Systems Theory is an empty shell, parasitic on the explanatory powers of whatever theories are drawn on to illuminate whatever individual organization theorists believe is the most relevant approach in their view.

While commentators such as Kast and Rosenzweig (1972, p. 459) believe that General Systems Theory "emphasizes a very high level of abstraction" they contend that it nevertheless provides a new paradigm for the study of organizations (and their environments). A less sanguine assessment comes from Herbert Simon

(1962, p. 482) in his discussion of "The architecture of complexity" where he notes that systems theory's popularity "is more a response to a pressing need for synthesizing and analyzing complexity than it is to any large development of a body of knowledge and technique for dealing with complexity. If this popularity is to be more than a fad, necessity will have to mother invention and provide substance to go with the name". (For further discussions of Simon's views regarding General Systems Theory see Agre 2003.) Simon proposes a different, and subsequently highly influential solution, as we discuss in the following sections.

## From environment to task environment

Simon's answer to dealing with complexity and uncertainty, more formally developed later with Allen Newell (e.g., Newell and Simon 1963, 1972, 1990), departs significantly from the solutions offered by other (organizational) systems theorists and is grounded first and foremost in his conception of human cognition as bounded, and what affordances the environment makes available by cognition so defined. We first consider Simon's notion of bounded rationality, how he conceptualizes 'environment', and importantly, the relation between the two.

While Simon shared with other organization theorists the concern over environmental complexity and uncertainty, as a cognitive psychologist, he (also March and Simon 1958) suggested heuristics and organizational routines as appropriate means to deal with complex environments because these methods permit simplification in the decision-making process. Reacting in part against the then prevailing view of 'economic man' (Simon 1955, 1956) whose decision-making was deemed optimally rational or 'Olympian' (Simon 1983), Simon argued as early as in *Administrative Behavior* (1947) that while rational decision-making was indeed the central part of administrative theory and core concern of 'administrative man', the (economic) concept of rationality was in dire need of revision: "Broadly stated, the task is to replace the global rationality of economic man with a kind of rational behavior that is compatible with the access to information and the computational capacities that are actually possessed by organisms, including man, in the kinds of environments in which such organisms exist" (Simon 1955, p. 99; for a helpful discussion on heuristics and satisficing, see Richardson 2006, Ch. 44).

Rational behaviour thus delimited, however, poses serious challenges for the individual decision-maker precisely because "… of the psychological limits of the organism (particularly with respect to computational and predictive ability)". (Simon 1955, p. 101). As a consequence, it is impossible for the decision-maker "…to reach any high degree of rationality. The number of alternatives he must explore is too great, the information he would need to evaluate them so vast that even an approximation to objective rationality is hard to conceive. Individual choice takes place in an environment of 'givens' – premises that are accepted by the subject as bases for his choice; and behaviour is adaptive only within the limits set by these 'givens'" (Simon 1947/1976, p. 79; for discussion see Agre and Horswill 1997).

Of critical importance in Simon's (1947/1976, 1955, 1956) and Newell and Simon's (1972) account of organizational/administrative problem-solving is that the major constraints the environment sets on decision-making are those of information which the decision-maker has to make sense of in order to accomplish the organization's goals. The decision-maker as a human organism in the Simon/March/Newell model is characterized as "a complex information-processing system" (March and Simon 1958, p. 9) or IPS, a conception of cognition that is at the core of the *Physical Symbol System Hypothesis* (PSSH) formally developed by Newell and Simon (1972). According to cognition thus defined, the operation of minds could then be likened to those of serial computers; rational thinking is symbol manipulation, and it is the symbol processing inside the mind/computer that matters. (For discussion of the influence of classical AI and modern cognitive science on educational administration see Evers and Lakomski 2020.)

Implicit in the preceding comments of problem-solving or task execution is the notion of 'environment' that now needs to be specified. The central concept here is what Simon describes as *task environment*, an original and brilliant proposal that both narrows and specifies the focus regarding what needs attending to in an organization's environment. In Simon's early work (e.g., Simon 1956; Newell and Simon 1963), 'environment' is formally defined as a set of choices it sets for an agent to solve a problem, such as finding food for a simple organism that has a single need. *Task environment* specifically:

> ... refers to an environment coupled with a goal, problem, or task – the one for which the motivation of the subject is assumed. It is the task that defines a point of view about an environment, and that, in fact, allows an environment to be delimited. Also ... we shall often distinguish the two aspects of the theory of problem solving as (1) demands of the task environment and (2) psychology of the subject. .... The two are in fact like figure and ground – although which is which depends on the momentary viewpoint.
> *(Newell and Simon 1972, p. 55)*

What makes an environment a *task* environment is delimited in the way that the agent constructs an internal representation of the task, that is, s/he constructs a problem space in her mind. It is the interrelationship between the internally constructed problem space and goal, and the agent's representation of the goal to the goal itself that is essential for the task environment because it allows the task relevant to be sorted from the task irrelevant (Lakomski 2005, p. 109; Kirsh 2009). While playing chess, for example, it would not matter whether the pieces are made of timber or displayed on a computer screen, whether I am a novice or an experienced chess player. The rules of the game, the order of moves, etc. are fixed, that is, the problem is well defined, and if there is a discrepancy in player capacity, players may just face different task environments (Kirsh 2009).

*Task environment* and *problem space* are abstract and formally elegant constructions, designed to present within cognitive psychology a methodological solution, that is, computational approach to problem-solving that was deemed applicable to *all* problem-solving.

The Simon-Newell model was relatively successful when it was applied to domains characterized by well-structured problems, such as the Power of Hanoi puzzle or games, but the attempt to extend their cognitive architecture to domains where problems are mostly ill-defined/structured, such as we encounter in everyday life, did not meet with much success. This was indeed recognized as a serious but solvable problem by Newell et al. (1996). (See Churchland 2007, Chs. 1 and 2, for why this problem is fatal.) Simon (1990, p. 4) correctly noted that there is little knowledge of "how the symbol processing capabilities of the human brain are realized physiologically. Information processing psychology explains the software of thinking but says only a little about its 'hardware' (or 'wetware'?)". At the time of this statement, however, these questions were already being addressed driven by advances in the 'new' connectionist cognitive science that developed mathematical models for artificial neural nets or parallel distributed processing (PDP) (Rumelhart and McClelland 1986a, 1986b). The advantage of these models was that they had the ability to model learning through pattern detection in the data, something that was not possible in the symbol-processing model of serial computing (Evers 2000, 1998, 1990; Elman 2006; Evers and Lakomski 2020; for broader critical discussion of the symbol processing view, see Dreyfus and Dreyfus 1988, p. 1994; Clark 2001, Ch. 2; Churchland and Senjowski 1994; Evers and Lakomski 2000, Ch. 3; Shanahan 2016).

Underlying the shift to 'brain-style' computation (Rumelhart 1993) was the realization that the differences between brain-as-computer and biological brain mattered, and that improved neuroscientific knowledge of the 'wetware' replaced the idea of the primacy of symbol processing with a more detailed understanding of neuronal pattern recognition and activation which could accommodate the importance of symbol processing. In everyday life, people do not solve problems according to the formal structure of the symbol-processing hypothesis and the narrow definition of task environment and problem space. Real-life problem-solving is not a matter of search in a narrowly defined problem space, constructed entirely in the agent's head and solved before any engagement with the world. Rather, as abstractions, the conceptions of task environment and problem space have artificially shrunk the external world to fit the former's specifications (see Hutchins 1996, Ch. 9, for an original account of how symbols got into the head in the first place). As we know, everyday problem-solving is far messier in that we usually need to determine first what the problem is, and this might change with changing circumstances, and we might identify the wrong problem to solve. Determining what the problem is and then going about solving it are separated in Simon's model, but this is not so in real life. Problem-solving, rather, is interactive, in that we rely on resources including other agents and cultural elements, all of which help understand the nature of the problem, what the constraints are, how big the problem is, and what options we have available. Also, we need to be able to determine whether or not we are getting to a solution.

Of importance for the present argument is to emphasize that once the 'real world' of cultural products, scaffolds, and artifacts is 'let back in' and acknowledged as the proper arena in which problem-solving takes place, it is evident that *task environment* and *problem space* are not only intimately connected but also considerably broader and more complex than supposed in the Newell/Simon proposal. An important consequence for the study of how humans think, solve problems, and organize, is that it can now draw on the empirical and theoretical resources of a whole array of sciences, including cognitive anthropology and archeology, and most recently, cultural neuroscience. While the strong coupling of agent and environment in terms of the agent creating her own problem spaces, and the fundamental insight of bounded rationality were important, it's just that Newell/Simon assumed an un-natural view of human cognition that expunged or 'redacted' the real world. Ironically, human cognition is indeed limited, but the source of that limitation is not where Simon looked for it. It could be said that he misdiagnosed the problem of cognition, and subsequently suggested the wrong remedy.

In the next section we consider some specific features in the world that are not simply aids to think with, but are 'cognitive' in their own right, and thus properly belong to what Hutchins (2014) calls the cultural ecosystem of human cognition. This is a further exploration of the biological fact that humans have limited computational and memory capacities, and how they rely on cultural manifestations such as structures, artefacts, and symbols as externalizations and extensions of minds.

## From task environment to activity space and thinking with things

Everyday decision-making in the cultural environments in which we live is rarely straightforward because the problems that need solving are often ill-defined and fundamentally depend on the resources afforded in the specific environments in which they are located. Here, it is useful to think of environment as *activity space*, following Kirsh (2000). Physical, as well as virtual spaces count as activity space that is "populated with resources, tools and constraints in which the agent operates. The reason the same physical space can support multiple environments or activity spaces is that the way an agent projects meaning onto a space partly *constitutes* it". (Kirsh 2000, p. 37).

What such activity space and problem-solving looks like is described in an empirical study by Tyre and von Hippel (1997) that details the transfer of new production equipment from laboratory to factory sites. Similar to Hutchins' (1996) cognitive ethnography of pilotage, Tyre and von Hippel (1997) describe what agents actually did while attempting to solve the problems encountered in the introduction of new production machines into two different factory sites (Lakomski 2008; also see Julian Orr 1996 ethnography of copier repair technicians). The authors focussed explicitly on the complexities of many situational features as they arose between multiple locations and agents, agents and agents, and objects and agents, which together made it possible to implement the new technology. More specifically, it was the successful *coordination* of the complex resources and constraints in separate physical environments that led to successful implementation. Although they did not employ the theory of distributed cognition, locating their work in the situated learning perspective (e.g., Resnick et al. 1991; Salomon 1997), Tyre and von Hippel's study demonstrates just how dynamic and interwoven the interaction is between what particular environments/activity spaces afford and the knowledge in agents' heads.

Activity spaces and the emergence of solutions via coordination in distributed cognitive systems is possible for one fundamental reason. The fact that brains are limited in terms of memory and computational capacities, requiring 'off-loading' to ease cognitive load, is well known. However, such easing of cognitive load is only part of the reason for making use of the environment, that is, the states, structures, and processes that exist outside the brain/body. As Sapolsky (2018, p. 49) explains, any time the frontal cortex has to work hard it expends a lot of energy and "has an extremely high metabolic rate and rates of activation of genes related to energy production". In this sense, frontal cortical neurons are expensive. When the frontal cortex gets overloaded when we have to make too many decisions all at once, our task performance declines immediately afterwards (Sapolsky 2018, p. 49). Generally, cognitive processes are carried out where it is less costly and requires less energy to perform them. For example, when a mathematical problem becomes too complex to solve in the head, a calculator, abacus, or pencil and paper do the job more easily and efficiently. Interacting with those external structures makes processing more efficient and effective than processing 'in the head' alone, where efficiency means speed accuracy, and effectiveness the ability to cope with harder problems (Kirsh 2010, p. 443), skills that would have been evolutionarily advantageous. So, changing "the terrain of cognition" not only changes the cost structure but also makes possible:

> a) access to new operators— you can do something outside that you cannot inside; b) you can encode structures of greater complexity than you can inside, external mechanisms allow us to bootstrap to new ideas and new ways of manipulating ideas; or, c) you can run a process with greater precision, faster, and longer outside than inside—you can harness the world to simulate processes that you cannot simulate internally or cannot simulate as well.
> *(Kirsh 2010, p. 442; Clark 2008)*

Here, it is useful to be reminded of what in the present context is meant by 'external representations'. Zhang (1997, p. 180) defines them "as the knowledge and structure in the environment, as physical symbols, objects, or dimensions (e.g., written symbols, beads of abacuses, dimensions of a graph, etc.), and as external rules, constraints, or relations embedded in physical configurations (e.g., spatial relations of written digits, visual and spatial layouts of diagrams, physical constraints in abacuses, etc.)".

Importantly, external representations, unlike things in the mind, can extend both in space and in time. We can manipulate them in many different ways, share them with other people, and apply tools to them. The role of external representations as "indispensable parts of cognition" (Zhang 1993, p. 775) has its roots in the evolution of the modern brain (see Dunbar 2017). According to Donald (1991, 1993), the emergence of new representational systems in the evolution of cognition made possible symbolic storage (via written language), and it is this third and most important stage that has made us into the modern, cultural cognizers we are.

But it is not just that external representations afford external memory that allows retrieval of experiences, as Donald (1991) pointed out. The interrelationship of our thinking processes with cognitive artifacts is *interactive* and goes back to the basic human need to associate conceptual structure with material structure. This relation is fundamental to cognitive life because conceptual structure needs to be anchored to something so that it is stable as well as constrained, and therefore publicly available. Hutchins' (2005, p. 1555) concept of *material anchors* encapsulates this relation. Such anchoring can take place in two ways which Hutchins (2005) combines: (1) conceptual structures are stabilized in cultural models that are created by inter- and intra-personal processes; and (2) such conceptual/cultural models or structures can be stabilized by associating them with material structure. When we "think with things" (Hutchins 2010a), that is, cognitive artifacts, we usually think in social contexts which means that the interaction system has become more complex in that multiple actors are involved so that new relations emerge, rather than new elements. This is what Hutchins means by a *cognitive ecology*. (See Hutchins' 2010a, p. 92, for the schematic representation.) When we think with things, such as in ship navigation, thinking does not just go on in the head; rather these activities are embodied as well as embedded and are thus *multimodal*. Multimodal representations, according to Hutchins (2010a, p. 97) "are likely to be more stable than single-mode representations", partly because they are anchored to durable material structures, partly because representations can also be anchored in the body and are thus 'somatic' anchors. It is in this way that external representations are stabilized and are available for manipulation. It seems a reasonable hypothesis, as Hutchins (2010a, p. 98) suggests that "all thinking and imagination have their origins in this interaction system", and that without it there would not be any cognitive life, or organization.

## Organizations as cognitive systems

From the beginnings of the formal study of organizations, the relationship between environment and organization was recognized as important, while its appropriate conceptualization has remained an issue of ongoing discussion.

Although open systems theory correctly noted the permeability of organizational boundaries and the cognitive limitations of agents in planning and decision-making as the central aspects of organizational functioning, its theoretical-epistemological framework does not have the resources to determine where 'organization' ends, and 'environment' begins. Combining both the importance of the environment refashioned as 'task environment' and the limited cognitive powers of the decision-maker constituted a significant advance in conceptualizing the relationship. But while the Newell/Simon model focussed squarely on human cognition as central to rational decision-making and problem-solving, it bound conceptualizing the environment to the abilities of the *individual* decision-maker where cognition is understood as information processing that takes place entirely in the head. Here, we can see that insofar as Simon's decision-maker is the senior organizational administrator bounded rationality implies a model of *hierarchical design* for problem-solving, deemed to flow from the top down. It is this model that has become so prominent in educational administration and leadership. But as bounded rationality in Simon's account is common to all humans, including senior administrators, this top-down model enables only a narrow and unchecked definition of the problem and its solution because of the absence of feedback loops. Organizationally speaking, this is risky business as problems are standardly misidentified, checks and balances are absent, and we are prone to solve the wrong problem in any case.

Once symbol processing has been allocated its proper and significant role on the basis of our growing knowledge of how the biological brain works, given what we currently know of the evolution of cognition, including the cognitive role of external representations, a much broader conception of cognition emerges, as discussed in the previous section. The organization/environment nexus can no longer be maintained as separate and distinct once it is understood just how complex the role of the environment is and how inextricably involved in both problem definition and solution. Organizations are neither organisms nor machines but are the culturally evolved external manifestations or material structures, of collective, coordinated, cognitive activity that both facilitate, as well as constrain, specified activities, such as teaching and learning. There is no 'prime mover', as claimed in traditional organization theory.

If organizational performance is in the end determined by and dependent on specificities of context, described as cultural cognitive systems comprising shifting alliances of the knowledge of different human actors in interaction with their environments and the affordances these offer, then organizational problem-solving is not only dynamic but also proceeds "from the ground up". This suggests organization design of a very different type, one which is in principle open to checks and balances because of the influence of environmental factors which shift and change according to context.

## Conclusion

Finally, implicit in our discussion of external representations or cognitive technology is yet another consideration that is worth highlighting, albeit briefly: the role and influence of the Web. It will have consequences as yet unperceived not only for biological cognition but also for our cognitive systems at large. The scope of cognition first broadened via tool use, then through spoken, followed by, written language as the most powerful cognitive tool, is radically expanded by the global reach of the Web. We might consider the development of the Web as a sort of turbocharged "mindware upgrade", to borrow a term from Clark's (2003) book *Natural-born Cyborgs*. The Web has become a "'Cognitive Commons' ... in which distributed cognizers and cognitive technology can interoperate globally with a speed, scope and degree of interactivity inconceivable through local individual cognition alone". (Dror and Harnad 2008, pp. 1–2.) As a "transformative technology" (Smart 2012, p. 446) the Web goes way beyond just influencing the social processes of daily interactions and may well further transform our cognitive and epistemic capabilities. Smart's (2012) basic point is that the Web is relatively new and still evolving and may well morph into what he calls the "*Real World Web*" in the service of the "Web-extended mind", a further development of the Extended Mind hypothesis (see Chapter 3). A Web-extended mind is "a bio-technologically hybrid cognitive organization that leads a dual life as *both* a Web-based system and an extended cognitive system" (Smart 2017, p. 359). This challenging proposal deserves more space and time than we can give it here. (See Dunbar 2012, for some implications of the internet for social cognition.) Suffice it to note that once the WWW has moved away from HTML-based, browser-accessible information to 'data-centric' modes of information representations (Smart 2012), driven by technologically advanced interaction mechanisms, implications for schools will be considerable, both in terms of their mission as purveyors of essential societal knowledge, values, and beliefs and the kind of organizational design/s most suitable to accommodate this practically unlimited flow of information.

While there are many uncertainties given the rapid development especially of technological tools and media in relation to social organizations such as schools, it is clear that the task of managing teaching and learning exceeds the mental powers of any one agent, or principal. Given the characterization of cognitive systems as constituted by shifting alliances of resources and constraints, successful problem-solving is a matter of *coordination*, that is, as aligning all those resources in a way that they actually solve a problem. How much of a role a principal plays, or is able to play, in any decision-making process is not a matter than can be stipulated *a priori* but will only ever emerge after investigation, not before.

# References

Agre, P. (2003). Review: Hierarchy and history in Simon's 'architecture of complexity'. *The Journal of the Learning Sciences*, 12(3), 413–426.

Agre, P., & Horswill, I. (1997). Lifeworld analysis. *Journal of Artificial Intelligence Research*, 6, 111–145.

Bertalanffy, L. (1950). The theory of open systems in physics and biology. *Science*, 111, 23–29.

Bertalanffy, L. (1972). The history and status of general systems theory. *The Academy of Management Journal*, 15(4), 407–426.

Bidwell, C.E. (1965). The school as a formal organization. In J.G. March (Ed.), *Handbook of organizations*, Chicago: Rand McNally.

Bidwell, C.E. (1979). The school as a formal organization: Some new thoughts. In G.L. Immegart, & W.L. Boyd (Eds.), *Problem-finding in educational administration*, Lexington: D.C. Heath.

Bidwell, C.E. (2001). Analyzing schools as organizations: Long-term permanence and short-term change, *Sociology of Education Extra Issue*, 74(5), 100–114.

Bidwell, C.E., & Kasarda, J.D. (1985). *The organization and its ecosystem: A theory of structuring in organizations*. Greenwich, CT: JAI Press.

Churchland, P.M. (2007). *Neurophilosophy at work*. Cambridge, UK: Cambridge University Press.

Churchland, P.S., & Senjowski, T.J. (1994). *The computational brain*. Cambridge, MA: The MIT Press.

Clark, A. (2001). *Mindware: An introduction to the philosophy of cognitive science*. Oxford: Oxford University Press.

Clark, A. (2003). *Natural–born cyborgs*. Oxford: UK: Oxford University Press.

Clark, A. (2008). *Supersizing the mind*. Oxford, UK: Oxford University Press.

Cyert, R.M., & March, J.G. (1963). *A behavioral theory of the firm*. Englewood Cliffs, NJ: Prentice-Hall.

Donald, M. (1991). *Origins of the modern mind: Three stages in the evolution of culture and cognition*. Cambridge, MA: Harvard University Press.

Donald, M. (1993). Précis of origins of the modern mind: Three stages in the evolution of culture and cognition. *Behavioral and Brain Sciences*, 16, 737–791.

Dreyfus, H.L. (1994). *What computers still can't do*. Cambridge MA: MIT Press.

Dreyfus, H.L., & Dreyfus, S.E. (1988). *Mind over machine*. New York, NY: The Free Press.

Dror, I.E., & Harnad, S.R. (2008). Offloading cognition onto cognitive technology. In I.E. Dror, & S.R. Harnad (Eds.), *Cognition distributed: How cognitive technology extends our minds*, Amsterdam/Philadelphia: John Benjamins.

Dunbar, R. (2012). Social cognition on the internet: Testing constraints on social network size. *Philosophical Transactions of the Royal Society B*, 367, 2192–2201.

Dunbar, R. (2017). Evolution of the human brain. In J.D. Wright (Editor-*in-chief*) *International encyclopedia of the social and behavioral sciences*. 2nd edition. Volume 11. Oxford, UK: Elsevier.

Egri, C.P., & Pinfield, L.T. (1997). Organizations and the biosphere: Ecologies and environments. In S.R. Clegg, C. Hardy, & W.R. Nord (Eds.), *Handbook of organization studies*, London: SAGE.

Elman, J.L. (2006). Connectionism, artificial life, and dynamical systems: New approaches to old questions. In W. Bechtel, & G. Graham (Eds.), *A companion to cognitive science* (pp. 488–505). Malden, MA: Blackwell.

Emery, F.E., & Trist, E.L. (1965). The causal texture of organizational environments. *Human Relations*, 18(1), 21–32.

Evers, C.W. (1990). Educating the brain. *Educational philosophy and theory*, 22(2), 65–80.

Evers, C.W. (1998). Decision-making, models of mind, and the new cognitive science. *Journal of School Leadership*, 8(2), 94–108.

Evers, C.W. (2000). Connectionist modeling and education. *Australian Journal of Education*, 44(3), 209–225.

Evers, C.W., & Lakomski, G. (1991). *Knowing educational administration*. Oxford, UK: Pergamon.

Evers, C.W., & Lakomski, G. (1996). *Exploring educational administration*. Oxford, UK: Pergamon.

Evers, C.W., & Lakomski, G. (2000). *Doing educational administration*. Oxford, UK: Pergamon.

Evers, C.W., & Lakomski, G. (2012). Science, systems, and theoretical alternatives in educational administration: The road less traveled. *Journal of Educational Administration*, 50(1), 57–75.

Evers, C.W., & Lakomski, G. (2020). Cognitive science and educational administration. In R. Papa (Ed.), *Oxford Research encyclopedia of education*. New York: Oxford University Press. doi:10.1093/acrefore/9780190264093.013.ORE_EDU-00604.R1.

Freeman, J.H. (1978). The unit of analysis in organizational research. In M.W. Meyer (Ed.), *Environments and organizations*, San Francisco: Jossey-Bass.

Hoy, W. (2019). Theory of the school as an open-social system. Available: www.waynekhoy.com.

Hoy, W.K., & Miskel, C.G. (2013). *Educational administration: Theory, research, and practice*. Ninth Edition. New York: McGraw-Hill.

Hutchins, E. (1996). *Cognition in the wild*. Cambridge, MA: MIT Press.

Hutchins, E. (2005). Material anchors for conceptual blends. *Journal of Pragmatics*, 37, 1555–1577.

Hutchins, E. (2010a). Imagining the cognitive life of things. In L. Malafouris, & C. Renfrew (Eds.), *The cognitive life of things*, Cambridge, UK: McDonald Institute Monographs.

Hutchins, E. (2010b). Cognitive ecology. *Topics in Cognitive Science*, 2, 705–715.

Hutchins, E. (2014). The cultural ecosystem of human cognition. *Philosophical Psychology*, 27(1), 34–49.

Kast, F.E., & Rosenzweig, J.E. (1972). General systems theory: Applications for organization and management. *Academy of Management Journal*, 447–465.

Katz, D., & Kahn, R.L.(Eds.) (1966). *The social psychology of organizations*. New York, NY: John Wiley.

Katz, D., & Kahn, R.L. (1983). Organizations and the systems concept. In J.R. Hackman, E.E. Lawler III, & L.W. Porter (Eds.), *Perspectives on behaviour in organizations*. New York, NY: McGraw– Hill. 2nd edition.

Kirsh, D. (1999). Distributed cognition, coordination and environment design. *Proceedings of the European Conference on Cognitive Science* 1999, 1–11.

Kirsh, D. (2000). A few thoughts on cognitive overload. *Intellectica*, 30, 19–51.

Kirsh, D. (2009). Problem solving and situated cognition. In P. Robbins, & M. Aydede (Eds.), *The Cambridge handbook of situated cognition* (pp. 264–306). New York: Cambridge University Press.

Kirsh, D. (2010). Thinking with external representations. *AI and Society*. 25, 441–454. DOI 10.1007/s00146-010-0272-8.

Lakomski, G. (2005). *Managing without leadership*. Oxford, UK: Elsevier.

Lakomski, G. (2008). Collective learning and knowledge transfer. In S.J. Armstrong, & C.V. Fukami (Eds.), *Handbook of management learning, education and development* (pp. 69–89). London: Sage.

Lawrence, P., & Lorsch, J. (1967). *Organizations and environment*. Cambridge, MA: Harvard University Press.

March, J.G., & Simon, H.A. (1958). *Organizations*. New York: Wiley.

Meyer, J.W., & Scott, W.R. (1992). *Organizational environments*. Thousand Oaks, CA: Sage.
Morgan, G. (2006). *Images of organization*. Thousand Oaks, CA: Sage.
Newell, A., & Simon, H.A. (1963). GPS: A program that simulates human thought. In E.A. Feigenbaum, & J. Feldman (Eds.), *Computers and thought* (pp. 279–296). New York, NY: McGraw-Hill.
Newell, A., & Simon, H.A. (1972). *Human problem-solving*. Englewood Cliffs, NJ: Prentice Hall.
Newell, A., & Simon, H.A. (1990). Computer science as empirical inquiry. In M.A. Boden (Ed.), *The philosophy of artificial intelligence* (pp. 105–133). Oxford: Oxford University Press.
Newell, A., Rosenbloom, P.S., & Laird, J.E. (1996). Symbolic architectures for cognition. In M.I. Posner (Ed.), *Foundations of cognitive science*, Cambridge, MA: MIT Press.
Orr, J.E. (1996). *Talking about machines*. Ithaca and London: ILR Press.
Parsons, T. (1956a, 1956b). Suggestions for a sociological approach to the theory of organizations, I, II. *Administrative Science Quarterly*, 1 (March), 63–85, 2 (Sep.), 225–239.
Phillips, D.C. (1969). Systems theory—a discredited philosophy. In P.P. Schoderbek (Ed.), *Management systems*, New York, NY: John Wiley & Sons.
Perrow, C. (1973). The short and glorious history of organizational theory. *Organizational Dynamics*, 2(1), 2–15.
Resnick, L.B., Levine, J.M., & Teasley, S.D. (Eds.) (1991). *Perspectives on socially shared cognition*. Washington, DC: American Psychological Association.
Richardson, R.C. (2006). Heuristics and satisficing. In W. Bechtel, & G. Graham (Eds.), *A companion to cognitive science*, Malden, MA: Blackwell.
Rumelhart, D.E. (1993). The architecture of mind: A connectionist approach. In M.I. Posner (Ed.), *Foundations of cognitive science*, Cambridge, MA: MIT Press.
Rumelhart, D.E., & McClelland, J.L. (Eds.) (1986a), (1986b). *Parallel distributed processing. Volumes I & II*. Cambridge, MA: MIT Press.
Salomon, G. (Ed.) (1997). *Distributed cognitions, psychological and educational considerations*. Cambridge: Cambridge University Press.
Sapolsky, R. (2018). *Behave*. London, UK: Vintage.
Scott, W.R. (1998). *Organizations*. Upper Saddle River, NJ: Prentice Hall. 4th edition.
Scott, W.R. (1961). Organization theory: An overview and an appraisal. *Academy of Management Journal*, 7–26.
Selznick, P. (1948). Foundations of the theory of organization. *American Sociological Review*, 13(1), 25–35.
Shanahan, M. (2016). The frame problem. In E.N. Zalta (Ed.), *Stanford encyclopedia of philosophy*, Stanford, CA: Stanford University.
Simon, H.A. (1947/1976). *Administrative behavior*. New York: Macmillan, 1947; 3rd edition, 1976.
Simon, H.A. (1955). A behavioral model of rational choice. *Quarterly Journal of Economics*, 69(1), 99–118.
Simon, H.A. (1956). Rational choice and the structure of the environment, *Psychological Review*. 63, 129-38.
Simon, H.A. (1962). The architecture of complexity. *Proceedings of the American Philosophical Society*, 106(6), 467–482.
Simon, H.A. (1983). *Reason in human affairs*. Palo Alto, CA: Stanford University Press.
Simon, H.A. (1990). Invariants of human behaviour. *Annual Review of Psychology*, 4, 1–19.
Simon, H.A. (1991). Organizations and markets. *The Journal of Economic Perspectives*, 5(2), 25–44.
Smart, P.R. (2012). The web-extended mind. *Metaphilosophy*, 43(4), 446–463.

Smart, P.R. (2017). Extended cognition and the internet. A review of current issues and controversies. *Philosophy & Technology*, 30, 357–390.

Tolman, E.C., & Brunswick, E. (1935). The organism and the causal texture of the environment. *Psychological Review*, 42, 43–77.

Tyre, M., & von Hippel, E. (1997). The situated nature of adaptive learning in organizations. *Organization Science*, 8(1), 71–83.

Zhang, J. (1997). The nature of external representations in problem solving. *Cognitive Science*, 21(2), 179–217.

Zhang, J. (1993). External representations: An issue for cognition. *Behavioral and Brain Sciences*, 16, 774–775.

# INDEX

Note: Page numbers in *italics* indicate figures, **bold** indicate tables and page numbers with "n" indicates the end notes in the text.

activity space 171–173
administration, science of 3–4, 8
*Administrative Behavior* (Simon) 8, 168
administrative-organizational theory 146
*Administrative Science Quarterly* 162
administrative theory: components of 3; ethics and 3–4; hypothetico-deductive structure of 3
Affect Control Theory (ACT) 135–136, 138
agency/structure issue 94
algorithmic information theory 65
Andersen, H. C. 60
Anderson, M. L. 16
antecedent semantic webs 63
Argyris, C. 82
Aristotelian view of motion 114
Armstrong, N. 119
Arrow, K. 25
artificial neural network mathematical models 9
Australia 37
autobiographical self 42
Axelrod, R. 28

Barrett, L. F. 132, 138–140
Bechtel, P. 40
belief/desire theory 26, 67–68
Bertalanffy, L. 164–166
best-fit models 117–118
Bidwell, C. E. 164
Biesta, G. 98
Boiger, M. 133–134
bootstrapping cycles 15
bounded rationality 12, 163
brain processes 9, 15, 26
Brunswick, E. 165

Caldwell, B. J. 22, 88
Caldwell and Spinks model 88
carbon dioxide ($CO_2$) 69–70
Carnegie Institute of Technology 162
cartesian dualism 39, 40
Cash, M. 49
center of narrative gravity 42
centralized mind 27–30
Ceres 65
Chaitin, G. 65
Chalmers, D. 29, 31, 43
chaotic behaviour 77
Chitpin, S. 6
Churchland, P. S. 11–12, 40
Clark, A. 15, 29, 43–46, 88, 89, 175
classical decision-making 147–149
*cogito ergo sum* 39
cognition: causal machinery of 145; characteristic of 32; conception of 38, 169; digital computer as a model for 8, 9; disembodied 38–40; distributed 14–17, 21, 25–26, 31–32, 38, 45, 64, 68, 163; educational administration

and 12–14; enculturated 46–48; indispensable parts of 173; inside/outside boundary of 43; leader 37–49, 163; mathematical 47–48; naturalism's treatment of 8; neural circuits of emotion 13; neural network models of 9; neuroscience and 8, 12–14; unifying view of 15
cognitive centrism 15
cognitive ecologies 42–46, 173
cognitive integration (CI) 47
cognitive practices 46–48, 112
cognitive prototype of leadership 62
cognitive scaffolding 31
cognitive simplification 12
cognitive system 15–16, 44–45, 163, 172, 173–174, 175
cognitive tasks 106
Cohen, J. 109–110
Cohen, L. 48
coherence justification 3, 4, 10, 11
coherentism 3, 93; *see also* naturalistic coherentism
collective intentionality 132
collectivist emergentists 28
communal prototypes 63
community optimum (CO) 81
comprehensiveness 5, 64, 93
computer context 9
confirmation bias 151
conscious feeling 13
conscious reason 39
constraints on learning: institutional 85–87; organizational 85–87
constructionist theory of emotion 132
context(s): characteristic of cognition in 32; cognitive 121; computer 9; dependent interactions 29; of education 24; Euclidean space 57; force 12; importance of 132; individuals in 83–85; of inter-agent communication 47; of justification and discovery 93; of knowledge 25; of the Korean War 59; leader cognition in 37–49; learning in leadership 10; of learning organizations 74; limits of comprehensiveness 5; of non-Euclidean space 57; non-leadership 70; organizational 92; particularities of 5–6; social-cultural 46; sociocultural 133, 134, 140
cultural ecosystem of human cognition 44
culturally adaptive emotions 133
cultural neuroscience 171
culture-based cognitive system 163
Cyert, R. M. 162

Damasio, A. R. 9, 13, 41–42, 151–154, 156
D'Andrade, R. 107
Davidson, D. 108
Decartes, R. 39
decision-making 13, 33; bounded rationality 147–149; classical 147–149; complexity of real-life group 14; educational 147–149; emotion for rational 9; human 12; neuroscience of emotion in 9; role of emotion in 12; to solve absenteeism 7; somatic marker hypothesis 152–156
Dehaene, S. 48
Dennett, D. 109
Dewey, J. 58, 74, 79–83, 85, 89, 149, 157
direct introspection 39
disembodied cognition 38–40
distributed cognition (DC) 43, 46, 64, 68, 163; cognitive cultural practices in 46; EM/C and 45; leadership and 14–17; methodological individualism 31–32
Dolan, R. J. 151
Donald, M. 173
Donmoyer, R. 4, 6, 8
dualism 39
Durkheim, E. 8, 23–24

Eccles, J. 40
educational administration 12–14, 22, 146, 164; administrative-organizational theory and 146; classical AI and 169; cognitive science in 40; emotion/values imbalance in 149; leadership and 64, 129, 174; modern cognitive science 169
*Educational Administration* (Hoy and Miskel) 8, 165
*Educational Administration Quarterly* 4
educational decision-making 147–149; bounded rationality 147–149; classical decision-making 147–149; emotional decision-making and 156–158; high reason 147–149; informed intuition 158; normative *versus* descriptive accounts of 146–147; overview 145–146; role of emotion in 145–159; somatic marker hypothesis 152–156
educational leadership 22, 62, 70
*Educational Leadership* (Hodgkinson) 58
*Educational Management, Administration and Leadership* 4, 22
effect size (ES) 68–71
electroencephalography (EEG) 153
Elster, J. 24, 26
emergence 27–30

Emery, F. E. 165
emotion(s) 13; constructionist theory of 132; construction of 134; culturally adaptive 133; defined 152; in education and educational leadership 129–131; from as essences to as constructions 131–133; mechanisms of 139; naturalizing 127–140; neural construction of 138–140; overview 127–129; role in educational decision-making 145–159; semantic pointer theory of 136–138; sociocultural construction of 133–134; sociological construction of 134–136
emotional consensus 14
emotional decision-making 156–158
emotional labor 135
encultured cognition 46–48
error elimination 100–103
ethics; administrative theory and 3–4; naturalism and 4, 8–9, 10–12
Euclid's first proof 113, *113*
Evers, C. W. 6
evolved self 42
explanatory individualism 25
extended mind 32, 42–46, 89, 163; *see also* Web-extended mind
*Extended Mind* or cognition thesis (EM/C) 43–44

Fodor, J. A. 118
force, defined 12, 62
functionally integrated systems 138
functional magnetic resonance imaging (fMRI) 153

Galileo's thought experiment 114–115, *115*
Gandhi, M. 58
Gardner, H. 58
Gauss 65
Gazzaniga, M. S. 41
General Conference on Weights and Measures 26–27
generality *versus* particularity 4–8, 9
General Systems Theory 163, 164, 166, 167
Gibson, J. J. 43
Gillett, A. J. 47
Gougu theorem 113, *114*, 121
Grandy, R. E. 119
Greenfield, T. 149
Gronn, P. 58

Hattie, J. 5, 68, 69
Hawking, S. 63
Hawthorne Western Electric plant 69
Hazlehurst, B. 47
Heise, D. R. 135–136
Hochschild, A. 135
Hodgkinson, C. 58, 149–150
Hollan, J. 45
Holland, J. 29
Hoy, W. 8, 12, 97, 145, 165
human-computer-interaction (HCI) 43
human irrationality 106–108
Hutchins, E. 44–47, 83–84, 107, 171, 173

individualistic agentic prototypes 63
individual learning 74, 80, 81–83, 85–89
individual organization 162
individual rationality (IR) 81
institutional constraints on learning 85–87
instructional leadership 5
*International Journal of Leadership in Education* 22
International Successful School Principalship Project (ISSPP) 37, 59, 63
Iowa Gambling Task (IGT) 155

James, W. 41
Johnson, M. 39–41
*Journal of Educational Administration* 4
*Journal of School Leadership* 22
Julius Caesar 59
*Just as I Am* (Gronn) 58

Kahn, R. L. 167
Kahneman, D. 107
Kajic´, I. 136–138
Kast, F. E. 167
Katyal, K. R. 6
Katz, D. 167
Kim, J. 28
Kincaid, H. 25
Kirchhoff, M. 47
Kirsh, D. 171
Kitcher, P. 74, 79, 80–81
*Knowing and Guessing* (Watanabe) 60
Kolmogorov/Chaitin definition of pattern 65
Krugman, P. 22

Lakoff, G. 39–41
leader: centrism 14, 21, 31, 92; learning from 58–59
leader-centric variables 70

leader cognition 37–49; cognitive practices 46–48; disembodied cognition 38–40; enculturated cognition 46–48; from extended mind to cognitive ecologies 42–46; overview 37–38; self as constructed 41–42
leadership: antecedent semantic webs 63; appearance of 27; attribution of 27; behaviours 62, 67; cognitive prototype of 62; development from uncertainty to social epistemology 74–89; distributed cognition and 14–17; educational 22, 62; effect size 68–71; evidence and 57–72; falsification and 63–64; inference and 57–72; instantiations of 5; instructional 5; learning through problem-solving trajectories 92–104; modelling learning organizations 83–85; organization and 14–17; preferred theory of 4; prototypes 62–63; school 5; search for patterns 64–68; self-learning 74; similarity in classification 59–60; social epistemology 79–83; social prediction 77–78; theory and 64–71; theory choice and 63–64; theory-ladenness 62–63; transformational *versus* instructional 5; uncertainty 77–78
*Leading and Managing* 22
*Leading Minds* (Gardner) 58
learning in leadership contexts 10
learning organization/institution 74, 79, 80, 82, 83–89
least squares method (LSM) 66
LeDoux, J. 41
Lindquist, K. A. 132, 139
*The Logic of Scientific Discovery* (Popper) 81–82, 93, 147
Lukes, S. 26, 27

MacArthur, D. 58
March, J. G. 162, 164
market-oriented individualism 22–23
material anchors 173
material self 41
maximal dynamic cohesiveness 119
Mead, M. 58
mechanisms of emotion 139
Meehl, P. 70
Menary, R. 47
Mesquita, B. 133–134
methodological collectivists 28
methodological individualism 16; centralized mind 27–30; distributed cognition 31–32; educational leadership and 21–34; emergence 27–30; individuals and structures 23–25; leadership 21–23; overview 21; problems 32–34; self-organization 27–30; social explanation 23–27
*Methodological Individualism* (Evers and Lakomski) 15
Millgram, E. 117, 147, 157
mind: as centralized 27–30; as extended 32, 42–46, 89, 163; unconscious 42; Web-extended 175
Miskel, C. G. 8, 145, 165
model emotional contagion 14
modelling learning organizations 83–85
Moore, G. E. 11
multi-criteria decision-making 101
multi-criteria decision problem 102
multi-criteria problem-solving 102
multiple anatomical and functional principles 138

Nagel, T. 118
*Natural-born Cyborgs* (Clark) 175
naturalism 3; affective 13, 131, 151; cognition and 8, 12–14, 26, 64, 67, 151; computational 147; critics of 10–12; ethics and 4, 8–9, 10–12; human subjectivity and 8; in natural science 4
naturalistic coherentism 3, 64
naturalistic fallacy 11
natural science 68; administration and 17; application to social science and 4; coheres with 3–4, 64, 67, 71; structure and processes of 4
Neill, A. S. 58
neural construction of emotion 138–140
neural network models 9, 84, 155
neural plasticity 15
neural reuse 15–16
neuroscience: affective and cognitive 13; of cognition 8; cultural 171; educational administration and 12–14; of emotion in decision-making 9
Newell, A. 8, 40, 163, 168–170
Newell/Simon model 171, 174
New South Wales government 33
Newtonian celestial mechanics 57
Newtonian mechanics 62
Newton's law of gravitation 65
Newton's second law of motion 12
Nickles, T. 11, 116, 117, 121
Nisbett, R. E. 110
Nobel prize 81
non-emotional activity 14

non-Euclidean space 57
non-leadership contextual factors 70
normative cognitive pluralism 112
normative patterned practices (NPP) 47
normative *versus* descriptive accounts of decision-making 146–147

*Objective Knowledge* (Popper) 93
Objective Knowledge Growth Framework (OKGF) 94
OECD Program for International Student Assessment (PISA) 22, 23
ontological individualism 25
*The Open Society and Its Enemies* (Popper) 10
Oppenheimer, J. R. 58
organization(s): activity space 171–173; as cognitive systems 173–174; as a discipline 162; environment and 164–166; from environment to task environment 168–171; epistemological problems 166–168; individual 162; leadership and 14–17; as machine metaphor 164; naturalistic view of 162–175; from task environment to activity space 171–173
organizational scaffolding 87–88

parallel distributed processing (PDP) 170
Parents and Citizens Association (P&C) 33
Parsons, T. 162
particularity *versus* generality 4–8
Pessoa, L. 138–140
Pessoa's recent model 138
philosophical responses 108–110
physical-symbol system hypothesis (PSSH) 8–9
Physical Symbol System Hypothesis (PSSH) 169
Piaget's theory of cognitive development 66
Pickett, K. 23
POEM (POinters–EMotions) 136, 138, 140
Popper, K. 6, 10, 40, 74, 79, 81–82, 85, 93–94, 115, 147
Popper Cycles 6, **7**, 11, 61, 70, 82–83, 84, 94, **95**
popular dualism 40
positional objectivity 118–119
positron emission tomography (PET) 153
*The Poverty of Historicism* (Popper) 75, 82
Prinz, J. 41

problem-solving trajectories: error elimination 100–103; example of 93–94, **95**; leadership 92–104; problems 96–98; tentative theories 98–99
prototypes 62–63, 108; *see also* specific prototypes
psychological constructionism 136
psychological primitives 132
Pythagoras' theorem 113, 116, 121

Quine, W. V. O. 11, 59, 61, 108

real business cycle 22
*Real World Web* 175
reasoning 106–122; cultural differences in 110–111; evidence for human irrationality 106–108; large-scale problems 117–121; normative cognitive pluralism 112; philosophical responses 108–110; problems, solutions, and objectivity 112–116
reflective practitioner model 93
Resnick, M. 27
Reynolds, C. 30
Robinson, V. M. J. 5
Rogers, K. B. 136
Rosenzweig, J. E. 167
Royal Family 84–85
*The Rules of Sociological Method* (Durkheim) 23–24
Russell, B. 71

Sapolsky, R. 172
scholarship 10
Schön, D. 82, 93
school-based management movement (SBM) 37
school leader 6
school leadership 5
*School Leadership and Management* 22
school leadership movement 37
*School Organization* 22
Schröder, T. 136–137, 140
science of administration 3–4, 8
science of society 23, 24
science of sociology 8
Scott, W. R. 165
Searle, J. R. 132
second law of motion (Newton) 12
seemingly ill-structured problem 97
selection task 106
*The Self and its Brain* (Popper and Eccles) 40
self as constructed 41–42
self as knower 41

self-as-process 41
self-organization 27–30
self-organizing social processes 134
Selznick, P. 164
semantic pointer architecture (SPA) 136
Semantic Pointer Theory of Emotion (SPTE) 136, 138
Sen, A. 118–119
Shanahan, M. 120
similarity in classification 59–60
Simon, H. 8, 40, 83, 113, 146, 148, 162–163, 168–170
Simon/March/Newell model 169, 170
Sims, K. 30
situated conceptualization 132
skin conductance response (SCR) 155
Smart, P. R. 175
social epistemology 85; development from uncertainty to 74–89; leadership 79–83
social explanation 25–27
social explanation and reduction 25–27
social prediction 77–78
social self 41, 42
sociocultural construction of emotion(s) 133–134
socio-economic status (SES) 5, 6
sociological construction of emotion(s) 134–136
sociology, science of 8
somatic marker hypothesis (SMH) 146, 151–153
Spinks, J. 22, 88
spiritual self 41
stability/plasticity dilemma 150
Starratt, R. 10
Stich, S. 109, 112
Strogatz, S. H. 84–85
structured problems 32–34; *see also* well-structured problems
substance dualism 39
super-empirical virtues 3, 10, 12, 64
Sydney Opera House 28
symbols 8
symbol/subsymbol problem 137
synaptic self 42

Tang, Y. 48
Tarter, C. J. 12
task environment 168–173
tentative theories 98–99
Thagard, P. 11, 117, 136–137, 140, 147, 156–158
Thatcher, M. 58
Theorem of the Ugly Duckling 64
theory choice: effect size (ES) 68–71; falsification and 63–64; leadership and 63–64; search for patterns 64–68
theory-ladenness 62–63
Thesaurus for Microsoft Word 62
Tolman, E. C. 165
totalitarianism 11
Trist, E. L. 165
Tversky, A. 107
Tyre, M. 171–172

uncertainty 77–78
unconscious mind 42
University of Waterloo 11
unpredictable novelty 29

ventromedial prefrontal cortex (VMPFC) 153–154
Verbeurgt, K. 117
*The View from Nowhere* (Nagel) 118
*Visible Learning* (Hattie) 5
von Hippel, E. 171–172
von Neumann machine 9

Wason, P. 106
Watanabe, S. 60–61
Watts, D. J. 84–85
Weber, M. 8, 24, 27
Web-extended mind 175
well-structured problems 96–97
Wilkinson, M. H. F. 78
Wilkinson, R. 23
Willower, D. 149

Zhang, J. 173
Zollman, K. J. S. 84–85

Printed in the United States
by Baker & Taylor Publisher Services